EXPERIENCING
the ENNEAGRAM

Edited by
Andreas Ebert and Marion Küstenmacher

Translated by Peter Heinegg

CROSSROAD • NEW YORK

1992

The Crossroad Publishing Company
370 Lexington Avenue, New York, NY 10017

Originally published as *Erfahrungen mit dem Enneagramm:
Sich selbst und Gott begegnen*
Copyright © Claudius Verlag, 1991

English translation copyright © 1992 by The Crossroad Publishing Company

Printed in the United States of America

Library of Congress Cataloging-in-Publication Data

Erfahrungen mit dem Enneagramm. English
   Experiencing the enneagram / edited by Andreas Ebert and Marion Küstenmacher; translated by Peter Heinegg.
      p. cm.
   Translation of: Erfahrungen mit dem Enneagramm.
   Includes bibliographical references.
   ISBN 0-8245-1201-4 (pbk.)
   1. Spiritual life—Christianity. 2. Enneagram. I. Ebert, Andreas. II. Küstenmacher, Marion. III. Title.
BV4503.E713 1992
248.2—dc20
                                  92–26317
                                       CIP

Contents

Part I
FOUNDATIONS

Part II
PSYCHOLOGICAL ASPECTS

Part III
PERSPECTIVES FOR SPIRITUALITY AND THE CHURCH

Preface

"The young man who cannot weep is a savage;
the old man who cannot laugh is a fool."

"Do we really need another book on the Enneagram?" I ask myself. "Do I have anything more to say?" I wonder. The answer to both is surely no. There is nothing more to say, only more concepts and clarifications, with an occasional hope of life-shattering insight. And perhaps tears or laughter. These break through the boring concepts and clarifications. Tears and laughter are worth waiting for. Teats and laughter might be the One Sure Way — when they proceed from the well of Grace.

I continue to trust the wisdom of the Enneagram and use it in the work of the Gospel because it leads many people back to that well where body and soul are still yearning for Spirit. For too long the religious and Christian West have tried to do an "end-run" around body and soul to get to God's Spirit, or even to get to our own transcendent spirit. A truly biblical anthropology saw the human person as tripartite. The oldest letter in the New Testament expresses it very well: "May the God of peace make you whole and holy, and may your spirit, soul, and body be kept complete and ready for the coming of our Lord Jesus Christ" (1 Thes 5:23).

Soon this more traditional model of spirit, soul, and body was lost as Paul struggles with his dualistic "flesh" versus "spirit." We have yet to recover from this confusing switch of lenses: flesh is bad, spirit is good, and never the twain shall meet. Now we finally say yes to body and soul, but often get trapped there for lack of experience and expertise. Conservative types, anxious to preserve Spirit/God/truth, tend to fear and avoid the messages of body and soul. Progressive types, enamored with their new discoveries of body-work and soul-work (psyche), tend to remain in the outer courts of Spirit, almost humiliated before the Transcendent. But both of us lose: the first is pseudo-spirit or empty religiosity, the second is psycho-spirit, trapped in the private self. Conservatives, who are usually not true Traditionalists, will avoid the wisdom of the Enneagram for fear of being waylaid. Liberals, who are often trapped in their own cultural moment, will often use Enneagram technique to avoid the scary encounter with the Not-Me.

But the trinitarian understanding of our human nature says that all three parts must be honored and respected: body, soul, and spirit. Quite simply, the Enneagram is soul-work, with some body manifestations. Its original purpose was to open us up to our own longing for God, where "Deep calls unto deep" (Ps 42:7). The Enneagram insight overwhelms one with his or her need for "salvation," his or her incapacity to change oneself by oneself, and the metamorphosis of grace that turns sin into gift. The Enneagram at its best is significant soul-work that relates one to their own spirit, which always longs for the eternal Spirit of God. The body stands as witness, antagonist, and truth-speaker to both soul and spirit.

We can only wait, desire, and, to use a dangerous old word, repent. It will bring both tears and laughter, tears that harrow hell and laughter that pierces the heavens. Finally it is the body that most rightly names both our soul and our wondrous human spirit. Don't be afraid of any of them.

RICHARD ROHR, O.F.M.
Center for Action and Contemplation
Albuquerque, New Mexico

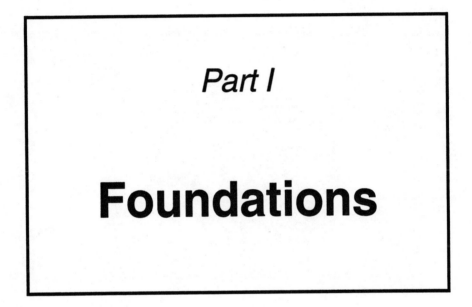

Part I

Foundations

The Enneagram: Vulnerable Community

Richard Rohr

Loving God, we thank you for this evening, and we thank you for all the hope and longing in this room. Lord, we are seeking wisdom. We are searching for you and for ourselves. We beg you to be our teacher and leader, to show us what we need to see and what we don't, what we need to hear and what we don't. We thank you for your patience, for everything has its time. You convert us slowly. And you call us to you slowly but surely. Help us to be just as patient with ourselves and one another. We put ourselves and this weekend in your hands — in the name of Jesus. Amen.

This is my final appearance after five weeks on the road. I hope that my fatigue won't interfere with what I want to do and what you deserve. But it seems to me that Enneagram weekends take care of themselves. It's obvious that people who come to these meetings bring with them a kind of inner longing or internal quest for which I only have to provide a little structuring. I'm sure that in your conversations and in group discussions there'll be at least as much going on as in my talks.

I'd like to emphasize that spreading the Enneagram is not my main activity. But I'm glad to keep doing it because I see that it bears so much fruit. I'd further like to stress that the Enneagram is not necessary for salvation. It's quite possible for anyone who is open and growing to reach many of the same conclusions entirely by himself or herself. I hope that I can at least help by labeling the experiences that we all have and so get a process started.

The Enneagram lets us name our "demons," and in a way that we normally don't allow one another to do. Enneagram conferences are the only kind of exercise where I'm allowed to rip people's "head" off, to tear out their "heart" and their "belly" — and they laugh. This tells me that a thoroughly spiritual wisdom is at work here. For many years I've been a counselor and spiritual advisor to a lot of men and women. In the ordinary course of pastoral care it would take eight months to build up enough confidence to tell somebody to his face the sort of things you can say the very first time with the Enneagram. For some reason the Enneagram seems to remove the element of personal confrontation, so that we can see ourselves as part of a pattern.

Keynote address at the Enneagram Workshop of the Protestant Academy of Tutzing, Würzburg, Germany, March 23, 1990.

Right from the start I'd like to underline the fact that in its original sense the Enneagram is a tool for conversion, for turning ourselves around. It's more than just another psychological curiosity for learning about ourselves. If we use it that way, we forfeit its true strength. Because then we're misusing it, pampering our ego instead of letting it go and giving it away. The Enneagram has no false pity for the ego, it will pay any price to uncover the games our ego plays.

At first glance the Enneagram's intention looks completely negative. That's why as a rule so few SEVENs come to Enneagram workshops: It's too hard for them to come to grips with the negative side of life. So I congratulate all the SEVENs who are with us today. On the other hand, these seminars usually attract a mob of ONEs — like myself. We're enthusiastic about finding a method for criticizing, if not slaughtering, ourselves.

I know that Andreas Ebert's and my earlier book, *Discovering the Enneagram,* maintains that the Enneagram derives from the Sufis, a charismatic movement in Islam. But in recent days it has become increasingly clear that this cannot be proved. Meanwhile some American specialists absolutely deny that it's from the Sufis. For this reason probably the most honest thing to say is that we don't know what its origins are. We can follow a few traces back in time, but we never get to the point of departure.

In 1971 when I first became acquainted with the Enneagram, I was told to use it exclusively as a personal spiritual tool for counseling and not let anyone know that I was familiar with it. It was a secret instrument for spiritual advisors, enabling them to read the souls of men and women. It was an oral tradition of wisdom that had been passed down exclusively from one spiritual leader to another. But, as you know, the Americans have broken with the oral tradition, which is typical of THREEs. We want to put everything into mass production. And I have no doubt that now, thanks to its being written down and publicized, something essential has been lost. Our book was based on the transcript of a live workshop. I'm not saying that to make excuses for the book but to stress that any Enneagram book is only second-best. There is something special about having the Enneagram transmitted to you *personally,* so that you get a sense of the energies that it's all about. In that respect I hope this weekend will be a help to everyone.

One more very important point. The depths of wisdom open up only in the course of time. It takes a while before you can get over the first impressions and external symptoms of a particular type and then distinguish the different energies. In this process we learn how our energies react to one another, how they attract or repel each other. We all know that two people can say the exact same words, but we find ourselves drawn to one person and repelled by the other.

In this sense we can call the Enneagram a tool for the "discernment of spirits," to borrow a phrase from Paul. When you've dealt with the Enneagram for many years, you'll find that you can read these energies in the gestures, facial expressions, and body language of other people. The body doesn't lie. The body is a window of the soul. But this mustn't be our starting point. I would just beg you to be patient and assure you that the longer you work with the Enneagram the deeper your insights will be. After dealing with the Enneagram for nineteen years now, I have to admit that I keep discovering new aspects of myself that point to the fact that I'm a ONE. Frankly this discourages me occasionally — so much so that there are times I could puke. And I'd like to help get you too to the point that *you'd* like to puke. Perhaps that's what the saints meant when they "wept for their sins." This has nothing to do with masochistic self-laceration. Rather it's a kind of knowledge that shakes you up and makes you realize, "I still have to convert. I'm still sitting in the trap. I still can't look truth in the eye. I still see everything through blinders or rose-colored glasses." The Enneagram helps us to take those glasses off.

There's nothing at all esoteric about the Enneagram; it's really quite traditional. It tries to do exactly what good spiritual advisors have always tried to help people do. You hear talk nowadays about developing a "third eye." This means the power to observe the self, as it were, objectively — not to judge or condemn, just to observe it. For those of us who have had a religious education this is very hard. Religion teaches us to judge before we've seen. This weekend we're not here to judge, but to observe. I hope you can see everything that we say in that context. Jesus says, "Judge not!" Don't attack yourself. Simply try to *see* and to *discern* what's authentic in your life and what's inauthentic, what's honest and what's dishonest — as Jesus would say, what's "built on rock" and what's "built on sand." Ultimately this will not lead you to hate and despise yourself, but to be able to really love yourself — without for a moment denying your dark side. This is further proof of genuine spirituality, because its final result isn't negative but liberating.

Here's what it's all about: Evil and darkness have only one way to influence our life and take control of it. They have to disguise themselves. And the best possible disguise is, of course, virtuousness. Thomas Aquinas says that we all chose something that *seems* to be good. With our internal logic we justify everything by saying there are good reasons for it. The Enneagram shatters our self-centered logic. You aren't free until you're free from yourself. And the first task of spirituality consists in breaking our dependency upon ourselves. Traditional spirituality would call this the "way of purification" or the *via negativa*. We first have to discover and take back the lie, before we can build on the truth.

For many years we have been living in an affluent society with a capitalist bias. For centuries now we have been reading the Gospel from the standpoint of this bias, which says that spirituality has to do with "having" or "getting": We supposedly get proofs of grace, we get salvation and spiritual wisdom. In this connection I'd like to quote the German mystic Meister Eckhart, who says that the spiritual life is more about subtraction (becoming less) than addition (becoming more). For hundreds of years we have been living with a spirituality of addition, while the much older tradition quite obviously deals with subtraction. The Enneagram is a way of subtraction.

But I can't make myself holy. I also can't "become worthy." I can't climb a ladder to God. The only thing I can do is let go of my false self — and let the true self appear. The spirituality of all great world religions deals with letting go, but for some incredible reason we have managed to turn this upside down. I think this fundamental egocentricity is the chief spiritual problem of the West. We all take endless pains and load endless burdens upon ourselves to make our private self feel good — or to punish that self because it's bad. We have to leave behind us the illusion of the isolated self.

The first stages of working with the Enneagram may look as if its object were precisely this isolated self. But anyone who continues to grow will increasingly see how much of this private self is an illusion. The private self takes its own thoughts much too seriously, it takes its own feelings much too seriously — as if these thoughts and feelings provided an objective access to reality. In fact they are only there to protect us. As a rule they're like a suit of armor for our character, designed to fend off reality. The Enneagram helps us to see that we don't need any such armor. It leaves us free to let go of the masks. They'll still be there, but we won't take them so seriously any more. We won't believe in them anymore. We'll learn to laugh at ourselves. That, by the way, is the first indication that you're on the way to freedom. Anybody who can't laugh at himself isn't free. And anyone who can't let other people laugh at him or her is certainly not free, but is taking himself or herself too seriously. Such people are trapped in themselves, as if they had cornered the market on objective truth. The Enneagram says: You are at best a ninth of the truth. And besides, there are thousands of different ways to be a NINE — or any other type. We are all only a small part of the truth.

Every point of view, as the phrase itself indicates, is the perspective from a quite specific point. We want to try to find out what our specific point is. What ground are we standing on? As soon as we know that it's only a small slice of the landscape, we'll see that we mustn't spend the rest of our lives defending this slice. That would make true love, community, and truth impossible.

We have all been through the experience of seeing the traditional explanations of the world come to grief. Let me just single out one example from recent Catholic history. I myself was trained after the Second Vatican Council. I studied during the Vietnam War and the days of Martin Luther King, Jr. Back then we thought that if everybody would just think the way we did, the world would look completely different in twenty years. We were the '68 hippies. We thought everyone in the world just *had* to think as progressively as we did. In the late '70s we began to get more and more disillusioned. And when Ronald Reagan came, the disillusionment got even worse. We realized that a progressively energized ego was just as bad as a conservatively charged ego. The key point is not to be "progressive" or "conservative," but to be free from oneself.

I have worked in a whole series of religious institutions, orders, and dioceses. After a certain amount of time there you notice that sometimes it doesn't make a bit of difference what theology the people have. I've met people who in my judgment have a horrible theology, but whose heart is free. They're not blocked off. You can get through to them, and they can open themselves and meet you. This is the best theology. And I have spoken with many theologians in our country who have a perfect theology and celebrate wonderful liturgies. Then I sit down and talk to them, and I notice that they can't come out in the open, can't get out of themselves, and they won't let me in. They're not free from themselves. Perhaps their pitfall is having to be right at all costs. Or maybe they're more in love with their theology or their position than with God.

That's why the Enneagram convinces me. The Enneagram is a thoroughly radical tool. "Radical" comes from the Latin word *radix*, meaning root. The Enneagram is radical, because it doesn't busy itself with symptoms, but with roots. It lays bare the basic causes. We might say the Enneagram unmasks our game. Every one of us plays a game. From the cradle onward it offered us a chance to survive. Many mothers have even told me that their baby had its Enneagram number while it was still in the womb. I don't know if that's true. But they claim that EIGHTs kick and shove more. I was present when a little girl was born who today, at twelve, shows every behavior pattern of a ONE. As she came out of the womb, she already had her fist clenched and her index finger raised. I really don't know where this comes from. But I do know that it's a survival tactic, and we employ it for many years. By the time we're thirty we're experts. Every atom of our body is so stamped by it that we ourselves can't see it — but everyone else can.

This is the reason why we have to develop the "third eye," or the capacity to stand over against ourselves, to see ourselves as others see us and as God sees us. This is why from the beginning our prayer has to aim at longing for and loving the truth, whatever it may cost. Otherwise we're turning the Enneagram into a new toy, not a spiritual tool for conversion. I believe the spirit is the gift that allows us to connect and relate to everything that exists. Therefore a spiritual person is anyone who has the freedom to let reality get through to him or her. An unspiritual person defends his or her own private reality and blocks out the big picture.

The great spiritual traditions of all great religions supply us with tools that can help us get rid of our false self. For instance, most of the great world religions have discovered the same three exercises of fasting, almsgiving, and prayer. All three are ways of letting go, ways of subtraction, not addition. Fasting means letting go of what my body thinks it absolutely needs; almsgiving means letting go of what my thirst for security thinks it needs; and real prayer, in my opinion, means letting go of what my understanding and emotions think they need. You need time to practice this, because prayer too has been turned into a spirituality of addition, instead of a spirituality of subtraction. God doesn't need our words. Jesus says, "In your prayers, do not go babbling on like the heathen" (NEB). God also doesn't need our thoughts, nor the warm feelings that we cultivate for him (or her). Instead, we need a way to free ourselves, once and for all, from our own ideas and feelings.

Twenty-eight years ago, when I was a Franciscan novice, we heard a lot about "the virtue of letting go." In the last twenty years hardly anybody has been talking about it — until the Enneagram came around. Because we've lost the art of letting go, we are finally producing the most dependent and addicted society the world has ever known. This can get to the point that people don't know who they are — apart from their dependencies. People don't know who they are — apart from their own thoughts and feelings. In this seminar I'd like to make it clear that we are more than our thoughts and feelings. On this journey we want to try, so to speak, to crawl back to the "clean place in the soul," as far as possible. I don't think it will work completely. But at least we can try to laugh at our own illusions.

The second experience, along with laughing at the self, will normally be the experience of the self being humiliated. Please don't be afraid of this. It's really a good sign that you've found the right number — and that you've seen the abyss carved out by the sin of this number. If you're totally enthusiastic about being a FOUR, then either you're not a FOUR or you haven't seen how dopey being a FOUR is. There is a fundamental experience of humiliation. Some of you — above all the FIVEs — won't want to share this with anyone. But perhaps at this workshop we can let ourselves become a vulnerable community.

Spirituality is less a given content or a pile of information than a process. If we understand spirituality primarily as a collection of carefully spelled out statements, we have undeniably fallen into the trap of denominationalism. True spirituality has a universal character. This in no way means that the central meaning of Christ is curtailed, but it will, I hope, contribute to the ability of Christians to see the whole breadth and depth of Christ.

Our sin and our gift are two sides of the same coin. To see the one we must simultaneously see the other. To taste the one, we also have to taste the other. We can't experience our gift in all its depth without at the same time discovering the dark and potentially destructive side of our gift. And when our sin has been transformed and redeemed, it will become our greatest gift. Most people are done in because they identify themselves too much with their gift. Too much of a good thing is bad, and the corruption of the best leads to the worst.

I'll use arbitrarily chosen numbers to illustrate my case: Let's just say that 70% of what we are is our gift. In between ages fourteen and twenty-five it's normal and downright necessary — and so it has to be allowed — for young people to identify with their gift. That's the reason why it's such a strain to be under the same roof with teenagers: They're living out their drives to the limit, and we have to let them do it. But we who are older have to leave this behind and grow up. Because in the long run if we identify too much with the 70%, our gift starts to go bad on us. As a rule you'll notice the rot setting in between age thirty and thirty-five — if you're in a growth process and receptive. If by fifty or fifty-five you're still self-addicted in this way, conversion gets very difficult. I always challenge people to convert while they're young. The older you are, the harder it gets, because you become increasingly dependent on yourself. The ideal time for a conversion is between age twenty-five and forty. Look at the age when Jesus worked. He didn't dare come out into the public eye until he was thirty. I think that because of purely psychic requirements it's impossible to understand the cross until you're thirty. But if you don't "take your cross upon you," as Jesus says, in good time, then you're building your whole life on a lie. Then the only friends you make are as narrow-minded and full of prejudice as yourself, people who don't tell the truth but let you cultivate your illusions. Spiritually speaking, they're not friends, but enemies. We need spiritual friends. The Enneagram points a way that makes spiritual friendship possible. But if we over-identify with our gift, that same gift destroys us.

As young people, we are generally rewarded for the constraints we impose on ourselves. For example, I managed to go through my entire career as a Franciscan seminarian without once getting called out on the carpet. I was a good ONE. I was always on time, I turned in my written assignments punctually, I was a good boy. And seminaries love good boys. But I was good from false motives: not for love of God, but because I was in love with my own perfection. They rewarded me for my sin. And I'm not the only one this happened to — it happened to all of you. We get regularly rewarded for our sin.

This is truer in some countries than in others. In the U.S. every young man thinks he ideally has to be a THREE. But, of course, most of them aren't. So they live through their adolescence, constantly thinking that something is wrong with them. And they try to be something they aren't. No wonder they take drugs and hate themselves. You should never talk someone into being what he or she isn't. And the Church, to be sure, has continually tried this too. Jesus allows us, thank God, to grow and be the person that we are. And we must always grant one another this freedom.

I remember that back when I got to know the Enneagram, I was initially afraid that it could make me even more critical and condemnatory. I was already

a ONE anyway, and I didn't need any more ways to pass judgment. But seriously, I beg you, don't be afraid. If you really stick with it, in the end the exact
opposite will happen.

First of all, the Enneagram serves to advance *my own* conversion and
not to pigeonhole *you*, to pin you down and explain you. And as soon as I
learned to be compassionate with myself and with the thousand different
possibilities of being a ONE, then I learned to give you the same freedom.
Today I do a lot less judging and condemning than twenty years ago. And I
think the Enneagram was one of the gifts and tools that have helped me do that.

When you learn the Enneagram, you naturally get obsessed with classify-
ing everybody. Frankly, that's the only way to learn it. But at first you'll make
serious mistakes, above all with the people who are especially close to you. In
the beginning it's very hard to assess your own parents or children. But when
you've known the Enneagram longer, it gradually moves from the forebrain to
the back of your head. There it's present as a silent advisor that helps us to size
things up, to enter relationships, or make connections. It operates much more
like a kind of unconscious intuition, and much less like a conscious method for
pigeonholing people and keeping them under our control. I can only ask you to
trust me on this — and keep at it.

QUESTIONS AND ANSWERS

Q. I located myself at a particular point in the Enneagram — until someone
came along and gave me an entirely different classification. Now I feel very
insecure. Can I trust myself, or should I trust the objectivity of other
people?

A. Ultimately both. But to begin with I would recommend that you trust
yourself. In the final analysis you have to recognize yourself and decide
for yourself. As a rule this is a genuine aha-experience that comes from
inside. Otherwise you'll never see the depths of your dependency. Naturally
you can ask your good and intelligent friends for help. But you can't adopt
their assessment before you yourself really know that it's right. Actually
others can only confirm what you yourself already see.

Q. Even though I don't belong to this generation with all its great opportunities, I still have a question: I too was at first fairly sure that I'd found
my type, but then later somebody else judged me to be an entirely different
type. I read up on it, and came to the conclusion that he was right. Can it
also be a form of letting go when you say: Maybe the others see things
better?

A. An outstanding way to put it. In confronting the Enneagram the issue is
    our self-image and our fixation on this image. It's a very humiliating ex-
    perience to find that we had committed ourselves to a specific image, and
    then it turns out not to be the right one. As a matter of fact, it sometimes
    happens that good friends have the true picture. And please don't take too
    seriously what I said about age. God can convert us at any time.

Q. What does "dealing with the Enneagram" mean, practically speaking, in
    everyday life? How do you manage to get the Enneagram into the back of
    your head? How can you live with it day to day?

A. In fact, you have to take the risk of exaggerating it for a while. During this
    time you'll become a terror to your friends and family. But eventually it
    has to shift out of your head so that it turns into an intuitive ability to dis-
    cern the truth. At first you'll pay too much attention to character traits and
    you'll make a lot of mistakes. But you have to make these mistakes to
    learn it. Gradually you'll become able to tell the various energies apart. It's
    a question of time and practice. Please remember that the Enneagram is
    first of all a tool for your own conversion and your own growth. And if
    you think you've correctly found your own number, then please don't get
    all hot and bothered trying to get a grip on the other numbers too. You
    have to start by tasting the whole sin of your own number.

Q. I noticed with myself that on my first try I went a long way from the
    number that I am. And in the end I had to take a more careful look at
    the numbers that I was steering clear of, because I liked them the least.

A. I can only say that this is a very frequent experience. It shows how the ego
    will bob and weave, so as not to look itself in the eye. I'm glad you men-
    tioned this, it'll help many other people.

Q. You said that the best time for repentance comes between twenty-five and
    thirty. I'm only twenty-one.

A. Then, as Martin Luther said, sin bravely! Some advisors try to teach the
    Enneagram to young people. As a rule, young people find it quite interest-
    ing and entertaining, but no real conversion takes place, because they
    haven't yet tasted how much their sin harms others. I'd like to ask all
    parents: Don't try to pin your children down with the Enneagram. Other-
    wise it will just turn into a pedagogical device for changing them, which
    would be catastrophic. A small child who is a FIVE must be allowed to be
    a FIVE. You can't drag children into a "redeemed condition." This process

has to go its own way. But I'm glad that as a twenty-one-year-old you're here today. Listen and get whatever you can out of it. Still I bet that one day, when you're as old as I am, it will mean a lot more to you.

Q. You've spoken several times about the "private self." Is there also a non-private self or a common self?

A. I believe every true religion ultimately has one. It helps us to overcome the illusion that we're isolated. Paul calls this teaching the body of Christ.[1] John speaks of the vine and the branches. Behind this lies the profound spiritual experience that unites us more than it divides us. If we do nothing but spin around our private, split-off ego, we dilute the Gospel and thereby lose a large part of its power. Then we're continually taken up with nursing our private guilt feelings and striving for our soul's private salvation. This effort has knocked western civilization off its moorings. I'd like to say that quite emphatically in this context, where we're dealing with the Enneagram. At first the Enneagram really looks as if it was aimed only at the individual self. For this reason, right from the start I want to relativize the individual self and put it into the context of the mystical body of Christ. I hope the implications of this become clearer in the course of the weekend.

Q. Can we work on the assumption that if you take the path of the Enneagram you'll find in yourself the part that's a part of God or Jesus?

A. I think this is exactly what you'll find. Ultimately you'll get somewhere that you'll know is a place of great dignity and strength. And yet this is no self-made value or self-begotten power. It has nothing to do with morally good behavior. It will feel like an encounter with objective reality, with a kind of objective goodness — despite all signs to the contrary. I believe this is at least one possible way of describing the experience of God in us. And yet at the same time you'll know that you're only one part and that your brothers and sisters reflect other aspects of God. This prepares us again for the teaching of the body of Christ.

Q. My friend and I have both had the same experience: We each find two typical patterns in us that seem to have nothing to do with one another. I can't decide whether I'm a ONE or a FIVE. But your book stresses that a person is one and only one type.

A. There are several possibilities. First, you're still young and you may not know yourself very well. Second — and this holds for all of us — it can happen that many of us who have been raised by a very strong parent find that our own personality is overlaid by the dynamics of that parent's personality. Then we think either that we're the same type as our father or mother, or that we *should* be that number. Some people experience this so strongly that they can't even imagine being another number than their mother wants them to be. The third possibility is that you're making a connection that we call the arrows (comfort and stress points). In your case this can't be right. Confusing ONE and FIVE happens frequently. For a while I too thought I was FIVE, for example, because I have a tremendous love of reading. But the question isn't *whether* I like to read but *why* I like to read. I read to perfect myself, to get more information about how I can be "good." I don't read without a purpose. I read novels for example, and I look for the hidden Christ figure. I'm constantly in search of the deeper meaning. By contrast, a FIVE will read purely and simply for the experience of gathering information. I cite this example only to show how there seems at first glance to be a link between different numbers. Perhaps I should put it the other way around: FIVES sometimes take themselves for ONEs, because both types have a strong inclination to harmony. Perhaps that hint will suffice.

Q. I can't imagine that I can grow on the path of the Enneagram all by myself and without direction. Do I need a group for this, or a spiritual advisor? Or is it actually possible to do it all by oneself with the help of a book?

A. A very legitimate question. I think you need either a spiritual director or a group — one or the other. That's what we mean when we say that the Enneagram is an "oral tradition." It's something that you have to talk through. You have to hear other SIXes talk about this energy — or outsiders who can recognize the dark side of SIX. You have to catch a galloping horse. This can come down to, for example, asking a friend for help: "Call my attention to it when I do that again." If they agree to this request and say, "Look! You're doing it right this minute!" we'll naturally get mad at them. Actually they would have to remind us every three minutes. That doesn't mean you need this person or group till your dying day. But for a certain amount of time it could be very helpful for sharpening your own perception. After an Enneagram conference in Munich four or five self-help groups were formed: NINEs Anonymous, TWOs Anonymous, ONEs Anonymous, etc. In this sort of group, where people of the same stamp come together, you get honest much more quickly, and for this very reason you can help yourself. In Alcoholics Anonymous all the participants are alcoholics. This makes for solidarity. Self-help in a group is also useful because right from the start it respects the autonomy of the individual person, and there's no guru who knows better than everybody else while he himself is invulnerable.

Q. Is it helpful for my spiritual advisor to have the same Enneagram number as I do? Does he have to know the Enneagram? Or do I first have to introduce him to it before he can advise me?

A. Different spiritual advisors have different advantages at different stages of life. I don't think that we have to be bound to one and the same advisor all our lives. A person who shares the same number with us and understands it will have a lot to give us. From another point of view it might not be so good. Looking at life as a whole I would rather recommend turning to a person who can see you more objectively — unless the advisor of the same type is very wise and objective. Normally we aren't much attracted to a person of the same type anyway. We hardly know of one example of a marriage where both partners belong to the same type — except for Nancy and Ronald Reagan, who are both THREEs. Altogether I would advise you not to tackle the whole business too feverishly, in all too deadly earnest. The thing will work itself out much more from your subconscious than from your consciousness.

Brief Summary of the Nine Types

Richard Rohr

TYPE ONE

As a ONE it's the easiest thing of all to describe my own sin. At some point in our early life we became convinced that only perfection is worthy of love. You have to earn the right to be loved. It's hard for ONEs to imagine that the imperfect and the broken also deserve love. But it's precisely this experience — of unconditional love — that helps us break through. We can't believe it. You can see how Paul and Martin Luther grappled with this — because they were both ONEs. Recently I was listening to tape recordings of my first talks, given back in 1973. Even then I was continually preaching unconditional love, because one always preaches first and foremost to oneself.

ONEs are constantly disappointed by reality, because they're always hoping: Now something perfect is finally on the way. But upon closer inspection it turns out that this isn't it. And disappointment thickens into rage, not directed at anything in particular, but a shapeless, universal irritation at the imperfect state of the world.

This anger naturally supplies us with a lot of energy for our attempts to improve the world. But it's aggressive energy. For example I became a retreat director in order to try to make people better. We all frequently do the right thing for the wrong reasons. Discovering this is very humbling, because I once thought I was doing everything out of love for God. Perhaps there was a bit of that mixed in, but I also did it because I'm Richard Rohr. God uses our sins for his own ends. That's why "no flesh can boast before God," as Paul says.

The rage of ONEs doesn't look like rage. At first blush it strikes us as idealism or zeal — as a virtue. And this rage is not only hidden from others, but from ONEs as well. ONEs are always quite surprised when they discover that their sin is anger. As a rule others see this more readily than we do. We're convinced that we're pursuing high ideals and noble goals. It's very hard for us to concede that they're only my high ideals and not necessarily objectively noble goals. This is the first thing we have to recognize if we want to become compassionate.

Talk given at the Enneagram Workshop of the Protestant Academy of Tutzing, Würzburg, Germany, March 24, 1990.

Deep down in ONEs lies a deep current of vexation that they don't recognize or admit. This current leads them to snap judgments. It all happens so quickly that they themselves don't notice that they've already passed judgment again. These snap judgments ultimately lead to a continual state of resentment. The process is quick as lightning: *irritation-judgment-resentment. Irritation-judgment-resentment.* That's why we have to reach in the moment irritation flares up: It's the only way to break the vicious circle. We have to acknowledge how deep and constant this rage is. And we have to stop calling it something else, "truth," for example, or "justice." We simply have to admit that we are damned furious. We find that hard, because model children aren't furious.

The self-image that ONEs are dependent on proclaims, "I am a good boy (girl)." We have to be model children either to gain the love of our parents or not lose it. I was my mother's favorite. To maintain this position I had to be "good." That's why, for example, I never admitted I was egoistic. My egoism had to disguise itself. I didn't allow myself to notice my own feelings. I felt what I was supposed to feel. And so my feelings were hidden — even from myself.

ONEs must first of all discover their true feelings and their own view of reality. This is hard because everything is constantly being overlaid and suppressed by commandments and prohibitions. ONEs must stop passing judgment, above all moral judgments. We are obsessed by moral judgments. Everything has to be good or bad, meritorious or sinful. If we learn simply to let things be the way they are, if we learn to see before we judge, then we'll arrive at a wonderful, cheerful tranquillity.

If all goes well, in the end we'll succeed better than anyone else in overcoming and transforming anger. At some point we get so tired of our rage and our strained seriousness that inner peace can become our greatest gift. Redeemed ONEs have a pronounced feeling for harmony and balance.

Normally people take us for very reasonable people, because our judgments let us see both sides of every case. But we have to stop constantly judging; we have to stop thinking that our judgments are really aimed at the truth. Instead of "all or nothing," we have to allow for "both/and." This brings redemption for ONEs.

TYPE TWO

At some point TWOs came to believe that they would be loved if they themselves loved. "If I serve you, you'll always love me." That's why TWOs look for security in the world of love. They go through life buying love. They see to it that you have to love them. They ingratiate themselves: "I'll love you in such a way that you can't not love me. And if you don't love me, you'll feel guilty." In all this they themselves don't notice how much pressure and guilt they're handing out. But everyone who lives near a TWO senses this constant, silent expectation. We always know that this person is looking for more attention, for a bigger response.

TWOs are the loving ones, the world's servants and helpers. This love takes on many different shapes. TWOs are also the co-dependents of this world. If you're loved by a co-dependent, some day you'll have to pay for it. Because there's always an ulterior motive, though it's hidden from the TWOs themselves. There's a hook in this love, there are always strings attached. Once TWOs acknowledge that, they begin to get liberated.

TWOs bear a deep sense of shame within them. Early on they discover how needy they are, and they want at all cost to prevent anyone from noticing how deep this feeling of indigence goes and how much they need other people. So they operate indirectly: They often satisfy their needs secretly. They become masters at this. They really give a lot, but they secretly keep track of it. They send out 500 Christmas cards — and make another list of who sends them one.

If some day they've had enough of not being loved back the way they themselves love others, they decide: "I deserve a reward." Then they reward themselves in some very concrete though often hidden manner. They could be addicted to chocolate: They have to get themselves something sweet, after giving so much sweetness away. They often go into stores and buy something they really don't need at all. But they're ashamed of these needs.

It's important that TWOs look the facts in the eye and see how deep their neediness and their shame go, so that their love can step into the light and become more honest. They have to learn to laugh at their exaggerated neediness. For them to recognize that a large part of their love has been dishonest is a profoundly humiliating experience. I've found that more than all the other types TWOs will cry uncontrollably when their pattern becomes clear to them. Their self-image has always been, "I am love in person." When this image is taken away from them, it almost tears them apart.

Here you can see how things stand with their sin, pride, and what the journey into humility means for them. They have to get to the sobering point where they realize, "I'm really not capable of love. I have to take back myself and let God love through me." If they learn that, they become very humble instruments of love. But first they have to recognize their own ploys and let go of them. That constitutes a heroic conversion for a TWO, which is why we use Mother Teresa as a symbol for TWOs. The motto she gave her sisters is, "Don't count the cost." When TWOs stop calculating, they're free.

The gift of cordiality is at the same time the pitfall for TWOs. It takes a long time for their hearts to be purified. Perhaps the simplest way to describe the path of redemption for TWOs would be this: Their world of feelings and relationships has to be purified. If TWOs travel this road, they become totally capable of love. Such people make wonderful friends.

But we also have to be on the lookout so that TWOs don't manipulate us. They are not just highly manipulative, but also highly manipulable. We all know that and thoroughly exploit it. We know that all we have to say to a TWO is, "I need you," and they'll jump. TWOs themselves know that they do this — and afterwards they hate themselves for it. And they hate you too, because they know that you're using them. We too have to be converted in our relations with TWOs, because it's a form of co-dependency. We profit from TWOs, and are happy to have them stay that way. So we have to quit playing this game ourselves. Especially in marriage it's the TWO's partner who doesn't want to stop that, because after all it's pleasant being waited on hand and foot.

TYPE THREE

At some point in their lives THREEs have been taken in by the lie that, "I'll be loved by you, if I deliver a product to you. You'll love me, if I'm successful." Perhaps they've had the experience of coming home and hearing Mom say, "You're good because you got an A." THREEs have learned that their accomplishments were recognized, but they weren't, not for their own sake. So they try their whole life long to bring home As and show you their report card. "Do you see how good I am? Do you love me now?"

I remind you: TWOs, THREEs, and FOURs all play the game of love, which is why we call them the heart types. They get their energy from your reaction to them. If you deprive them of the reactions from other people, TWOS, THREEs, and FOURs lose their energy.

THREEs have to experience success somewhere, because success gives them the certainty, "I am valuable and good." On the other hand, they have a very hard time living through failure. Even when they objectively fail, they have to turn the unsuccessful project into one more success.

As you know, I like to use Ronald Reagan as an image of THREEs. His father was an alcoholic, but Reagan never talked about that. He never admitted the pain of this childhood experience. Even Nancy confirms that he never talks about it. If he had been able to live through this pain and this blot on his life — really live through them — then he might have been able to break through this pattern of an unredeemed THREE. But instead he took up a typical THREE profession: He became an actor. The actor constantly has to produce images of success, rather than experience ordinary life with all its flops and failures.

The THREE game represents a great temptation in an affluent society and a culture dominated by advertising and images: the temptation to *seem* rather than *be*. That is why THREEs must struggle to attain depth. THREEs can shun the depths in favor of quick successes. They have to be encouraged to go inside themselves, into the silence where there's no feedback and where they simply are what they are. Otherwise THREEs are in great danger of falling victim to ego-inflation. At their worst they can be characterized as hollow or superficial. As a rule THREEs change only in the context of a sickness or a breakdown that can no longer be smoothed over.

It's amazing how many THREEs are attractive and good-looking. They quickly notice how appealing they are to others, and so the first thing they sell you is themselves. This makes an impression — you can't help being impressed. It's not their fault for noticing, "It works! This is how to do it!" And they know that once you've "bought" them, you'll buy their product too. So they're not just actors, but salesmen too. They ensnare us. They normally get three times as much done as the rest of us — and probably six times as much as a NINE.

Without THREEs a lot of good things would never happen. And many good things would at least not be well made. If you want a job done professionally, you have to hire a THREE. This is a gift. Even Paul counts the gift of "ministry" as one of the charisms or gifts of the Spirit. Today he'd probably call it "good management."

THREEs and SIXes represent the capital sins that are lacking in the classic Christian-western catalogues. This is my explanation for the fact that they've managed to spread with so little resistance, and that we're not in a position to deal with them. We've failed to develop any tools to crack them. If the demon remains disguised and goes unnamed, we can never get complete control of him. For a long time we've failed to recognize the dark side of THREEs.

This holds true above all for the U.S. The THREE model is so impressive. In my country of all the types THREEs have the hardest time converting. There's no incentive for them to change. On the contrary, you get rewarded for being a THREE. And all young people think they've really got to be THREEs. This is why when we strip off the THREEs' disguise, we have to use a firm hand. The same holds for SIXes.

In conclusion, one more good thing about THREEs. If THREEs realize their self-deception, they learn more than all the others to love truth and integrity. Then they search for this uprightness with their whole heart. They strive for honesty with all the goal-oriented energy of a THREE. They know that their temptation is appearance, so they yearn to really be.

TYPE FOUR

FOURs are marked by a deep longing for something that's more beautiful than what's actually there. The present is always somehow or other ugly. Early in their lives FOURs have learned to head for fairer skies. They've developed an incredibly blooming imagination. When the outside world gets ugly, they know where they can escape it. There they create plays and poems and music, and feel deep sensations.

The feeling that energizes them the most is longing or melancholy sadness. Yearning for a lovelier world somehow provides them with the capacity for creating beauty. We outsiders don't understand this dynamic. FOURs strike us as depressive or unbalanced or at least highly eccentric. And while they're young, they are in fact very self-involved, because they have to enter their fantasy world to get energy. And if we don't fit into this world, they find us boring.

Parents tell me that it's very difficult to raise FOUR children, because they're constantly withdrawing into their beautiful inner world and continually playing with their own moods. Sometimes they seem manic-depressive, because they try out every emotion. They attempt to experience what sadness and ecstasy feel like. And when they sample these emotions, FOURs find them very real.

For FOURs ritual is identical with reality. The symbol is the same as its content. Symbols and images are more exciting than the real thing. The rest of us don't think so. This puts FOURs in a class by themselves, and they know it. They like this, they thoroughly enjoy it, because they enjoy being something special. In America FOURs are usually the easiest type to recognize by external features: For example, they like to wear black.

FOURs' path to redemption begins when they lose their fascination with being different from everybody else, and when they learn to use their creativity to see and elicit special qualities in other people. FOURs are good at "animating" or "empowering," because they discover, name, and promote other people's potential. This step toward making other people important redeems FOURs from self-centeredness.

The wonderful old churches in Europe, to my mind, show that in earlier centuries the Church must have greatly prized the gifts of FOURs. In an era when uniformity and rationalism were in less demand, FOURs must have felt very happy in the Church. Nowadays FOURS don't feel at home there — except if they're allowed to design beautiful liturgies. FOURs have a natural access to the sacramental world, because, as mentioned, symbol is more important to them than substance.

Redeemed FOURs are in a position to compress the broad spectrum of their emotions, so as to plunge into the depths with a few feelings. This makes the difference, for example, between the would-be artist and a great artist. Redeemed FOURs stop playing around with feelings and start really feeling. At this stage they have a lot to give us, because they have a sensibility we lack. But they have to stop being in love with their own sensitivity. That is, they have to enter a depth dimension at one point. They must experience a feeling through all its stages, instead of collecting more and more agony and ecstasy.

TYPE FIVE

FIVEs are characterized by a deep experience of emptiness, a bottomless abyss that seeks to be filled. FIVEs would like to find fulfillment through intelligence. They find security through understanding and explanations. FIVEs want to understand everything, and they make a beeline for explanatory models.

During an experience they often don't know what feelings they're having. The feelings don't get "developed" till a few days later, because FIVEs take in a situation with their heads, where it remains for a while. Only later can they let it sink in deeper and truly feel it. The symbolic plant of FIVEs is lettuce, which has its heart in its head.

Of course there are also FIVEs who permanently bar the entrance to their hearts and stay forever in their heads. These FIVEs are caught in deepest point of this pitfall. For them intelligence becomes the censor or control center that admits only the kinds of information that fit the logic they have on hand. Such FIVEs can be very rigid, narrow-minded and — in the bad sense — conservative. When their logic is very narrow and designed strictly for self-defense, they never make the breakthrough to genuine *wisdom*, but remain stuck in one set of opinions or another, with which they over-identify.

But if they let authentic wisdom integrate head, heart, and gut to name their sin and gift, they really have a lot to teach us — precisely because they don't stick to their own ideas, but can free themselves from them.

With FIVEs we sometimes use the same word to designate their sin and their gift: *distance*. They keep their distance, which can lead to their losing touch with reality. But this same distance can give them objectivity in the good sense, an objectivity that we others, who are too caught up in things, don't have.

If their logic has breadth and a solid foundation, they can in fact become very well-balanced and wise men and women. The best symbol for the redeemed FIVE is the Buddha. Buddhism naturally strikes FIVEs as much more immediately sensible than Christianity. Jesus is too bloody, too committed, too earthy, too concrete. Buddhism, by contrast, places greater stress on distancing oneself from the world and is much more serene. Nevertheless the classic statue of Buddha has one hand opened upwards and the other hand touching the ground. This is the SIX wing of FIVEs. FIVEs have to keep their hand on solid ground, planting both legs on the earth and "remaining true to the earth," as Dietrich Bonhoeffer, himself a FIVE, once said.

Another symbol for FIVEs is the "unbelieving" Apostle Thomas, whom Jesus challenges: "Touch me! Place your hand in my wound, in my pain." FIVEs would prefer to stay in their heads and come up with a definition of pain. FIVEs have to learn to accept the Incarnation, the becoming-flesh. Then they'll stay realistic and well-balanced.

FIVEs gather their energy through their eyes. They often wear glasses from an early age, because their eyes get worn out so quickly. They have to be observing all the time. They take in life through their eyes — but you can't be certain about what they're going to do with it. Sometimes they make nothing at all of their lives except to gather still more information. That's why we call their sin covetousness: collecting information for the sake of collecting. If they don't get out of themselves, so as to do something with all their knowledge, such people can become very sick and eccentric, and the rest of us will no longer take them seriously. They become cranks, spinning webs of airy fantasy. Needless to say, many great thinkers and philosophers have been FIVEs.

TYPE SIX

Please remember, meanwhile, that we are in the domain of the head, the center of which is type SIX. It's important to recognize that the grounds for fear lie in the head. Most of us probably think that fear is something emotional. But anxious types are governed by apocalyptic thought patterns about how everything might go wrong.

Their sin can best be described as fearfulness. There's an endless stream of anxiety in their head. Early in their lives someone told them that they couldn't trust themselves. For this reason they're very short on healthy self-confidence. They feel, "I should trust someone who's smarter than I am." And so they look for an authority they can trust. But we have to keep on telling them that they can and must trust themselves. SIXes have to be told that every day.

Unfortunately the churches, like politicians and the military, have hitherto staked and built their operations on the energy of SIXes. It has been estimated that half the population of the U.S. is SIXes. This type takes on many shapes and forms. And it's no accident that we find one statement more frequently in the Bible than any other: "Fear not! Fear not!" Nevertheless we in the Church have made people afraid and told them, "Be afraid!" In the Catholic Church we've said, "Don't trust yourself, trust the Pope." The Protestants have said, "Don't trust yourself, read the Bible."

In this way both of us, each in our own way, have produced fundamentalism, which is firmly ensconced in the head and reflects pure, unredeemed SIX energy. It's accompanied by a collection of little fixed expressions that *explain* reality so that there's no need to *encounter* it. SIXes have an exaggerated need for security.

Still I would also call SIXes the "glue" of the world. They are the world's working masses. They have no ambition, they're content to be ordinary laborers. Under all circumstances they'll protect and support what they believe in — whatever that may be. They're loyal servants of the cause they believe in. They don't demand any special recognition. They have no grand plans. SIXes hold all this world's institutions together. They're the silent, industrious servants who do what they're told.

And just as we all exploit TWOs, we exploit the SIXes too. We build on their fear, because we know they have a need to obey us. So we also have to free ourselves from co-dependency on the SIXes, although politicians, the Church, and the military are only too glad to make use of their energy.

I've just come from visiting a U.S. army base. When they introduce themselves the GIs first tell you their rank and place in the military hierarchy. SIXes want to know where they belong: "Tell me where my place is, and I'll stay there."

Oliver North, the man who diverted U.S. government money to finance the Contras in Nicaragua, said at his trial: "When my commanding officer tells me to stand on my hand, I stand on my head." This is false loyalty, false courage.

In redeemed SIXes, on the other hand, we meet a person who is courageous and reliable in the best sense of the word. That's why it's important that SIXes find something that deserves loyalty and fidelity.

We describe Germany as a SIX country. That doesn't mean, of course, that all Germans are SIXes, but that down through the history of this country SIX energy has been esteemed and supported. And perhaps even today people here are rewarded and considered good Germans if they're SIXes. That's why it's probably very important for *all* Germans to take a very thorough look at SIX energy.

I'm glad that many people in this group have already recognized and have been able to admit that they are SIXes. It is very important to discover the features of a redeemed SIX. We have to see people who live the redeemed side of SIX, so that we can acknowledge what's wrong with the unredeemed part. A redeemed SIX is the most reliable and trustworthy friend. And God knows the world needs such people. Maybe that's the reason why he made so many. The rest of us would spend all our time just pursuing our own interests. I call the SIXes glue, because they hold the world together.

TYPE SEVEN

The domain of SEVENs is the head too, but at first glance they don't look at all cerebral. The disguise is perfect. But all SEVENs would concede that they're head people. We also call them "planners." They plan the whole day and they plan their entire future — taking care to maximize joy and minimize pain.

The self-image of SEVENs is, "I'm a happy and cheerful person." But in saying this they don't acknowledge that their deeper motive is fear of pain. This holds for mental as well as physical pain. They're afraid of the dark and painful side of reality. As children they were often afraid of the dark, and they often develop a lifelong love of things that are light and gaily colored.

As soon as you start talking about serious things, they change the subject. And even when they have to cry, they still laugh through their tears. They don't let themselves really feel the pain.

If they're religious, SEVENs are fascinated by heaven. They like to look up, because "beyond the clouds freedom must be boundless." In Albuquerque I lived with three Franciscans who were all SEVENs. One day I came home, and they were all flying kites. They waved and called out to me, "Come on, Richard, join us!" As a stern ONE I could only ask, "What good is that?" Actually, SEVENs are very good for ONEs, because they keep us from taking everything with such deadly seriousness.

SEVENs often look younger than they really are. They look at life with the eyes of children. In some ways they'll never grow up. Their patron is Peter Pan. In America they're the eternal scoutmasters, the professionally young. There are sixty-year-olds in our Church who are still working with young people. Deep down they feel more at home with adolescents than with grownups. It's certainly a great gift for humanity that such people exist.

But SEVENs also have to taste pain. They also have to look the dark side of life in the eye. But most of the time SEVENs will do everything humanly possible to avoid it. Normally they never voluntarily face the darkness, only when there's no other choice. They can always withdraw into their brains and find a reason for not doing that. But this explanation always serves simply to promote their own ends and their need for self-protection.

Please remember that we've also labelled the FIVEs, SIXes, and SEVENs the "self-preserving" types. Their first reaction is always to pull back from reality, to try to keep it at arm's length: FIVEs pull back into their heads, SIXes pull back into their fear, and SEVENs pull back into their false joy. The joy promised to us by the Gospel is Easter joy, which is the other side of pain, joy after pain. SEVENs would like to have joy without pain. This is a false and superficial joy. The rest of us notice it right away and speak, for example, of "nervous laughter."

You can immediately tell the difference between a superficial SEVEN and one with a deep foundation. The joy of a "deep" SEVEN is infectious and makes us merry too. For this reason I call *St. Francis of Assisi* the patron of redeemed SEVENs. His life was a search for perfect joy. But he found his way to this joy by looking pain in the eye and kissing the leper instead of avoiding him.

TYPE EIGHT

EIGHTs can often be recognized right off by the fact that they're larger than life. They make their presence felt, and they make you pay attention to them.

They come rumbling into the room, and you know they've arrived. They know it too, and they like it. They get their energy from experiencing their strength. They are bundles of energy. EIGHT energy is reflected in their gestures and their faces — and it puts a strain on us.

After spending a half hour with an EIGHT, you feel like taking off. It's too much, simply too much. That's what we mean when we speak of EIGHT's "lust." They exaggerate everything they do. And they do it in a way that the rest of us would label "negative."

They meet reality in a confrontational fashion. The rest of us have no feeling for this "muscular intimacy." Their advances consist in picking a quarrel with you. The rest of us think, "This person can't stand me." But this is only the EIGHT's way of trying to get close to us. And they wonder why we draw back from them. Deep down EIGHTs are often very sad, they ask themselves, "Why can't anybody stand me?" But they still don't change their methods. They always make the same attempt to "turn us on."

If ONEs are the model children, EIGHTs are the bad boys and girls. Their self-image is, "I'm bad." And they like being bad. Can you imagine how many problems these people have with the Church, where you're always being told, "Be nice and sweet and good and pious"? EIGHTs don't get it; to them, "good people" are nothing but doormats or jellyfish.

I know a terrific woman who's an EIGHT. She told me it took her forty years to learn to trust Jesus. Because the way Jesus was presented to her — as a blond, blue-eyed softy, sweetly smiling down at the little children — said nothing to her. This Jesus wasn't worth her love. EIGHTs want someone who will grapple with them, someone who stands for something.

EIGHTs have an inborn sense of justice. They see the stupidity and injustice of the world and love to rip its mask off. They want to wipe out wrongs. Without EIGHTs nothing in this world would change. We would resign ourselves to the most idiotic systems.

My mother is an EIGHT, and I know that I've inherited her passionate nature. I now see that this is the gift she has handed on to me. When the whole family is sitting in peace and harmony at Christmas dinner, and we're all talking about all sorts of pleasant things, she'll suddenly fling a hand grenade out onto the table. When we were children, we used to say, "Oh no, mama, not again!" She'll abruptly bring up some political subject, something about injustice. It's her way of inserting herself into the group. Or if we're together in public anywhere, she'll suddenly point to somebody and launch into a commentary. I'll go, "Psst!" But fighting with EIGHTs only gives them more energy.

Don't get into an argument with an EIGHT — you're wasting your time. If you raise your voice, EIGHTs raise theirs even more. They love combat, and under no circumstances will they retreat or admit defeat.

The key to EIGHTs is to see the little boy or girl that lies inside them. I promise you, this little child is always there. There's no doubt about it. Normally in the course of their life they'll show it to only two or three other people. But then the secret's out, and they all know it. When EIGHTs go around roaring like wild animals and you'd prefer to knuckle under or take flight, I recommend that you simply speak to the little child inside them. Work on the assumption that it's there.

EIGHTs never stop trying to protect the little girls and boys of this world, everything that's tender and vulnerable. In the Third World I've met many missionaries who are EIGHTs. They're ready to put up with endless unpleasant and repulsive things. They accept the greatest privations, they sleep on the bare ground, simply to help a poor child. Their love for the weak, for little people, is boundless.

On the other hand, if you try to puff yourself up, then they prick your balloon. But if you come to them in real weakness and vulnerability, they will take endless, passionate pains over you. So please don't hate the EIGHTs. By the end of their lives they're usually dragging around a heavy burden, because so many people can't stand them, and they themselves have hurt so many others. And that's true. As a matter of fact, they often do trample on others. Their passionate nature is at once their sin and their gift. This means that they have to break through their destructive passions in order to reach their life-giving ones.

My mother, for example, is now close to death. At first she didn't want me to travel to Europe for five weeks. But when she knew that I'd have to take the trip after all, she said: "I won't die till you're back." And she won't. She's seventy-five, and now, at the end of her life, she's very close to the little girl within her. But it took her all her life to get to this point.

TYPE NINE

The NINEs stand at the "top" of the circle, and that's because with NINEs we're dealing in a sense with original human nature, with Adam and Eve. NINEs are the way we all were before we got complicated. That's why, I think, so many of us like and envy NINES. We long for their simplicity and straightforwardness, although it gets on our nerves and may drive us up the wall to see all the things they *don't* do.

NINEs have a very hard time finding and pursuing a clear purpose. They're everywhere and nowhere. They make mountains *into* molehills: They can turn genuinely big deals into trifles. Nothing is really all that important. Even when they're objectively faced with a problem, they refuse to see it. That's what we mean when we talk about their "laziness." NINEs simply don't know how to concentrate their energies.

NINEs are often quite active in all sorts of hobbies and activities. But if you look closely, you'll notice that many of these activities are fairly meaningless, and the NINEs don't invest a lot of energy in any of them. NINEs fill the soccer stadiums of Europe — they're in the spectators' seats. And they can jump up and cheer and get all enthusiastic over nothing.

NINEs are especially prone to addiction. These are usually rather minor dependencies, like nicotine and coffee. But NINEs always need some stimulant or other to help them feel their own juices flowing. Andreas Ebert and I both have friends who are NINEs and who drive motorcycles or trucks. It's as if they had no motor in themselves and so had to plant one under their backsides. Meanwhile the direction they're headed in is of no particular importance.

We ONEs take the shortest road from here to there. NINEs go off on side-trips, detours, roundabouts, stay put, turn around, and then . . . Well, NINEs aren't so sure they want to go there after all. They're not so sure they want to go anywhere. Which is why they can be so unnerving to other people. Sometimes you want to shake them and ask, "Who are you, and what do you actually want?" They just don't know what they want — it's all the same to them. That's what we mean when talk about their "laziness."

Most of us like NINEs. This comes from the fact that they follow our impulses and our energy, whatever form they may take. If you're a THREE, they join in your "THREE-ery" — even if they're out of "sync." They play whatever game is going on. For this reason they're "easy to care for," they have a quasi-congenital friendliness.

We also call NINEs "passive-aggressive." Don't forget that we're in the center of the "gut" types. We ONEs want to reform reality. EIGHTs rebel against it. But NINEs just sit there and say, "It's all baloney. It's just not worth wasting time on all that." When you get to know a NINE better, you'll notice that this trait is always there. It's a kind of cynical passive-aggressive view of the world.

But this also means that NINEs can achieve a great deal if they manage to concentrate their energy. Because they never fire straight at the target. As persons they're nice and peaceable, but pay attention to both their wings, EIGHT and ONE. Each has an acute sense of value and a great deal of emotion. And so it can sometimes happen in the middle of an aimless conversation that NINEs will suddenly say something that contains a tremendous truth and is profoundly convincing. And in this way, because they're so nice and trustworthy, and because you drop your defenses when you talk with them, NINEs can out of nowhere strike deep into your heart.

The man who was my host just now at the U.S. army base is a NINE. Last week he went to his commandant and quite calmly explained to him that the U.S. military is corrupt, and so he wanted to quit and return home. He told me, "I was very surprised that I talked that way." His commandant didn't believe his ears. This is the "decisive action" of a NINE.

NINEs are uncomplicated. Their intentions are quite clear and transparent. All of a sudden they reach a point where everything is crystal clear to them.

Then they make a decision that they'll stick to, whatever it costs. You can take the donkey as the symbolic animal of NINEs. Once they've rammed their hind legs into the ground, they stay right where they are and can't be budged an inch. The rule of thumb here is: What you see with a NINE is what you get. There are no hidden intentions, which is another reason why NINEs are so beloved. We know that they're showing us their true faces — even if there isn't a lot of energy there. But if you can help them to concentrate that energy, they will, as a rule, do one or two things in their life really well. And God probably expects no more than that from any one of us.

Empirical Studies of the Enneagram: Foundations and Comparisons

Markus Becker

1. THE HISTORY OF THE ENNEAGRAM

The Oral Tradition

"One of the main problems with introducing the Enneagram is that its exact origins are lost to history. No one really knows precisely who discovered it or where it came from."[1] Riso places this remark at the head of his extensive research and reflections on the origin and history of this typology, and it should serve as a warning against getting carried away by speculation.

Attempts have been made to date the beginnings of the Enneagram as far back as the 5th or 4th millennia B.C. in Mesopotamia, but this can be classified as mythmaking. More down-to-earth proposals trace the origin of the Enneagram to some Sufi brotherhoods, members of a mystical sect of Islam. It remains unclear, however, whether the Enneagram existed then in something like its present form or was instead an abstract model, resulting from the numerological speculations of Arab mathematicians. Its formal structure does at any rate point to a non-European source for this system.

Riso maintains that,"The credit for transmitting the Enneagram goes to George Ivanovich Gurdjieff (ca. 1874–1949), an adventurer, spiritual teacher, and seeker of what might be called practical secret knowledge of human nature."[2] Still, the source of his teaching remains as enigmatic as the man's life story.

In this context, though, we find once more an indication of the system's Arab roots: "The central symbol of the Gurdjieff work, the enneagram, is certainly of Sufi origin."[3] Actually the only undoubted thing here is that Gurdjieff concealed the origins of his knowledge, and his disciples filled in this lacuna.

All that we know for certain is that Gurdjieff taught a system that is quite similar, *formally speaking,* to the Enneagram. For his point of departure he obviously took certain metaphysical speculations, in which a connection between cosmic laws (the Law of Three and the Law of Seven) was represented in a diagram that occupied a central position in Gurdjieff's teaching: the Enneagram. On the other hand, it wasn't really used as a personality model, but as a universal symbol. "The enneagram can be used in the study of all processes, since it must be present in all sequences of events. The days of the week can be laid around the circle, with Monday at one and Sunday at point nine."[4]

Here too points 3, 6, and 9 are considered central, along with the idea that a person reacts like a *machine* and is determined by three *function centers*, "the thought, feeling, and movement centers."[5]

These elements are quite similar to the Enneagram in its present form, but they undergo further development in Gurdjieff, and he modified them to suit his purposes.

In summary, then, some formal features of a rudimentary or original "Enneagram" were familiar to the Gurdjieff circle. Likewise the methods applied and the principles, such as the notion of man as a machine, the exercise of self-scrutiny,[6] and several others are strongly reminiscent of the contents and terminology of the Enneagram as we have it now. But none of this can establish the probability of a direct derivation.

Another line of tradition is more important for the present form of the Enneagram. It goes back to Oscar Ichazo, the director of the Arica Institute in Chile. But, like Gurdjieff, Ichazo conceals the origin of the typology with a veil of mystery. He supposedly got to know the system while working at the University of La Paz, from a man whose name was never revealed.[7]

Ichazo undertook a busy round of travel, studied esoteric lore and eastern religions, and combined these experiences with psychological traditions in the Enneagram to produce a comprehensive model of personality. We can recognize in this system, both in its form and content, a clear precursor of the recently published versions of the Enneagram.

In the early 1970s a group of Americans learned the Enneagram from Ichazo and spread it across the country through the newly founded Arica Institutes in New York, Los Angeles, and San Francisco.[8] An important link in this chain of tradition was Claudio Naranjo, a Chilean psychiatrist who worked at the Esalen Institute in California developing new forms of therapy and who became well known for his research on the possibilities of a drug-supported short-term psychotherapy. Naranjo founded small groups everywhere in the country, and thanks to him the Enneagram also made its way, through the mediation of Rev. Robert Ochs, into Jesuit circles.

The Jesuits were the most active in continuing the tradition of the Enneagram by handing it down and using it in pastoral care, counselling, and the Spiritual Exercises. The reason why its beginnings and its paths of transmission lie deep in the darkness of the past derives from the nature of the Enneagram itself, which until very recently was passed on orally as "secret knowledge."

The Written Tradition

The written reports, investigations, and descriptions of the Enneagram can in each case be traced back to one of the three lines of tradition: Gurdjieff, Ichazo, or the Jesuits.

J. G. Bennett's *The Enneagram* (1914) (see the revised edition, entitled *Enneagram Studies*[9]) is the first demonstrable, explicit publication on the Enneagram. It also gave rise to extensive and far-reaching queries about the early history of the Enneagram.

In 1978 *The Enneagram of the Man of Unity* was published. The author was I.B. Popoff, a woman who, like Bennett, belonged to the circle of Gurdjieff's disciples and who adopted his reading of the Enneagram.

Charles Tart's *Transpersonal Psychologies* (1975) contains both a chapter on Gurdjieff's work with individual elements of the Enneagram, as well as remarks on the work done at the Arica Institute, that is, the Ichazo tradition. This tradition, contrary to that of Gurdjieff and his disciples, transformed the Enneagram into a psychologically oriented system. Ultimately Jaxon-Bear invokes this tradition too in *Die neun Zahlen des Lebens* (The Nine Numbers of Life).

The Enneagram: A Journey of Self-Discovery (1984) reflects Jesuit tradition and a Christian understanding of the self. It was written by a group of religious: M. Beesing, R. J. Nogosek, and P. H. O'Leary, S.J.

Yet another writer who draws upon this tradition is Richard Riso, who is an ex-Jesuit. In *Personality Types: Using the Enneagram for Self-Discovery* (1987) he presents sketch-like notes on the "Jesuit material,"[10] out of which he develops his consistently psychological approach to the Enneagram.

In *Emotions and the Enneagram* (1990) Margaret Frings Keyes refers to the Jesuit, Robert Ochs, as part of her investigation of Enneagram typology in the light of Jungian psychology. The same author has also written an amusing book called *The Enneagram Cats of Muir Beach* (1990), in which she presents the nine personality types in allegorical stories about nine cats and their character.

In a roundabout fashion Richard Rohr and Andreas Ebert likewise draw upon the same source in their *Discovering the Enneagram: An Ancient Tool for a New Spiritual Journey* (1990). Rohr, a Franciscan priest, and Ebert, a Lutheran minister, work out a Christian-ecumenical perspective in which the Enneagram is understood as an instrument designed to help people on the way to mental and spiritual growth.

In the summer of 1991 I concluded an empirical study in which I tried to elaborate and scrutinize the *psychological* content of the Enneagram. My results were then correlated with the findings of modern psychology of personality. The test at the end of this book is one such result.

To sum up, we can say that each of the authors or teachers mentioned has developed a particular approach to the Enneagram and rounded it out in his or her own way. Gurdjieff's interest was of an esoteric and spiritual sort, while Ichazo and Naranjo tried to work out more therapeutic and psychiatric components. All subsequent presentations of the Enneagram have been in one form or another a combination of these two basic tendencies.

2. THE TRIADS

Three Authors, Three Models

All three descriptions of the Enneagram (by Riso, Jaxon-Bear, and Rohr/Ebert) share a common point of departure: three "basic types," from which they derive the nine previously mentioned personality types. But here too the individual authors use very different terms, which are sometimes imprecise and even confusing. Hence the three systems and their terminology will be sketched out separately.

According to Riso there are triads of *feeling, doing,* and *relating,* each of which comprises three types. "In each Triad, one of the types overdevelops the characteristic faculty of the Triad, another type underdevelops the faculty, and the third is most out of touch with the faculty."[11] Some initial confusion arises from the fact that each of the *primary personality types* — namely the THREE, the SIX, and the ONE — either lacks the qualities of one of its triads or has them in the least developed state.

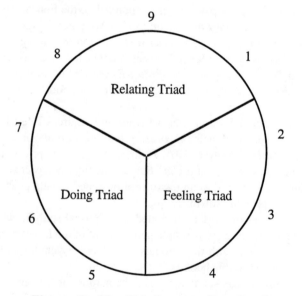

Figure 1: The Triads according to Riso

Thus Riso provides the following characterization of the nine types.

In the "relating" triad the capacity for relationships, immediate contact, orientation to reality and confrontation with the world are:

> *overdeveloped* in EIGHTs,
> *lost* in NINEs,
> *underdeveloped/ambivalent* in ONEs.

In the "feeling" triad the life of feeling, in the sense of immediate access to one's own emotional reality, is:

> *overdeveloped* in TWOs,
> *lost* in THREES,
> *underdeveloped/ambivalent* in FOURs.

In the "doing" triad the capacity to act, understood as direct translation of inner impulses into deeds is:

> *overdeveloped* in SEVENs,
> *lost* in SIXes,
> *underdeveloped/ambivalent* in FIVEs.

"All three faculties operate in an ever changing balance to produce our personality."[12] But everybody has a *basic tendency* that he or she follows and that determines his or her possibilities and limitations.

Jaxon-Bear calls the three main groups the *anger, image*, and *fear* points, but he too derives from them the nine individual types. "There is in each case a central point and two variations of it, the inner and outer version."[13]

In the anger triad rage and aggression are the central theme, but they are experienced and processed differently:

> *externally* in EIGHTs,
> *not at all* in NINEs,
> *internally* in ONEs.

In the image triad status, the role society demands that people play, is of crucial importance. This leads to insecurity about one's identity. Each type experiences his or her sense of self differently:

> TWOs *externally*,
> THREEs *not at all*,
> FOURs *internally*.

In the fear triad, how to deal with fear and anxiety is the central problem, which each type localizes differently:

> SEVENs *externally*,
> SIXes *not at all*,
> FIVEs *internally*.

This situation is manifested in one of the "three bodies" — physical, emotional, or mental — which each person, depending upon his or her type, makes excessive use of.

A similar distribution is a basic part of the third system.

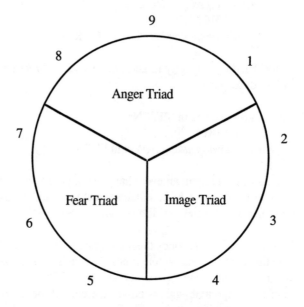

Figure 2: The Triads according to Jaxon-Bear

Rohr and Ebert likewise describe three centers, on whose *energy* each of the nine types primarily lives. These are the *head*, *heart*, and *gut*. "The Enneagram presupposes that every person is dominated by one of three natural impulses. Thus for each of the nine types there are three subtypes."[14] And then each particular life situation helps determine which aspect of their own personality the various types live out.

Jaxon-Bear likewise starts out from the assumption that every person is familiar, in one way or another, with all these problems, but that once placed in a stressful situation, he or she will most of the time act impulsively, prompted by his or her fixation.

In Rohr and Ebert this triadic arrangement has, we should note, a *double function*: On the one hand it gathers the nine personality types into three groups, while on the other it differentiates each of the types into three *subtypes*: self-preserving, social, and sexual.

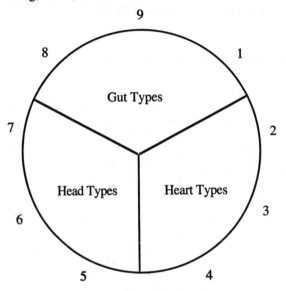

Figure 3: The Triads according to Rohr and Ebert.

The *head area* roughly matches the doing/fear–triad, the *heart region* resembles the feeling/image–triad, and the *gut region* more or less corresponds to the relating/anger–triad.

Here too, as in the systems of Jaxon-Bear and Riso, we can discover a certain patterned structure: The gut types live on an elementary physical energy, a "sexual" power that invades alien regions, conquers, gets things going, and creatively changes situations, but that is often perceived by others as hostile. This energy is at work *excessively* in EIGHTs, *not at all* in NINEs, and *ambivalently* in ONEs.

The heart types are shaped by a social energy that is directed at others and is interested in the maintenance of community and the flow of communication. This energy is at work *excessively* in TWOs, *not at all* in THREEs, and *ambivalently* in FOURs.

For the head types self-preserving energy has pride of place. They tend to protect themselves and to withdraw in anxiety. This energy is at work *excessively* in FIVEs, *not at all* in SEVENs, and *ambivalently* in SIXes.

This schematic summary was put together after our authors' work appeared, but it closely adheres to their explanations. In surveying it one is struck by the fact that for the head region the actual central point is SEVEN, because in it — as with NINE and THREE in their triads — the corresponding energy is not at work. But this sharply contrasts with the theory of the Enneagram, which arranges the nine types around the Enneagram-circle in a strictly prescribed order, and which considers NINE, THREE, and SIX the central points.

The following terms are constitutive for our authors' triads:

	Jaxon-Bear	**Riso**	**Rohr/Ebert**
Type 8, 9, 1	Anger	Relating	Gut/Sexual
Type 2, 3, 4	Image	Feeling	Heart/Social
Type 5, 6, 7	Fear	Doing	Head/Self-preserving

The individual types are all described in the triads under this specific *aspect*, either because it is their main problem (Jaxon-Bear), or because it best characterizes their behavior (Riso) or their primary energy (Rohr and Ebert).

The Relationship–Triad: Types EIGHT, NINE, and ONE

What the Enneagram calls "relationship" and describes as crucial for this triad does not mean the "communicative process." It refers instead to the way that the three types (EIGHT, NINE, ONE) generally relate to their environment, how they as persons enter into relationships with it: "Eights by dominating it, Nines by finding union with it, and Ones by striving to perfect it."[15]

Type EIGHT confronts the world *directly* by dominating it. Type NINE *does not* confront the world, but identifies and unites with it. Type ONE confronts the world *indirectly* by following an abstraction (ideal) and trying to realize it. That creates the specific problem vexing this triad: anger and the concrete way that it deals with its rage and aggression.

With NINEs aggression seems to be missing. It becomes visible only when the repressed rage explosively vents itself. NINEs prefer to direct their rage against themselves, or "they distance themselves from the body — a strategy by which they try to avoid the feeling of anger."[16]

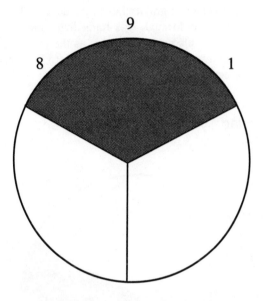

Figure 4: The Relationship-Triad

They perceive even the normal ability to assert themselves as aggressive. Fighting for something or taking something in the teeth of resistance from others doesn't fit their self-image as loving and satisfied people.

EIGHTs are altogether different. They often report that even back in childhood they were "bad" boys or "fresh" girls, confronting the world belligerently, wildly, decisively. In the ghetto the refrain of Michael Jackson's song, "I'm bad," is tantamount to "I'm good," because strength, self-assertion, and ruthless determination are vital attributes there. This says something essential about the basic attitude of EIGHTs.

With ONEs, on the other hand, the approach to aggression is split. "[They] get furious and then blame themselves. They don't know how to handle anger appropriately."[17] They also clearly sense their own aggression, but at the same time think they have to justify it. This can be expressed in a rigorous moralizing, and harden into a general attitude of righteousness and dogmatism that mercilessly enforces their principles. Here their latent aggressiveness raises its ugly head.

The great fear this type has of losing control is connected with the conflict between sensing anger on the one hand and being unable to release it on the other. But this is precisely how their anger turns into their defining force. It oozes from their every pore, so to speak, and from their sarcastic remarks anyone can sense how fed up they are. The repressed anger makes ONEs hyper-critical — but self-critical too.

The *gut people,* as Rohr and Ebert call the types of this triad, are character-ized as follows: "Their center of gravity lies in the underbelly, where the 'raw material' of our existence is located. It is immediate, spontaneous, felt, and intuitive. (In this sense we also speak of them as the group of *sexual types.* They don't filter reality through the brain or heart first.)"[18] Hence they have as little access to introspection as they do to their fear.

The Feeling-Triad Types: TWO, THREE, and FOUR

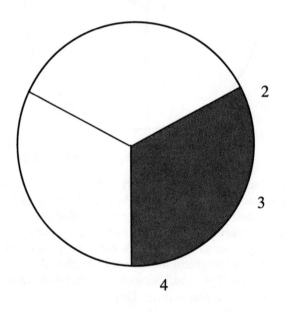

Figure 5: The Feeling-Triad

"These three personality types have common assets and liabilities which involve their *feelings.* When these types are healthy, their feelings are the focus of what is admirable about their personalities, enabling them to become highly valued for their interpersonal qualities."[19]

They are fundamentally differentiated from one another by the way they live with their *inner terrain,* their feelings, their moods, and emotional energies: TWOs experience their world directly by expressing their feelings in relation-ships. THREEs have largely lost access to the world of their feelings. FOURs often confront their emotions *indirectly* by expressing them *artistically.* But their attitude toward the irrational sides of their personality is also ambivalent, because the irrational makes them particularly insecure.

This is the source of the specific problem spots in this triad. For individuals who belong to it have learned from basic experience — or deep feeling — that they cannot be loved for their own sake. This leads them to develop a broad spectrum of strategies to earn the love of their fellows or, somehow or other, to handle their own shortcomings. "These people have given up their real nature so as to match the image that society seems to demand of them. Often they are the most beautiful people in the Enneagram: They have created themselves in the image (as they have learned) that we love." [20]

This is why this triad is also called the Image-Triad, and its central problem is identity. With THREEs, the central *image* point, contact with their own feelings has largely been lost, because they aim all their energy at building up their social position, their *image*. Their fear of deeper emotions results from a mistrust of their own person and from the conviction that they will be lovable only if they behave in accordance with others' expectations, if they achieve or produce something. All their feelings of self-worth, the justification of their existence, derives from incessant productivity. For this reason they're always busy tinkering, repairing, producing. They are real workaholics, and work is the key to their lives.

They are ready to sacrifice a large part of their nature, their inner identity, to the image of themselves that they impart to the world around them, and for which they want to be loved.

TWOs behave quite differently. Their preferred field of operations is the home, relationships, their circle of friends, in short wherever they can express their sensitivity and solicitude. "TWOs would like to be loved by you, because they take such good care of you."[21]

This type tries to make up for their lack of self-worth by engaging their positive feelings, making themselves indispensable to *others*, taking on the role of *helper* and thus guaranteeing themselves the attention that they need so badly because of their inner deficiencies.

FOURs are in immediate contact with their feelings, but their profound lack of a sense of personal *worth* makes them insecure about their social role and relationships. They want to be *genuine*, they want to experience their own deep emotions, and in the process they plunge themselves — but still more those around them — into a tunnel where the winds blow alternately hot and cold.

This serves to program disappointments directly into the system, which in turn worsens the problems of self-worth and makes it still more difficult to build up an image, a socially acceptable identity.

These three types are labelled heart people. For them the crucial thing is to be in touch with their subjective feelings. They focus on how to shape their interpersonal relationships, even if at first blush, with THREEs for example, it might not look that way. They are, for the most part, interested, intent on intimacy with, and understanding or recognition from, their fellows; hence they live primarily on *social* energy. "Outwardly they strike people as self-confident, gay, and harmonious, but inwardly they often feel themselves empty, incompetent, sad, and ashamed."[22] The way they deal with tension between *inside* and *outside*, between the urgings of their own emotions and the expectations of those around them, determines how they solve the problem of identity.

The Doing-Triad: Types FIVE, SIX, and SEVEN

The types in this triad can be distinguished by their motivation and capacity for action, their ability to translate impulses and ideas directly into deeds. One thing they have in common is that they all live "in a strong polarity between thinking and acting."[23]

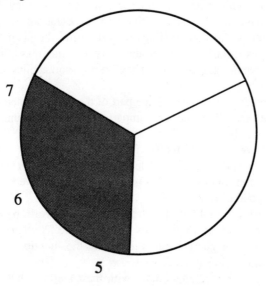

Figure 6: The Doing-Triad

FIVEs like to do abstract analyses of the world around them. In other words they prefer *thinking* to *doing*, and they are often out of touch with the practical side of life. Their ability to translate their own impulses into action is *under*developed.

SIXes "have the weakest connection to the ability to make decisions and to act on their own, without appealing to someone else, especially a figure of authority, in the form of a person, an institution, or a belief system."[24] In extreme cases they can lose the capacity to act autonomously.

SEVENs are primarily oriented to external reality, whose impulses they need for their own stimulation. In their hyperactivity they keep looking for new stimuli, so that their activity appears overdeveloped.

This is the source of the problem spots specific to this triad: The determining motive for these people is fear. "With the fear points their fixation crystalizes in the mental body. Their intelligence is used here to protect themselves from a threatening world."[25] In order to escape real or imagined dangers they develop various strategies so as not to be exposed to this fear.

SIXes try above all to find security by picturing the future, reflecting back and forth on its possibilities, and to this end carrying on endless conversations with themselves. Or they orient themselves to the outside world, seek protection and support from authorities and institutions, in the "bosom of the family" or in unshakable dogmatic convictions.

SIXes hide behind religious principles and general guidelines, so that they don't have to confront their primitive instincts, above all their animal impulses. But by doing so they risk losing immediate contact with this crucial side of life. The consequences of this approach are doubts and hesitant behavior. The fear of making their own decisions and then translating them into action ultimately becomes greater and greater, thanks to this external orientation.

FIVEs protect themselves from fear by gathering knowledge and information and *withdrawing* into their intellectual world. There they feel secure, because *thinking* makes it easier to reduce all difficulties to manageable proportions, and this gives FIVEs the reassuring sense of being in control. They love to observe their environment from a safe vantage point, and they are "among the most sensitive persons in the Enneagram. Their problem lies in the fact that they are short of external defense mechanisms. They retreat into a rich internal dream life, leaving behind to the world an almost invisible phantasm. Their skin is frequently prone to sunburn and rashes, which is metaphorically suggestive of their tender sensibility, which has to be protected from a harsh world."[26] But by retreating they are inevitably rendered incapable of having more than a handful of positive experiences of how problems can also be mastered by *action*. This leads to more fear and insecurity.

SEVENs avoid fear through activity. Pain and rising unrest are repressed by a constant supply of fascinating ideas, charming impressions, and interesting novelties. These people deal with fear by simply being optimistic, preferring to face a promising future rather than a problematic present, and always believing in the bright side of life. But any serious confrontation with fear is vigorously avoided.

These three types are labeled head-people, and their energies are directed toward *self-preservation*. This means that they have a tendency to retreat, right from the start, in every new or threatening situation, so they can *contemplate* the matter in tranquillity, soberly and objectively. All information first has to be thoroughly scrutinized "in their heads," and once everything is "in *order*," they may feel secure enough to act. Those around them often see them as convincing, clever, and self-assured, but this is often just a protective device, because deep down they feel confused, uncertain, and isolated.

Their passionate need for independence derives from fear of being too greatly and too directly involved in the world. Because that's where the center of their vital energies is, these people panic at the prospect of somehow or other "losing their head."

Critique

Merely by reviewing the descriptions of the Enneagram we can see that it was not developed systematically, and that any sharp demarcation between the types or even the triads can be made only with difficulty. At this point supporters of the Enneagram often bring in the concept of its *"dynamics."* The Enneagram, they say, is alive, it's as if we were speaking of a living being. This certainly does justice to the fact that a personality model has to be *dynamic* if it is to describe people in their complexity, multi-layeredness, and dynamically inter-related characteristics as comprehensively as possible.

But "dynamics" is all too often invoked when what we really need is clarity and critical analysis. Otherwise misunderstandings and unsupported claims will get unscrupulously spread around.

It does the authors credit when they relativize their own observations. "These examples correspond to the author's subjective estimate and make no claim to be authoritative."[27] Of course, this is a commonplace that holds for any psychological or philosophical model. But the use of unclear terms is irritating, because it confuses readers trying to familiarize themselves with the thought world of the Enneagram.[28]

Thus, while the anger, image, and fear triads match well the gut, heart, and head triads, the relating, feeling, and doing triads do not always fit into this system so well. For example, Jaxon-Bear writes of types TWO, THREE, and FOUR: "This group is also called the group of *relationships*"[29] — but Riso says that EIGHT, NINE, and ONE belong to the relating triad.

Above all it's not clear *why* the triads are divided up along the lines of precisely these criteria. We could just as well call the feeling triad the relating triad, because the capacity for relationships is overdeveloped in TWOs, lost in THREEs, and underdeveloped in FOURs. Similarly, in descriptions of the individual TWOs, THREEs, and FOURs we are dealing with "relationships" far more than in the case of EIGHTs, NINEs, and ONEs, the actual relationship triad. This shows that these terms are partially interchangeable, especially in Riso's terminology.

But Jaxon-Bear's system limps in a few places. He considers THREE, SIX, and NINE the central points, although paradoxically they are the *least* representative of the qualities in their triad. This makes sense only in the anger triad.

Anger triad: NINEs do not act out their aggression (EIGHTs do so externally, ONEs internally/ambivalently).

Image triad: THREEs go to extremes in cultivating their image (TWOs do so in an externally-oriented, FOURs in an internally-oriented, ambivalent fashion).

Fear triad: SIXes deal ambivalently (phobically-contraphobically) with fear, they are in any event "not afraid." (FIVEs flee inwardly, SEVENs outwardly.)

By their very terminology Rohr and Ebert dispense with a strictly systematic approach. *Head, heart,* and *gut* are terms that can claim different jurisdictions. But here too tensions emerge: According to the Enneagram theory types THREE, SIX, and NINE are supposed to be "central," that is, they have *not* developed the key theme of their triad or they don't act it out. This is true in two cases: In the gut region NINEs do not act out their sexual, hostile energies. In the heart region THREEs do not act out their social, other-oriented energies. But in the head region SIXes *do* act out their self-preserving, "retreating" energies. According to the description of the types, SEVENs are much more likely not to develop or act out such energies. Theoretically this shouldn't be so — one almost gets the impression that two adjacent types on the circle have been inadvertently switched.

3. TYPOLOGIES

Introduction

The Enneagram speaks of nine personality *types*, thereby falling back upon the concept of "typology" to construct its model. For this reason it makes sense to begin with a brief historical retrospective of some other typologies. These will then be integrated into the context of present-day psychology. Against this background their form and content can be discussed and a clear picture sketched of what "type" means in the first place.

History

People have always tried to describe, to classify, and whenever possible to explain the variety of individual differences in human beings. "Typologies" are an early expression of this attempt and can be found as far back, for example, as ancient Greece. Thus in his medical writings Hippocrates (ca. 460–377 B.C.) distinguishes among four human characters according to the predominance of one of the four bodily "humors" (blood, phlegm, yellow and black gall) and calls them *sanguinary, phlegmatic, choleric,* and *melancholic.*[30] Each type is assigned certain qualities, which then characterize the four temperaments, so that one can speak of light-blooded sanguinary types, heavy-blooded melancholic types, warm-blooded choleric types, and cold-blooded phlegmatic types.

Early on an attempt was made to coordinate different systems and categories, such as the four temperaments of Hippocrates with the four elements of *earth, water, fire,* and *air:*

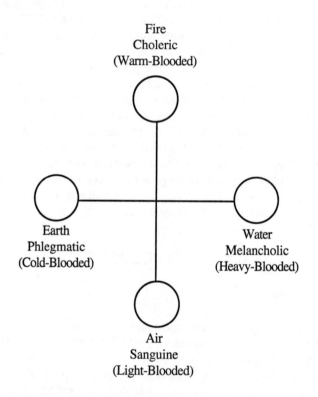

Fire
Choleric
(Warm-Blooded)

Earth
Phlegmatic
(Cold-Blooded)

Water
Melancholic
(Heavy-Blooded)

Air
Sanguine
(Light-Blooded)

Figure 7: The Four Elements according to Hippocrates[31]

Another well-known, but much more recent, typology is the *constitution typology* proposed by the German psychiatrist Ernst Kretschmer (1888–1964). It can "be characterized as a system of total typology, which embraces every area of the personality and physical appearance."[32] This is in contrast to a *partial typology,* which attempts to describe only individual aspects of the person. (Thus a driver who engages the clutch with jolts and jounces, and then lets the motor stall, may be a "typical" beginner in the domain of cars, but he might at the same time be highly competent, a "typical ace" in some other domain.)

Kretschmer takes descriptions of body structure as his point of departure, and distinguishes between *leptosomatic (asthenic), athletic,* and *pyknic* types. But the most interesting feature is the connection that Kretschmer makes been different body types and the psychiatric diagnosis of his patients. He observed that, "With more than random frequency pyknic types suffer from manic-depressive psychosis, while leptosomes are more prone to schizophrenia. Athletic types, the third category, are said to present the phenotype of epilepsy."[33]

The crucial point, therefore, is that here types are not simply *described*, but the fact of a person's belonging to a type enables us to predict the likelihood of his or her getting certain diseases.

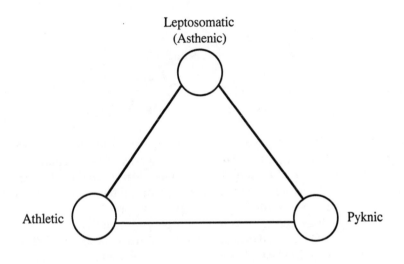

Figure 8: Kretschmer's Typology

Yet another approach was taken by C. G. Jung (1875–1961), who does not attach his typology to any physical phenotypes, but to the basic functions of the psyche. Among these he enumerates *thinking* and *intuiting,* or *feeling* and *perceiving,* along with a tendency to react in a specific way.

Jung, therefore, characterizes types by two factors: first, when one function is superimposed on and dominates its opposite, for example when *thought* is more sharply defined than *intuition,* or *feeling* is more pronounced than *perception.* On the other hand, types arise from the predominant manner in which each individual tends to react to inner or outer situations. For Jung, in other words, the types are not polar extremes, but are determined by the predominance of one or another function.

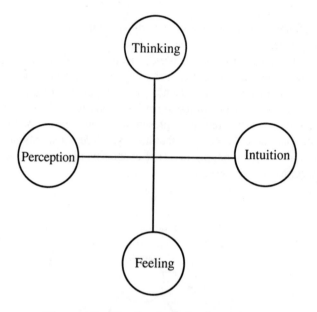

Figure 9: C. G. Jung's Typology

To a certain extent some *religious* descriptions of human beings are also typologies. For instance, the Old Testament speaks of the "godless" or "the wicked" and "the just." Each of these is a type characterized by quite specific behavior patterns, attitudes, and motives. Frequently they are even applied as stereotypes, lumping together whole groups or nations.

This typology generally considers a person's religious stance the all-determining factor. Beyond explaining events, it tries to make *predictions*, as in Psalm 1, "The LORD watches over the way of the righteous, but the way of the wicked is doomed."[34]

Figure 10: Example of a Religious Typology

There are also typologies oriented toward the Humanities. One such approach, developed by E. Spranger (1882–1974), from the school of Wilhelm Dilthey, attempts to "understand" mental phenomena present in, say, philosophy, psychology, education, history, and literature. In short it tries to grasp what constitutes "culture." "Spranger coordinates interest types with these subsections of culture. Individual aspects of culture seemed to be evaluated differently by different individuals, and Spranger's typology results from this subjective evaluation of particular sections: Spranger distinguishes six ideal types of personality: the aesthetic person (art), the theoretical person (science), the religious person (religion), the social person, the power person (politics), the economic person (economy)."[35]

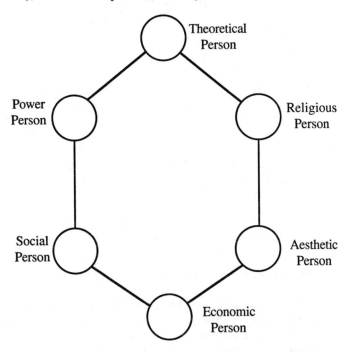

Figure 11: Spranger's Typology

The list of typologies could be continued indefinitely, because every new way of seeing the world creates new and different descriptive categories. If one views people primarily from the physical standpoint, typologies like Hippocrates' seem persuasive. If one deals with psychiatric phenomena, a typology such as Kraepelin's will be found helpful. If one takes psychic dynamics and the events of the unconscious to be the essential determinants of human personality, a depth-psychological typology such as Jung's may be convincing.

Religious persons keep harking back to biblical or other old typologies, and anyone studying human beings as "cultural creatures" will be able to work well with Spranger's system. The decisive issue for each typology is both the interest that drives it as well as its "background," and, not least of all, the approach, in other words its method of dealing with its material.

The same holds for the Enneagram. The history of this nine-point typology (see above) shows all too clearly that it contains features of an explanation and description of the world that differ sharply from one another, depending on which tradition lays claim to it.

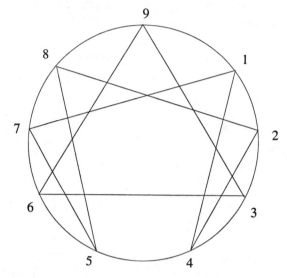

Figure 12: The Typology of the Enneagram

The only thing that actually remains the same over the course of time are certain formal elements — such as the nine points arranged around a circle and interconnected in a certain way. In esoteric groups the Enneagram is made into a typology of the unenlightened person. Christian tradition recognizes in this pattern the nine "root sins" of human beings, the expression of their alienation from themselves and God. Finally, psychology turns it into a typology of personality, which it tries to link up with other scientific findings. The only peculiar thing about this is that the Enneagram seems to have served as a structural element for the typologies of such varied disciplines and over such a long period of time.

The Concept and Formal Elements of Typology

The term "type" is used in the worlds of both everyday conversation and science. It is defined as "in general either a group of individuals characterized by a specific complex of features" or "a person who has all the features of his or her group in a particularly pronounced fashion."[36]

This double use in daily life and scientific discourse lends this term several qualities that make it problematic. Nevertheless down through history, as we have seen, people keep returning to it when they want to describe human personality. One of the strengths of typology seems to be the way it grasps precisely those aspects of human beings that to the psychological layperson seem to make up the "essence" of personality. This usually means factors concerning temperament and motivation, the emotional and social components of behavior — in any event less the "objective," "measurable" data than the *exact way* all this happens.

Turning to the dictionary for help, typo-logy, in its original Greek etymology, means talk about the "visible replica," "form," or "model." The reference here is to the image of a person stamped on a coin or to a model worked on in the course of technical production.

So in this sense typologies are to some extent subjective presentations that attend to (human) reality in a largely simplifying fashion. Hence the derivation of the term from the context of minting coins is interesting because this represents a transition from barter to a monetary system, that is, a form of economic abstraction, a cultural achievement. Like a money economy, typologies demand the capacity for abstraction. One disregards immediate impressions and circumstances, and puts them to use for the benefit of an abstract order.

Apart from this both money economies and typologies have to be constantly examined with regard to their value, in other words their truth and reality content, in brief their "validity."

A further assumption made by typologies is that human behavior and attitudes, above and beyond all the different situations, are relatively consistent. Types cannot be described without a temporally and spatially stable construct.

Scientifically speaking, typologies come under the heading of "differential psychology," which attempts to systematize individual differences, describing them and also, where possible, explaining how they came about. But this is exactly what prescientific typologies were aiming at: to bring order to the bewildering variety of modes in which human differences appear and express themselves by summarizing them in simple and readily graspable categories.

The simplest model imaginable is, of course, the *dyad*, as in the already mentioned example of the "godless" and the "righteous." One of the most frequently used schemes in the modern psychology of personality is the contrasting pair of "extroverts" and "introverts." But one also often encounters *triad*-typologies such as Kretschmer's leptosomatic, pyknic, and athletic types, or the triad proposed by Karen Horney, a friend of Freud. She initially postulated four modes of neurotic self- defense: "gaining affection, being submissive, attaining power, and withdrawing." But in her later publications this was reduced to three types, the compliant, the aggressive, and the detached, which shows that all these classifications are relative and, to a certain degree, arbitrary.[37]

The most widespread taxonomies are the *four-part* schemes. Thus in many important typologies we find the four temperaments (Hippocrates), four psychic functions (Jung), four anxiety characters (Riemann), and so forth.

If the number of categories or types in a given model goes higher, there is a danger that the system will become unwieldy. It will no longer be possible to take it in at a glance, and this runs contrary to the original intention of such schemes, namely to simplify the confusing multiplicity of phenomena. Spranger's six "life forms" or "basic interests" suffer from this defect, and one is intuitively tempted to group certain categories together, so as once again to reduce the system to a handy, easily remembered size.

From this standpoint, the Enneagram is an unusually complex typology, whose use requires a long initiation period and a lot of practice. Why shouldn't there be, for example, five temperaments? Or why does the system speak of just two, instead of three, types of reaction? The closer one looks at a simple typology, the more obvious its imprecision becomes. Thus it has proved extremely difficult to come up with empirical proof of certain connections, such as the one between bodily features and characteristic personal qualities.

One very seldom finds "pure" types, and the features postulated as defining the type are often only partly present or not in the expected configuration. At the same time we are apparently incapable of perceiving or describing such complex units as the system we call "man" without models that simplify the data. At this point logical-rational thinking presses against its limits. "Hence types are often 'scanned,' that is, intuitively grasped, with an accompanying analytical check by means of individual indicators."[38]

This method or form of knowledge, which scientists often later systematize and make more explicit, is called *phenomenology*. "It is the method of thought chosen by many philosophers, among others the existentialists, but by many psychologists as well. Phenomenology is the intuitive art of scanning the essence of things in their outer manifestations. In practicing it one must abstract from the external form or phenomenon, applying as it were a series of filters, in order to grasp the essential core."[39]

All this shows that the Enneagram, like other such models, operates in a dialectical tension between the two poles of intuition and empirical data. So even if the content of typologies defies a purely rational approach, it makes sense to define more precisely at least a few of their formal elements.

Within the context of the psychology of personality typology can be defined as a special variety of *dimensional* approaches. These attempt to classify the different kinds of persons within a grid of features, whereas typologies aim to attach the individual differences to characteristic, sharply defined, and hence "typical" personalities. These types form the cornerstones of the system into which one tries to fit individuals as snugly as possible.

The two methods operate differently, as we can see from the way they "distribute" the individuals in their specific mode of "graphing" features. Unlike the dimensional approach, typology proceeds on the basis of extreme distributions, that is, improbably high accumulations at both ends of the spectrum of characteristics. The following illustrations should make this clear:

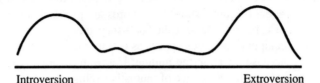

Introversion   Extroversion

Figure 13: Typological Mode of Distribution

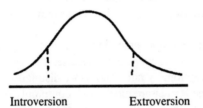

Introversion   Extroversion

Figure 14: Dimensional Mode of Distribution

Typologies and Modern Methods of Personality Research

"People often regret that psychology is such a flimsy science, indeed that it isn't a science at all in the sense of the natural sciences. This is manifested in the fact that psychological terms and situations are formulated in everyday language. Psychological theories allow for contradictory statements, and often one can't actually say whether two psychological statements are reconcilable or contradictory. This lack of firmness and tightness in psychological theories — and especially in theories of personality — has various causes. One reason for it is the failure to 'operationalize' constructs and the way psychologists jump too quickly to abstractions too high up in the air. Behaviorism tries to avoid this mistake — but in so doing Skinner (1954) has evidently acquired the reputation of being primitive. In contrast psychoanalysis is imposing, thanks to its highly concentrated speculative hypotheses, but it lacks empirical content, and it stagnates as it goes on developing more and more theories.[40]

For the reasons cited above the psychology of personality has witnessed a transformation that has even left its mark on the typologies. Moving away from the traditionally rather *qualitative* approach of early systems, psychologists nowadays are trying harder to use a *quantitative* typology to avoid the difficulties that inevitably crop up. Individual differences are ascertained numerically, with the help of tests, and "objectified."

Strictly speaking, the theory of a bimodal distribution (Figure 13) cannot be maintained because statistical studies offer solid proof that most personality features are unimodal (Figure 14), in other words are grouped along a continuum of "normal distribution," the so-called bell-shaped curve.

From this standpoint the types appear as extreme manifestations of a distribution that otherwise peaks in the middle. Hence in practice typologies do not start out by positing the existence of mutually exclusive categories. Instead they assume that every personality is to some extent a mixture, even when the fundamental framework is based on polar opposites (for example, extroversion/introversion). There can sometimes be vacillations between the two poles, but in this case one of the two extremes dominates and so is "typical" for the individual in question.

But if we want to grasp a person intuitively, it seems to be easier to orient ourselves to the extreme forms of any characteristic — even if in reality such "pure" forms are exceptionally rare. And so we distinguish between "real types" and "ideal types." The former are much more commonly found, but they display the features ascribed to them only in a more or less distinctive form, so that we constantly have to make adjustments where they deviate from the description of the ideal form. Ideal forms, by contrast, are abstractions that present a clear-cut model of personality, but in real life they apply to most individuals only when modified.

This is the crucial problem for any model of personality that aims to be universally descriptive or explanatory, but particularly for typologies. For the sake of a clear classification one puts up with inaccuracies, because when we study persons thoroughly, we inevitably find that the closer we look at the individual case, the more nuances we have to include in the description.

Thus on the one hand there is a danger of sacrificing reality to simplicity, on the other we risk drowning in the abundance of particulars. In the first case we go off into sheer speculation, in the second our understanding remains totally baffled. Hellpach has formulated this dilemma in his "type-scanning rule": "In our eyes groups of living beings are resolved into types, the more distant or alien they are to us. And we see them dissolve into individuals, the closer or more familiar they are to us."[41]

Nevertheless, if it is not to open the door wide to arbitrariness, every typology has to render an account of the "essential," indispensable characteristics of its types. Just as there are more or less typical representatives of a type, there are also more or less central, distinguishing features that give each type its "profile."

So, for example, the extroverted type can be described as sociable, lively, dominant, and active, but also as irritable and impulsive. But can we still talk about such a type, if some of these features are missing, if the individual is active and lively, but not sociable and dominant? We must further define in how pronounced a *degree* the features have to be present for us to be able to speak of a type.

But since there are no objective norms, the "boundaries" of the typology always remain hazy and shifting. In one way this can be interpreted as perfectly adequate, given human nature, but from the empirical-scientific point of view it keeps creating headaches.

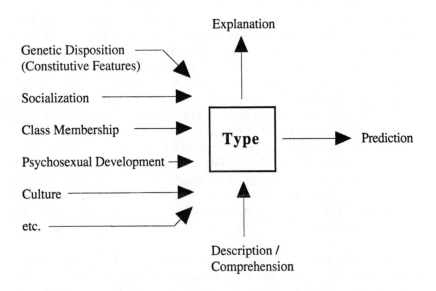

Figure 15: Typologies as Descriptive and Explanatory Models

Finally, two main motives can be found for the formulation and use of typologies: Humans obviously have a need to break down the all too confusing variety of phenomena and to lodge it in a simple, readily understandable system. This allows us to attain a clear comprehension as well as a plausible explanation (see Figure 15).

In the first place we evidently feel inclined to create the sort of *clarity* that gives us an *overview* of things, we want to make structures and schemas — ultimately, no doubt, to master our insecurity. This whole field of exploration, whether conducted humanistically or scientifically, can be understood as one of the many forms of behavior motivated by that drive or compulsion. While science has precisely defined methods, such as tests, to comprehend behavior, attitudes, self-image, or specific qualities, intuition is a more "homey" method for grasping types.

In the second place, typologies claim, for the most part implicitly, to give explanations by abandoning the plane of pure description and speculating about the underlying causal factors. This second motive of typologies aims, in a practical sense (for example in medicine, pastoral counselling, and psychotherapy), to come up with hypotheses that can serve as a foundation for therapeutic intervention. But just how valid are such practical connections? This is as a rule the most controversial and speculative element in many typologies.[42]

Only with the emergence of recent computer-aided methods of psychometrics have we been able to quantify the abundance of data that the human brain can comprehend "intuitively." Still more important, we can now organize these data, classify them, and investigate their underlying structures. A rapprochement between phenomenology and empiricism, between qualitative and quantitative methods now seems to be entering the realm of possibility.

Both perspectives have weaknesses, but strengths as well, that must be made reciprocally fruitful, without trying or actually managing to dissolve one standpoint into the other. For the typology of the Enneagram in particular this can mean that we may be able to examine critically the clusters of characteristics that the various authors define so differently. This might lead to greater coherence and validity in the system, although it has already given rise to fractious disagreements among the authors. Riso, for example, speaks in an unusually critical tone about a newly published book on the Enneagram by Helen Palmer: "I consider it both confused and confusing. I believe it is profoundly flawed and full of all sorts of mistakes."[43] An empirical study of the typology of the Enneagram can help at least to lower the number of such grey areas.

On the other side, the possibilities opened up by an intuitive perspective can be made useful even for the scientific or clinical- therapeutic domain. For many people the intuitive approach can still lay claim to a certain obvious validity, which, if we look beyond the horizon of empirical research and hypothesis-testing, is saying a great deal.

There is no room here for a detailed account of the development and progress of the quantitative methods, or of the criticism that has been leveled at them. But one branch of research should be mentioned, and that is factor analysis. This technique has played an exemplary role in the evolution of the psychometric methods, and is of particular importance for the empirical investigation that I have used in this article.

"A major goal of empirical investigation of personality is the desire to grasp not just all the nuances and behavioral realms of the personality, but beyond that to point up the structure and reciprocal dependency of the descriptive dimensions."[44] Researchers attempt to do justice to this aim with the methods of factor analysis, which are not weighed down by any theoretical baggage worth mentioning, of the sort that psychoanalysis, for instance, carries with it. The leading names in this line of exploration are J. P. Guilford, H. J. Eysenck, and R. B. Cattell, but these researchers have subsequently taken pains not just to understand personality from the standpoint of factor analysis, but to generate models from it that adequately describe personality in its entirety.

The goal of factor analysis, as originally developed by Charles Spearman, is to reduce a vast number of somehow interrelated variables to a smaller number of "factors," of which the variables are composed and which in a certain way "explain" these variables. Thus we are looking here for a structural order underlying the data, so as to reduce the mass of information and possibly connect it to theoretical concepts.

The data are collected through tests. During this stage some very important presuppositions are made, such as the level of interval scales (for example, deciding what constitutes "passing") or the assumption of linear connections, that are often methodologically debatable. But the questionnaires themselves are also sources of possible mistakes in measurement. Testing experts try at least to control distortions by intelligent design, individual steps that can be carefully checked, and observing the criteria of good tests.

A major problem for the quantitative methods of data collection — and this is especially true of factor analysis — is how the results are to be interpreted. Because of the impressive mathematical complexity of the findings, people sometimes all too readily fail to notice their lack of relevance and significance. Only a few constructs, such as the extroversion-introversion dyad, have proved over the course of time to be stable, replicable, and above all interpretable, despite the many different authors who have applied it.

The more quantitative methods, which are doubtless more exact, must continually be measured against such broad considerations. This brings us back again to the qualitative approach, in particular typologies, whose concern after all is to organize, describe, and explain the varied mass of data in a model that the individual can interpret and intuitively grasp.

4. THE ENNEAGRAM AND OTHER PSYCHOLOGICAL MODELS

Introduction

In his book[45] Riso makes an interesting attempt to integrate the Enneagram into the context of psychological, and especially psychoanalytical, science and theory. This points *one* way for further investigations. It is a way, of course, that once again cannot be measured empirically and contains a high degree of speculative elements.

Riso's examples definitely encourage further exploration and reflection, but for this very reason I should like in a brief concluding critique to point out some weak points and superficialities in his presentation.

Freud and the Enneagram

Freud, as we know, argued that there were three stages of psychosexual development in childhood, the *oral, anal,* and *phallic* phases. In Riso's scheme one member of the three Enneagram triads is assigned to each stage. In this way each type of a triad comes to represent one form of psychosexual fixation.

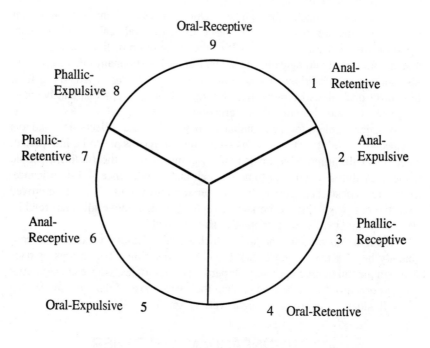

Figure 16: The Enneagram and the Stages of Psychosexual Development

Borrowing from neo-Freudian terminology Riso expands the model around three general dispositions of psychic energy — *receptive, retentive,* and *expulsive* — which once again differentiates each of the three stages of libidinal development. Riso's arrangement thus looks like the sketch in Figure 16.[46]

In addition to comparing the Enneagram with the psychoanalytical theory of character formation, Riso connects the *structural* concepts of Freudian psychology with the types of the Enneagram.

According to Freud there are three "authorities" that determine the structure of our mental life: the *id,* from which the biological drives primarily derive; the *super-ego,* which internalizes the norms of parents and society; and the *ego,* which stands, as it were, between the first two and develops its own capacities while playing the role of mediator between instinctual impulses and the *reality principle.* The figure projected by this psychic structure can be described in the broadest sense as "character."

According to Riso's scheme the following constellation emerges moti vated by that drive or compulsion.[47]

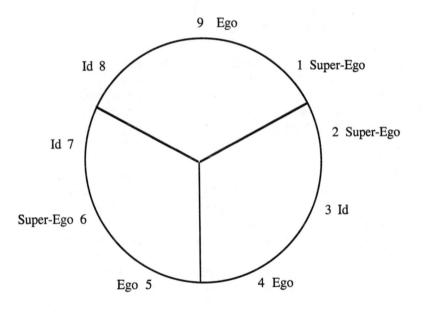

Figure 17: The Enneagram and Freud's Ego-Authorities

C. G. Jung and the Enneagram

Jung's model of the personality builds on three dimensions. Along with the predominant focusing on the *introversion-extroversion* scale, there are four additional psychic functions, namely, *thinking-feeling* and *intuition-perception* that stamp the personality.

This leads to the emergence of eight possible combinations, if we assume, as Jung does, that in each case one function of the allied pair of functions has the upper hand (in parentheses the matching Enneagram types):

> extroverted thinking type (ONE)
> extroverted feeling type (TWO)
> extroverted intuitive type (EIGHT)
> extroverted perceptive type (SEVEN)
> introverted thinking type (FIVE)
> introverted feeling type (SIX)
> introverted intuitive type (FOUR)
> introverted perceptive type (NINE)

One immediate problem in coordinating both systems naturally arises from the fact that Jung has only eight types and the Enneagram has nine. But Riso has an explanation ready. "There is also a certain poetic appropriateness to the fact that the Three (whose personality is so unfixed and changeable) does not correspond to one of the Jungian types. As the most adaptable of the personality types, the Three is treated in several of the Jungian types without having a category of its own."[48]

In his doctoral dissertation J. Wagner explores the connection between Enneagram types and Jungian typology, by comparing the raw values gathered from an Enneagram test with those of the Myers-Briggs Test (a Jungian type test). He comes to the conclusion that there is a highly significant difference between the nine Enneagram types and their values on the Myers-Briggs raw value scale.[49]

He also finds some further correlations between the Enneagram triads and the Jungian types: Heart types are more likely to be extroverted perceptive and feeling types. Head types are more likely to be introverted, intuitive thought types. Gut types are in general more likely to be intuitive types.[50]

Karen Horney and the Enneagram

On the basis of her clinical-therapeutic observations the psychoanalyst Karen Horney (1885–1952), as mentioned before, concluded that in every situation a person has in principle three possible ways of reacting: He or she can move away from people (the *detached* or *withdrawn* types), turn against people (the *aggressive* types), or move toward people (the *compliant* types).

Riso relates these fundamental modes of movement to the nine Enneagram types, so that in each triad there is one of the types described by Horney[51]:

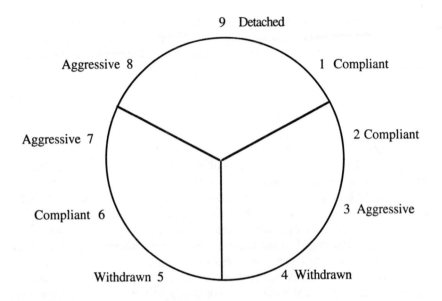

Figure 18: The Enneagram and Karen Horney's Typology

The *DSM III* and the Enneagram

Riso ends his comparative studies by coordinating the Enneagram types with the psychiatric categories of the *DSM III* (*Diagnostic and Statistical Manual of Mental Disorders,* which attempts to outline and classify all psychic diseases on a purely descriptive level).

Riso himself views the arrangement cited below as a working hypothesis and stresses that it "should be taken only as the roughest of approximations, since a great many distinctions would have to be made to sort out the correspondences in any clear-cut way."[52]

Type ONE	compulsive personality disorder
Type TWO	histrionic personality disorder
Type THREE	narcissistic personality disorder
Type FOUR	phobic personality disorder
Type FIVE	paranoid schizophrenic personality disorder
Type SIX	passive-aggressive, passive-dependent personality disorder
Type SEVEN	manic-depressive, histrionic personality disorder
Type EIGHT	antisocial personality disorder
Type NINE	passive-dependent, passive-aggressive personality disorder

In this arrangement the idea is to underline the *neurotic* developmental tendencies in the Enneagram types, in other words the condition of disintegration. Their psychiatric manifestation would thus be expected to follow the pattern described above.

Critique

One ground for criticism arises out of Riso's more than free treatment of the authors he cites. In a mixture of quotation, interpretation, and allegation he follows a double strategy. Models are cited, on the one hand, to support the validity of the Enneagram, but on the other to be criticized and "corrected" from the standpoint of the Enneagram. Riso does the latter in the sense that he either arbitrarily draws upon supplementary material, for example, neo-Freudian literature, to make the model fit the Enneagram better or, where the other models and the Enneagram don't agree, he relies on conjecture.

One must surely admit that Riso's book lacks the space needed for an exhaustive discussion. But this casual way of treating other models of personality will have to face the question of how adequately he deals with the subject. A few brief examples should make this clear:

On the one hand Riso finds confirmation of the nine types in Horney, but then he fills in the missing or contradictory facts by speculating that Horney's clinical observations had led her to almost the same conclusion. This culminates in the daring conviction that "Horney was independently on the way to discovering a three-times-three personality typology."[53]

As for Freud, Riso acts as if Freud had only *three* phases of psychosexual development, probably because this number suits the Enneagram better. The latency and genital periods are not even mentioned, prompting the suspicion that Riso first gets a different personality model to "fit," so as to present it as "proof" for the correctness of his own model. But if he uses only *parts* of the Freudian model, this should be frankly stated in some fashion.

Riso also takes a very free hand with C. G. Jung. His discussion of the problem of having to convert the eight Jungian types into the nine types of the Enneagram culminates in the statement that,

> While Jung did not have a separate category for the Three, he must have been aware of this personality type from his clinical and personal experience. In a sense then, Jung inadvertently described some elements of the Three without considering this type as a separate psychological entity, something which would have thrown off the symmetry of his two-times-four theoretical framework.[54]

First of all, this is, of course, putting words into Jung's mouth, and in a dubious argument to boot, when divergent information threatens to shatter Riso's own "theoretical framework" — of a three-times-three typology.

The clearest example of the "offense is the best defense" sort of argumentation is the way Riso coordinates the Enneagram and the *DSM III,* in an effort originally intended to prove the validity of the typology. Despite a few qualifying remarks he criticizes the compilers of the psychiatric manual because they "erroneously, albeit understandably, combine traits from one personality type with another, with the results that the brief schematic descriptions they offer are sometimes confusing."[55] This sort of argument, unfortunately, is not apt to help people appreciate the accuracy of the Enneagram or the features that render it comparable to other typologies.

5. RESULTS OF AN EMPIRICAL STUDY OF THE ENNEAGRAM

In the summer of 1991 the author conducted an empirical investigation of the typology of the Enneagram as part of his doctoral work at the University of Tübingen. One result of this is the Enneagram Types Test at the end of this book. But the development of the test inventory was only a first step in exploring the inner structure of the Enneagram and its pronouncements. To this end, along with the use of complex mathematical procedures, such as factor and cluster analysis, I also collected simple statistical characteristic values designed to throw light on the distribution and frequency of individual types.

Some of the findings will be presented as briefly as possible in the following pages.

Frequency Distributions

To start off, one item that attracts our interest is the comparison of the "frequency distributions" for the types, in other words the issue of whether certain types occur more frequently than others.

In general the Enneagram doesn't provide us with specifics here, but we might suspect that there would be more members of certain professions in some of the types, because the demands or peculiar conditions of certain activities match the characteristic features of these types. Thus, for example, some authors have surmised a connection between type TWO and the so-called "helping professions," but this could *not* be confirmed by my findings. Another connection concerns type SIX, which, it has been argued, is particularly well represented (at least in Germany). But Figure 19, which shows the frequency distribution of all the types as determined by the Enneagram test, indicates that type SIX is not especially numerous, and in fact is the closest of all the types to the expected value (under the theoretical assumption of equal distribution).

Number of
Test Subjects   (*N* = 320)

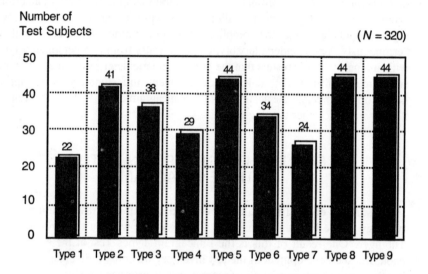

Figure 19: Frequency Distribution of the Types

The results become clearer when we differentiate the distribution of the types by *gender*:

The first thing that catches our eye is the fact that among women the distribution is more even. Only in type TWO is the proportion of women distinctly higher than elsewhere; the second most frequently registered type for women is SIX. Men, on the other hand, are found with disproportionate frequency in types THREE, FIVE, and EIGHT.

These results are exactly what one would expect. Type TWO is described as social and altruistic, type SIX as socially-oriented and in need of support, which matches the role expectations usually assigned to women. This raises the question of whether the types mentioned contain particularly stereotypical views of female roles.

But the findings are still more pronounced for the men. Thus type THREE is described as oriented to things and success, as a person especially concerned with achieving social status. Type FIVE is characterized primarily by rational and distanced modes of behavior, and type EIGHT by aggressive self-assertion.

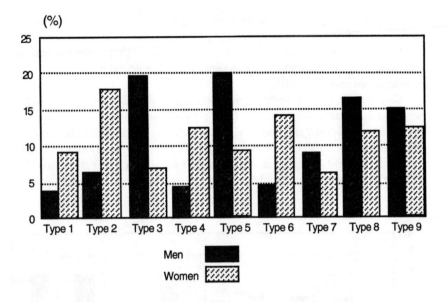

Figure 20: Frequency Distribution of the Types among Men and Women

By contrast, type SIX, as mentioned, is marked by insecurity and dependency, type TWO by social involvement, and type FOUR by exceptional access to the irrational sides of human life. The first two characteristics cited can readily be identified as typically "masculine" attributes, while the last two types represent behavioral roles that men are not commonly encouraged to play.

This suggests that the distribution results could be overlaid, or at least explainable, by gender-specific role stereotypes. (The only findings that are hard to interpret — the gender imbalance in type ONE — might reflect distortion by the relatively small sample pool for this type.)

In addition, a comparison of the frequency distribution of the types among different *age groups* yields meaningful results. Only two categories were used here, under and over thirty-five, first to keep the number of persons in any subgroup from becoming too small, and second for reasons peculiar to the Enneagram: In the literature on the Enneagram "mid-life" plays a special part. In our younger years, the claim is made, we live our particular type more unequivocally, because in the course of ageing new psychic territories get integrated into our personality. This can also be seen in the fact that during the first half of life often only one of the two "wings" is developed. "One of the tasks for the second half of life is to turn to the as yet underdeveloped second wing. Even people who know nothing of the Enneagram will do this unconsciously."[56]

Needless to say, "mid-life" comes at widely divergent times for various individuals, and even from the standpoint of developmental psychology it can be determined only with difficulty.

So I made a pragmatic decision on the basis of three factors: The oldest person tested was eighty-one, so, from a purely arithmetical point of view, "mid-life" would come at around forty. In addition, if we divide up the group by this criterion (39.5 years, to be precise), we are left with two groups of almost equal size, namely 170 persons older and 150 persons younger than forty. Finally, selecting this age as "mid-life" also has an intuitive plausibility.

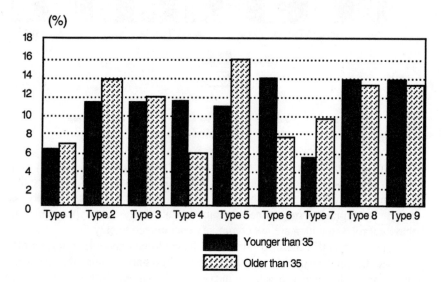

Figure 21: Frequency Distributions according to Age

The sharpest percentage differences are found in type FOUR (6.47% vs. 12%), type SIX (7.64% vs. 14%), and to a lesser degree in type FIVE (15.88% vs. 11.33%) and type SEVEN (5.33% vs. 9.41%). These results can be explained as follows: Type FOUR is described as maladjusted, insecure in social contacts, and in search of identity. All this actually fits in better with a younger person's understanding of his or her role. Type FIVE is characterized by cool reflective action — a quality that one would expect to find more frequently in the older group. Type SIX is marked by fear of autonomy, a strong feeling of belonging to a group and phobic/contraphobic avoidance of anxiety. Here it is difficult to correlate the disproportion to age-specific role stereotypes. Finally type SEVEN is described as materialistic, carefree, and resilient. It might be that the lower proportion of under-35s here is due to the fact that younger people are still uncertain about their social role, are still "seeking" and thus less stable.

The Types and Their Coordination with Countries and Animals

In various Enneagram authors we find a series of correlations of types to countries, animals, or colors. In *Discovering the Enneagram* Rohr and Ebert provide an overview of this approach, and make some interesting and helpful associations.

Statements such as, "Fours are often Francophiles,"[57] are admittedly catchy and people are glad to retail them. But we have to ask whether they aren't individual observations that describe a very limited correlation, as opposed to a matter of fact that necessarily applies to FOURs. In any event, I also checked to see if these coordinations could be confirmed.

Statistically speaking, the validity of these statements could be established only in scattered cases. Thus, for example, it's fair to say that people belonging to type SIX do tend to name Germany as "their country," but the association of France with FOURs did not hold up.

Apart from the fact that a very large number of test subjects would be needed to get any clear proof on this point, there are basic conceptual difficulties with it. For example, the identification of certain types with animals focuses on the congruence between qualities of the types and features commonly ascribed to animals. But that creates a double problem. First, what people take to be characteristic of animals varies with culture, experience, and individual preference. Thus one person may think of elephants (type NINE) as in the German expression, "an elephant in a china shop," another as the embodiment of a good memory, and a third a symbol of strength and inner repose.

Second, one has to ask which feature of the type in question is the comparison aiming at. Is the rhinoceros an image of the aggressiveness of type EIGHT, or does it illustrate EIGHT's "protective instinct"? Or if the chameleon vividly symbolizes the adaptability of THREEs to their environment, the laziness of this animal is quite atypical of THREEs. Hence such identifications with animals apply to only one area of the very complex construct that types as a whole describe.

We are working here in a very subjective and associative field that is hard to systematize. A given image will seem persuasive to one person but not to another. As mentioned, these correlations are scarcely susceptible to statistical proof. And the same holds for attempts to correlate Enneagram types to countries and colors. Nevertheless there are some interesting observations that bear mentioning.

Enneagram Types and "Their Animal"

Types THREE and EIGHT are described by the Enneagram as particularly self-assertive, aggressive, and "gripping." When these types are asked to name their animal, with far more than random frequency they mention all sorts of predators, from lions to eagles. Thus the characteristic qualities of these types do appear to find a conspicuous correspondence in their animal identifications.

Enneagram Types and "Their Country"

As far as prediction goes, the test simply established that type SIX produced the highest (absolute) number of people answering "Germany." But much more interesting is the fact that certain types do not choose certain countries. Thus, for example, the statement, "FOURs are Francophiles," cannot be proved, but the results of the Enneagram Test allow us to put it this way: Persons who attain the highest point totals as FOURs do not identify with "Germany." In other words FOURs tend to be "Germanophobes." By contrast, ONEs evidently have little feeling for the "French" way of life. These observations fit in quite well with the characteristic qualities ascribed to the types/countries. And so does the fact that FIVEs make conspicuously frequent mention of many northern and central European countries, but do not once mention "Italy" or any other southern European country. This can be construed as meaning that persons who show high numbers as FIVEs — who are described as being especially sober and distant — dislike identifying with southern European countries, preferring instead the northern and central countries. The latter, of course, are associated more with "cool distance" than with "fiery temperament."

But even with these associations we have to remember that it remains unclear whether the mentality, the landscape, or the language of the country in question is the decisive factor in the identification.

In addition the writers on the Enneagram come predominantly from the Anglo-American cultural domain, and this surely plays a role in choosing coordinations. For instance, in the U.S. the "Mexican siesta" is a widespread image that can readily be used to illustrate the "laziness" of NINEs. But the average central European, on the other hand, would generally not be very familiar with Mexican culture; and so the comparison would not be especially meaningful for him or her.

Factor Analysis

It is considerably more difficult to present the results of factor analysis in a way that is both brief and readily graspable. Hence I shall cite only one example to clarify the complex possibilities of classification and interpretation that it opens up.

Very broadly speaking, one can say that the nine types, as described by the Enneagram, are not "independent" quantities, but are interconnected in a variety of reciprocal relationships. Practically, this means that qualities which play one role in one type can also belong to the essential characteristics of another type. For example, EIGHTS display a high degree of "aggressive self-assertion," but the same is true of THREEs.

The Enneagram tries to take this complexity into account by speaking, for example, of the "wings" or the "stress points" and "consolation points." But it appears doubtful that this attempt is an altogether fortunate one. *One* of the factor analyses (principal axes analysis with four-factor solutions and varimax rotation) resulted in the following four factors:

Factor 1 (34.39% extracted variance): problems with self-doubt and self-criticism

Factor 2 (21.09% extracted variance): interest in and openness to people, ideas, and new experiences

Factor 3 (19.54% extracted variance): oriented to achievement and success; tense

Factor 4 (24.98% extracted variance): willingness to engage in conflict; capacity for self-assertion

To oversimplify, we can say that these "factors" are dimensions that to a certain extent "explain" the characteristic elements of the types. The individual types thus stand in a stronger or weaker correlation (load) to these factors.

Type ONE: with factor 1 and 3
Type TWO: with factor 2
Type THREE: with factor 3 (factor 2 and negatively with factor 4)
Type FOUR: with factor 1 (tends to correlate negatively with factor 4)
Type FIVE: with factor 1 (tends to correlate negatively with factor 4)
Type SIX: with factor 1 (tends to correlate positively with factor 4)
Type SEVEN: with factor 2 (tends to correlate negatively with factor 1)
Type EIGHT: with factor 4 (tends to correlate negatively with factor 3)
Type NINE: with factor 4 (tends to correlate with factor 1)

On factor 1 types FOUR, FIVE, and SIX "load" the highest
On factor 2 types TWO, THREE, and SEVEN "load" the highest
On factor 3 types ONE, THREE, and EIGHT "load" the highest
On Factor 4 types EIGHT and NINE "load" the highest

Thus type ONE is shaped above all by tension, orientation toward achievement and success, high motivation in work, and on the other hand by self-criticism and pangs of conscience.

These play no role for type TWO, which is marked chiefly by an interested openness, especially to people.

Type THREE, like type ONE, has a hard time winding down, because THREEs are workaholics and extremely success-oriented. They are connected with TWOs by their interest, which is, however, more oriented toward things. Their almost uniformly negative values on factor 4 show that they are sufficiently self-assertive and have enough coping mechanisms.

Type FOUR, FIVE, and SIX are largely characterized by self-doubt and insecurity. FOURs are primarily insecure about their role and identity, FIVEs are limited in their capacity to make social contacts. SIXes by contrast are strongly related to their social environment, but shy away from confrontation.

Type SEVEN is capable of enthusiasm, with many interests, and open to new experiences. Self-doubt and anxiety are lacking here.

Types EIGHT and NINE are the antipodes on the level of conflict avoidance versus self-assertion.

A further result of the factor analysis raises the question whether the types describe not so much neutral characteristics and kinds of behavior, but rather "clinically" relevant quantities, such as "aggressive inhibitions," "social competence," "construction of coping mechanisms," or "anxiousness."

Cluster Analysis

Simply put, cluster analysis allows us to describe how "close" the individual types are to each other. Here too, depending on the method chosen, there will be different results and possibilities of interpretation, but some observations are still relatively constant. Thus, types ONE and SIX display a greater similarity than, say, types ONE and NINE.

More important, however, is this general observation: When we combine the types in "clusters" — that is, groups formed according to the criteria of similarity — the same types do not necessarily appear in the same clusters.

This means that under certain circumstances individuals of the same type are less similar to people of a different type. Thus a TWO can be far more similar to a FIVE than to another TWO.

This finding naturally calls into question, to some extent, the Enneagram's general notion of itself and its predictive power. The Enneagram typology works on the assumption that it can adequately and completely describe people by assigning them to their type. In any case we can say that the types are not such fixed quantities as may have been assumed.

6. THE ENNEAGRAM TYPES TEST

The Enneagram Types Test (at the end of this volume) is an empirically scientifically constructed personality test, whose criteria of quality are quite satisfactory for a questionnaire of this sort. A retesting study carried out six weeks later resulted in a stability index (reliability) of over 0.8. This means that the rest measures with sufficient accuracy and in addition registers relatively stable characteristics — in other words, *not* short-lived moods, but long-term "typical" qualities of a person.

Comparison with another personality test, one widely known and respected in Germany, the Freiburg Personality Inventory (FPI-R), shows that the Enneagram Types Test registers quite precisely the qualities used to describe the types (validity). This might sound trivial, but it is a criterion that many so-called tests cannot meet. Evidence for this is provided by the observation that the test results agree all the more closely with the self-estimations (for example, "I am a NINE. . . ") the better the person knows the Enneagram.

The following are a few highlights of the very wide-ranging investigation that should lead to discussion, dialogue, and exchange of experiences: It seems necessary, for instance, to reflect critically on the "wing theory." Does the assumption of a "main type" and its "wings" (one or two "wings," depending on the author) at all tally with our observations and experiences? Are "stress points" and "consolation points" actually more closely connected to each type than other points of the Enneagram? Should we understand the types as "statistical" quantities ("I am a FOUR and nothing else. . . ") or as "dynamic descriptive dimensions," in which case identifying oneself with a type would be the beginning and not the end of a process?

These are not academic questions, but necessary reflections, if we wish to handle the Enneagram responsibly and, above all, if we use this model to counsel people in pastoral and therapeutic work.

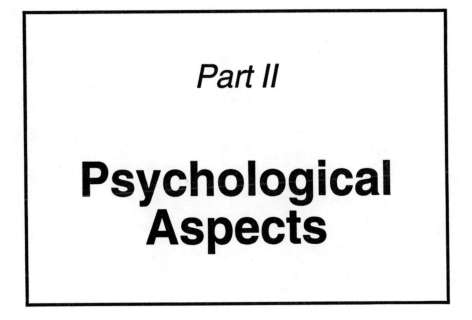

Part II

Psychological Aspects

The Enneagram and "Focusing":
A Map and a Path for Personal Change

Hans Neidhardt

I would like to begin this article on the attempt to link the Enneagram with the psychological process known as "focusing" by breaking a minor rule: "One" doesn't start off this kind of essay with "I." But I myself very much like to learn a few personal details about the author of a paper or a book I'm reading. That way I have a rough sense of the nature of the beast I'm dealing with.

I am an academically trained psychologist and psychotherapist with my own practice. Previously I worked for nine years directing a telephone counselling service with a large staff of volunteers. My professional roots lie in the person-centered psychology and philosophy of Carl Rogers. "Focusing" is a consistent technique that sticks close to the body and experience and that further develops Rogers's approach. This realm of humanistic psychology is where I have now come — after some years of apprenticeship and travel — to feel most at home.

My spiritual roots stretch back further, some of them all the way to my parents and grandparents, but above all to my youth. This was a time when I, like many other people, was fascinated by the new Protestant orders and communities. Later I was swept away by the first stirrings of the charismatic movement, and finally I worked actively at building up an ecumenical base community. The fact that these varied spiritual roots bore fruit in my profession of psychotherapy and not, say, in the ministry, surely derives, to a large extent, from my personal fixation: My main interest has always been directed at what goes on "in" people — and above all, of course, "in" myself.

In 1989 when I first came into contact with the Enneagram at the Craheim conference, I was extraordinarily skeptical — and not just because person-centered ideology tends to be hostile to diagnoses on principle. Some of the nine categories of the Enneagram didn't fit very well into what I already knew about theories of character. Other categories seemed to be using different words to say what had already been been systematized elsewhere. And I found all the juggling with the nine numbers decidedly fatuous.

Since then I have become thoroughly convinced that in the Enneagram we have at our disposal not just an extremely accurate "map of the soul," but that this old system, as a "mirror of the soul," also has the power to promote personal and spiritual growth.

The Enneagram turned into a valuable aid for my work with myself. As before, I remain skeptical about the people who feel they have to shove this "mirror" into other people's faces, and who think that they can hastily consign themselves and others to one of the nine pigeonholes. Quite apart from the fact that one can easily make terrible mistakes — what's the use of such mechanical categorizing?

I would like to try to present a way of working with the Enneagram without any pigeonholes. What I will be describing are first tentative steps. I hesitated for some time, uncertain whether it might not be too early to publish something on this topic. But ultimately I got the impression that it could be worthwhile to launch a discussion on the Enneagram and "focusing," even though my material is provisory and incomplete.

To start off our orientation I want to pick up the image of the map once again. It's useful to have a good map when you want to take a trip, to make it clear where you are before and during the trip, as well as to look back on the distance you've covered after you've gotten home. Of course, no matter how good the map is, it can't replace the trip itself. And staring at the map too often during the trip may prove to be a hindrance. "Focusing" is one of many modern psychological methods that can help us to journey into the landscape of the soul.

Focusing

"'Focusing,'" writes Johannes Wiltschko, "as you all know from photography,

> is the point at which something becomes sharply and clearly visible. Anyone who's ever taken a picture knows that you have to go through several steps in the right order to get the shot you want. First you select your subject, get the camera ready, chose the proper angle and composition. You find the right focal length by turning the appropriate ring around the lens till you see the picture clearly in the view-finder. Only then can you take the picture and develop it later.
>
> This path from noticing a subject to the finished picture can be called a process with several steps. This is exactly what we do in focusing. Only there our attention is directed not outside but inside, to the experiences going on within the body. Focusing means directing my inner attention to something that happens inside me, in my inner self, and gradually fine-tuning my attention until I perceive a clear inner image, feeling or words, so that we can learn to understand our-

selves better and cope with our problems independently and autonomously."[1]

So focusing means, on the one hand, a quite specific, clearly describable inner attitude, a standpoint from which we relate to our experience; and, on the other hand, the inner experience that evolves through a process when we translate the focusing attitude into reality.

Over the last twenty-five years focusing has been studied, described, and developed, both as a theory and a method, by the Vienna-born psychotherapist, Eugene Gendlin. Gendlin, who used to be a coworker of Carl Rogers, now teaches psychology and philosophy at the University of Chicago. So focusing goes back to the tradition of Carl Rogers's person-centered philosophy and psychotherapy.

The crucial question that led to the development of focusing was, why do some people profit from psychotherapy while others don't? Through a meticulous study of countless tape-recorded sessions with psychotherapists from the most varied schools of thought, Gendlin discovered that the success or failure of therapy depended on neither the therapist's technique nor the client's problems. The decisive factor proved to be (among other things) how the client stood in relation to his or her own experience. The precise way that people relate to their experience when they make constructive changes in their life is what Gendlin called focusing. He described it in detail and discussed under what conditions and by what steps this process of change occurs.

Focusing is by no means limited to the domain of psychotherapy, it is a general theory (and practice) of human change.

THE FOCUSING ATTITUDE

The focusing attitude can be clearly described (and practiced). It is characterized by three features:

Inner Attention

We direct our attention within (we "look," "listen to," and "sense" what is happening in the internal space of our experience). It may seem at first as if there was nothing there, or only something very vague and hazily perceptible to which we "normally" pay no attention. But if we are patient and continue to be inwardly alert, we will gradually discover more about what apparently goes on in us at every moment (just as we are "normally" unaware of our breathing and heartbeat), and something like an inner "landscape" will open up. Here we feel a faint pressure on the chest, there a stirring in the hand, an inner picture spontaneously comes into view, words and sentences "run through our heads." In the focusing attitude we can attentively track all this, we can look at it and listen to it: "Being inwardly attentive means being a sympathetic observer of my inner world."[2]

Attaining this special quality of attentiveness to inner experience requires certain external conditions. I can't become inwardly aware unless I feel reasonably secure in my outward environment at that particular moment.

The "Right" Distance from Experience

Focusing means relating to what is currently happening within me. The rule of thumb here is that I have to have some distance from what I am experiencing — hence I should neither plunge completely in, nor perch myself so far away that I can no longer perceive anything at all. I must create a relationship with my inner world that is accepting and understanding, interested and perhaps somewhat curious too.

This inner relationship roughly corresponds to what Carl Rogers has described as the elements of interpersonal relations in psychotherapy that are relevant to change, and that hold true for any good interpersonal relationship: Don't get too close (the "clinch," or excessive responsibility for the other) and don't go too far away (breaking off contact, no more bridges of understanding), in other words the perfectly appropriate level of appreciation.

One of the most important activities in focusing is the continual fine-tuning of one's inner distance from immediate experience so as to get it "right" (correct for that moment).

"Unintentionality"

In the focusing attitude we try not to want anything from our experience. Focusing means (actively) letting things happen: We observe with inner attentiveness what's there, and . . . we wait and see what happens next.

Inner attentiveness — the right distance — "unintentionality": Perhaps this can be illustrated in a "landscape image" that Gendlin likes to use. I imagine that I'm safely ensconced on the bank of a great river. I just sit and effortlessly watch all the things that float past me.

THE PROCESS OF FOCUSING

There have been solid scientific studies of what goes on inside a person who turns to his or her present experience in the focusing attitude, and what are the regular patterns followed by the spontaneous flow of the focusing process.

I "pick" a theme (a question, a problem, a dream, a particular person, etc.), direct my attention within, and wait to see what sort of physical resonance starts to form, first as a vague, not yet definable inner quality prompted by this theme. In the language of focusing this inner resonance is called the "felt-sense" or "the implicit." "Implicit" because while the physical resonance to the theme already bears its meaning within it, this meaning has not yet unfolded or been made explicit. The vague, physically perceptible whole of the "felt sense" then freely produces inner images, clear emotions, bodily impulses, thoughts (the explicit). And I can continually connect these spontaneous materials to their implicit "source," until the meaning spontaneously flowers in an "aha-experience."

The focusing process is a natural one that we don't actually have to learn, but need only discover. Each of us has already experienced (more or less accidentally) this process of change in everyday life, for example when we deal with a problem and find a creative solution, accompanied by a release of physical tension, a sigh of relief, and a clear inner "feeling" of "That's it, that's the solution, that's how I want to do it." Eugene Gendlin has earned our gratitude for carefully studying this natural process and thereby making it teachable and learnable.

SUMMARY: WHAT IS FOCUSING?[3]

Focusing

— describes the basic process of personal *development* by which people *change* their experience and their actions

— allows us to have experiences that hitherto were at best imaginable, and to become *capable of acting* in areas that were hitherto inaccessible

— brings us into contact with what we *actually* feel, think, and believe beneath our pre-programmed concepts and strategies

— helps us to *clarify* and concretize unclear feelings and thoughts, and to bring forth *creative new* material from the *wealth* of our inner world

— shows us, along with what we have experienced and learned in our personal evolution, the pathway to the *transpersonal* overtones of our lives

— gives us comprehensive support in *resolving conflicts* over people and things

— lets us *understand* other people more fully and relate to them more *deeply*

— teaches us to perceive situations *more accurately* and to react to them *more diversely* and appropriately

— *links together* experience and action, thought, feeling, and fantasy in a holistic method, grounded in the life of the body, that enables us to cope creatively and effectively with conflicts and crises in everyday and professional life.

THE ENNEAGRAM AND FOCUSING: FUNDAMENTAL CONSIDERATIONS

Focusing is a psychological method designed to gain access to the spontaneous experiential process of development and change that always occurs when a person moves in a constructive direction.

The Enneagram is a system that describes nine character fixations. In other words it deals with the (apparently) "hardwired," permanent structures of the person. It is rooted in a completely different source in intellectual history from that of focusing. I would like to show how this *path* of personal change and this map of the soul can complete and correct each other in work with people.

I shall begin this rather theoretical section with a brief glossary. I can only agree with Christian Wulf when he stresses how much we need to clear up the vocabulary used in the context of discussing the Enneagram.[4] Terms such as *ego, character, personality, self,* etc. either become synonymous or are used irregularly to mean completely different things. So I would at least like to indicate here how I understand and apply these terms.

Glossary

Person: By this I mean the physical-psychic-spiritual totality of human beings in their conscious and unconscious aspects. *Person* is thus a kind of collective term for everything that constitutes a concrete man or woman (the "whole landscape").

Ego: This is what I call the partial aspect of the person that is conscious: *I* (*ego* in Latin) think such and such. I'm reading this essay just now. While doing that *I* feel . . . (what I consciously perceive in the "landscape").

Character: In my definition this means a complex internal system of basic assumptions about one's own person and the world, resulting from certain fundamental experiences. "Normally" this system is unconscious (and hence very effective). *Character* can be recognized by the way a person organizes his or her outer and inner experiences, by the personal meaning that his or her outer and inner experiences have for him or her, and by the "strategies" (intellectual, emotional, and behavioral habits) with which he or she regularly, as if "automatically," reacts to situations in life. *Character* is therefore a kind of inner organizational pattern for a person, which, thanks to its regularity, makes it possible to be oriented and feel secure. But, on the other hand, it also impedes and disturbs because it prefers certain ways of reacting (both internal and external) while excluding or at least interfering with others. The Enneagram describes nine such organizational patterns and claims that every one of us is "fixed" (character fixation) in one of them. As Eli Jaxon-Bear says: "Each of us has all the models, hence you will discover a small part of yourself in every fixation. But there is one point that describes most precisely your fixation pattern. We don't change fixations."[5]

(To return to the earlier metaphor: *Character* is that place in the "landscape" that is my "home," and from which I select the scenes in the landscape that I want to avoid and the ones that I prefer to visit.)

Personality: This is what I call certain visible manifestations of character, in other words what is accessible to the *ego* (and other *egos*) — the "phenotype, as it were — the ways of behaving, qualities, etc., that can be observed on the "surface."

Anyone, for example, who reads a book about the Enneagram will surely try at once to place himself or herself in one of the nine fixations with the help of the qualities described there. But because such a reader is operating on the level of *personality*, this attempt can go awry: One and the same character fixation can manifest itself in the most diverse ways. Or similar personality characteristics can belong to quite different fixations (the obvious characteristics, easily visible to myself and others) of my "home" in the "landscape."

Self: By this I understand the "depth dimension" of a person (somewhat as C.G. Jung uses this term), hence the innermost region of our person that constitutes our *essential core*, the "site" where we open ourselves to transpersonal experiences. I mean "transpersonal" in the double sense of the word: first the experience of unity and connection with (all) other people, nature, and the cosmos. And second the "inner place" of our relationship with God, as the "image and likeness of God (Gen. 1:26), the supporting foundation on which the whole landscape rests.

"CHARACTER FIXATION" AS A SYSTEM OF UNCONSCIOUS BASIC ASSUMPTIONS

I am especially concerned with distinguishing clearly between *character fixation* (an unconscious system of basic assumptions) and *personality* (the "outside" of character, the part visible on the surface). Judging by what I have seen, the source of many misunderstandings about the Enneagram seems to lie in equating these two concepts.

Here is one (greatly simplified) example by way of explanation: If we try to imagine a newborn baby whose parents are not at all sure that they even want this child, and who also, in the way they hold the child, carry it and care for it are unsure (either too harsh or too careless), then this child will somehow sense: "Something's wrong here. Am I welcome? Do I belong?" The question of belonging will become an unconscious problem as the child grows up. And a basic assumption will take shape, along such lines as: "The world is hostile, I have to withdraw to protect myself. I got here by some kind of mistake. I should head back where I came from."

A person who in the course of his early years develops such an unconscious basic conviction, will later in life continually "have to" behave as though his environment were cold and hostile. This will in fact cause other people to reject him, which will again confirm his basic assumption. The character fixation in this example (a FIVE) is built up not through a one-sided "stamping," like a coin, but through the interrelationship of the child and its environment. In the final analysis the crucial factor is how the little child *experiences* his or her environment.

One of my own children, who was joyfully awaited and welcomed, has given my wife and me all sorts of trouble on account of his extremely low stimulus threshold and high irritability. Now a ten-year-old, he occasionally displays very clear FIVE features. And I think this is primarily because his special quality (quite different from his older brother, who was a happy, satisfied baby) continually overtaxed us.

The Enneagram literature I am familiar with is extremely deficient when it comes to statements about the conditions under which the individual fixations come about. Linear explanatory models that claim cause-effect connections (if you have X-psychic trauma, then you'll get Y-character fixation) are simply out of place in the psychic domain. The most plausible notion to me is that the various experiences of a child while interacting with his or her environment gradually form a kind of inner matrix out of which the character fixation is fashioned. From this point of view, character is always a "creative achievement" of the whole organism, so as to help it find the subjectively best possible way in situations it experiences as burdensome, threatening, or otherwise difficult. "Every character is in its own way a 'hero'."[6] Hence I believe we should be careful not to look at character fixations in a one-sidedly diagnostic manner through the lens of psychopathology.

We learn very little from the Enneagram about the conditions prompting the fixations, and this may leave both the professional psychologist and the interested lay person feeling unsatisfied. For immediate work this is less important, because the crucial thing after all is to track down the unconscious basic assumptions. Experience has shown that being able to explain *why* things are a certain way doesn't do very much for personal development anyway. Margaret Frings Keyes[7] follows a theoretical approach that is of some interest from a psychological perspective: She tries, among other things, to connect the Enneagram models with the "script" theory of transactional analysis.[8]

NON-IDENTIFICATION
WITH THE CHARACTER PATTERN

The "Reflexivity" of Consciousness

One of the special qualities of human consciousness is that it is "reflexive." We can think back on our own thinking, become aware of our feelings, form an opinion on them, observe our behavior, and have thoughts and feelings about our behavior, etc.

This peculiarity of human consciousness can also be discovered in the so-called reflexive verbs: know oneself, ask oneself, feel oneself, cheer oneself up, and so forth. This kind of expression presupposes the existence of at least two "parts" within a person, for example, the part that gets asked and the part that does the asking. Actually this phrase is often either a rhetorical question, which doesn't expect an answer, or a question directly aimed at one's interlocutor. But genuine "asking oneself" can also bring about "answering oneself" in internal dialogue, which is what constantly happens in the focusing process.

If our consciousness couldn't reflect on itself there would probably be no way for our human possibilities to develop. Directed by unconscious codes of behavior, we would simply function like well-programmed thinking, feeling, and behaving machines — which is exactly what the Enneagram maintains we tend to do.

Critical Self-Observation

When we get to know the Enneagram, the first and subjectively most important question is naturally to which one of the nine points our own fixation belongs. We study the fixation, read Enneagram books, go to workshops, talk with friends and partners, and get more or less insecure, irritated, sad, relieved or enthusiastic over the new discoveries. Busying oneself with the Enneagram seems to establish a kind of authoritative critical observer within the person that strives for more awareness of one's own usual thinking, feeling, and behavior. And this is certainly a good thing.

But it is by no means unique to the Enneagram. When as a young student I read Riemann's *Fundamental Forms of Anxiety,* I would critically observe in myself and others every trait that was "hysterical," "depressive," compulsive," or "schizoid." And after a while I found myself in a situation supposedly common in medical students: They discover that they have all the symptoms of the diseases they're studying at the moment.

Critical self-observation can in fact lead us into the dead end of hypochondria, which limits self-observation to registering the symptoms of the character fixation in question and ends by overloading the "authority" of the inner observer with all the energy of the fixation — without the person's noticing. (For example, a ONE gets angry at his damned perfectionism, or a FOUR turns exploring her subjective internal world into an end in itself.)

Self-Labeling as a Dead End

For this reasons I would argue that the statement, "I am a . . . (ONE, TWO, etc.)" is not without its dangers. I would propose instead, "You are not! That's your pattern, your program for thinking, feeling, and behaving. You're just used to imagining that you are your number. That's because you normally get your sense of identity from this pattern."

I don't believe that the purpose of the Enneagram consists in supplying us with new and more precise diagnostic labels and then in "fixating"[9] us in self-diagnosis all over again.

I'm reminded of one of my clients, who was given the diagnosis of "schizoid personality" in a psychiatric report a full fifteen years ago. Just now we're studying the effect of this "label" on the way my client deals with himself and his everyday experience, and he's beginning to discover how severely this ("correct") old diagnosis limited his perception of himself and others and colored everything "schizoid" for him.

When I say, I "am" a SIX (instead of, for instance, "my central character pattern is SIX"), I may be running the risk of losing the ability to perceive myself except through the lens of the Enneagram. That narrowing of self-perception could be fatal.

Eli Jaxon-Bear remarks quite properly on this point: "The great danger with this system lies in the fact that it can be used to justify falling into an even deeper sleep. This happens when we use the recognition of a pattern to keep this pattern going in us. That way we justify being stuck in the melodrama of our life."[10]

Attentive Self-Observation

If we want to work with the Enneagram without using it to diagnose and label, then we ask the questions differently, such as: What unconscious basic convictions do I use to organize my experiences so that, for example, I keep getting "nervous" in the same situations — or "aggressive" or "sad"; that I keep on making the same "stupid mistake"; that I keep on getting hurt in relationships in the same characteristic fashion? And what "motives" provide the energy for these automatic patterns?

This sort of access to our unconscious basic convictions, operating as a process and offering the opportunity for change, now strikes our ego's everyday consciousness as either impossible or very difficult. This is because the character fixation derives developmentally from a time in which the little child lived in a different conscious state (diffuse mood qualities, magical thinking, etc.) and grown-up ego-consciousness had reached only a very rudimentary stage of formation.

For this reason I am convinced that Enneagram work needs to be extended and completed by focusing or other methods that work not with everyday consciousness but with "inner attentiveness" (katathymic imaging, concentrative movement therapy, hakomi, or something similar).

Focusing strikes me as especially appropriate, because the focusing attitude helps to break out of the identification with character patterns, and at the same time to observe the way they function, to understand the underlying early "convictions," and in all this to experience the fact that character fixation is not destiny, once again in keeping with the principle that, ""This character pattern is something I *have*, not something I *am*."

The well-known psychotherapist Martin Siems addresses this point in his book on focusing:

> It's as if we were climbing down from the stage of our life into the auditorium, so as to watch our "act" from the audience. Perhaps we're a bit scared, perhaps we'll become a little sad, perhaps we also have to grin, but this view from a distance also gives us the possibility of clearly and accurately perceiving what we in fact keep on doing there. And from the spectator's vantage point it's easier to make "directorial" suggestions, in case we want to change or improve our performance. Through this perception, then, we identify not so much with ourselves as actors on the stage, but with ourselves as directors of the entire play.[11]

In the focusing attitude I have all the leisure I need for beginning to observe and for learning to understand my automatic, characteristic habits of reacting. In the focusing process I can test new options and give the new forces for growth a chance to work. Ron Kurtz, the founder of hakomi (body-centered psychotherapy) takes a similar line:

> Without mindfulness, you won't be in touch with your beliefs and dispositions. Without paying attention, without awareness, you will be operating out of habit, out of reaction and automatic behaviors. You will be moving, perhaps, getting things done, but you won't be learning, changing, growing and becoming freer. If you are not mindful, you cannot know or change yourself. . . . Inner awareness clarifies. . . . But to give up preferences, you must first know you have them and what they are.[12]

But beyond this the focusing process gives us inner experiences "alongside" and "beneath" our character fixations, a new relation to everything new and fresh that's stirring in the person/organism. Focusing makes the "landscape" more colorful and surprising (which isn't always fun, at times it can be painful or frightening). It opens up access to our potential beyond the ruts of character fixation; it can bring us into contact with our *self*.

THE RELATIONSHIP ASPECT:
A CRUCIAL EXPANSION

For simplicity's sake (because the subject is already complicated enough) I have up till now spoken as if the *person* with his or her character fixation and the internal experiential processes was a self- contained whole. In this I have simply been echoing the age-old western intellectual tradition that glorifies the *individual*.

This sort of notion may well be extraordinarily practical, but it denies the underlying fact that we humans (like all organisms) are creatures of relationships. The idea of the person as a closed-off totality bounded by a membrane of skin (or do clothes count too?) proves upon closer inspection to be an illusion: On the physiological level, for example, the lungs and the circulatory system make absolutely no sense without the oxygen from the air around us, just as the digestive system is meaningless without the food that we buy, prepare, and eat. And the rule that holds for these basic life functions obviously holds all the more for the "landscape of the soul." "Our conception, birth, and further development are all the result of relationships. What we call the soul essentially consists in the lived relationships that we internalize."[13]

This sort of "ecological" view (defining ecology in its most general sense of the "theory of interrelationships") makes a decisive change in our perspective. Thus, for example, we can see that the focusing process doesn't take place simply within an "individual," but always in a network of relationships grouped together by the focusing advisor as he or she works with that individual. And even if I focus on a question or theme just for myself, it makes a big difference whether I am sitting at my usually messy desk or if I first create a pleasant setting for myself.

I would add that the attentive self-study of my character pattern can be expanded by careful observation of what happens interpersonally, or, to put it another way, how my "fixation" — like a motor — starts up and overheats in interaction with other people. But I should also note what different facets of my *person* are experienced positively, depending on whom I am in contact with at any one time. Psychoanalysis has intensively investigated and described these processes that it calls *transference* and *counter-transference*.

With the help of the Enneagram we can readily "locate" whatever happens when we fall prey to individualistic bias. It can also help us — especially in the so-called "unredeemed" or "normal" mode — when we act as if our subjective view of any (relationship-)reality were the "measure of all things," depending on how our character fixation warps the perspective. Because then we set up in our relationships exactly the same patterns of experience that keep on confirming our unconscious basic assumptions.

This is where the Enneagram could become a sort of map for our world of relationships and help us to understand the typical entanglements (and possibilities for disentanglement and growth) in our relationships with other people.

When we discover that each of us is wired a little differently, and that in carrying out the same task everybody goes through a different process, then it becomes possible to forgive. We can begin to forgive ourselves, our partners, our parents, and our children. We can stop demanding of the people in our life that they be different from the way they are. We can stop expecting to get apples from a pear tree.[14]

From this "ecological" standpoint we finally recognize that anything like "personal development" or "self-realization" cannot possibly exist without development in our relationships as well.

Biospiritual, Development-Oriented Work with the Enneagram

Klaus Renn

I've been giving some thought to how to find the appropriate way to communicate with you. I invite you to enter with me into a space and an atmosphere that will let us be honest for the moment. I wouldn't want to pretend to know everything about the Enneagram or, God help us, about life. I just want to address, to offer, and point to what strikes me as worth noticing.

Precisely because I am contacting you right now only intellectually through the printed word, and you as a living reader have presumably switched on your head, there's only a slim chance that anything will really happen. Presumably you'll pick up some ideas from me, which you'll understand from the viewpoint of your value system — and that will be that. In any event on this level, though you may have a few aha-experiences, the Enneagram will not particularly touch your life. The chance we take in this sort of encounter is clearly greater than usual: We risk being stifled under a mighty mass of ideas, thoughts, and constructs without having had the least experience. In so doing we go hunting away on the surface of life, gathering information about the Enneagram and ourselves, and deducing from it further meaning — constructs for ourselves. But without immediate experience we really don't know anything, and we aren't living in reality either. Only through experience can anything change in our lives. Later reflection may interpret, extend, and generalize this experience. Hence it is at bottom impossible to come to a real change in life simply through reflection and exchange of ideas.

That is why it's very important for us to leave behind the level of conceptual thought in order to encounter our type in a truly experiential way. Because a great deal of what makes up my type is unconscious and automatic. If we want to be able to grasp, to touch, and to sense ourselves more closely, we have to encounter ourselves. That means we have to connect with a level of consciousness that makes us accessible to ourselves. This path leads to what is implicit, but only rarely explicit, to our person. This implicit element of our person is what depth psychology calls the unconscious. To make this somewhat clearer I suggest a little experiment, which you can try out even as you read.

Please slow down your reading speed and as you do take a deep breath that lets you perceive your body. Meantime become conscious, "I am reading this book." And ask yourself: "What am I longing for now?" But please don't ask yourself this in the usual way. Aim the question, "What am I longing for now?" in the direction of your chest and gut. It's a good idea to spend some time here, to put aside the book for one or maybe two minutes, and to wait: "I'm longing for . . . " Whatever emerges now, simply let it come: thoughts, memories, feelings, sensations, perhaps too a vague atmosphere: "What do I need in my life?" And I let this question fall into my body as well. Perhaps it's nothing very rational, perhaps only a sense of putting something down so as to see it more clearly. Before we end this brief experiment, I suggest you pose yet another such question in the direction of your gut: "What's alive in me right there?" Or "What is there just a little bit new for me?" Again give yourself some time, go toward yourself with the waiting-just-a-bit technique.

In the communications channel of our book this experiment surely has few chances of working. But perhaps you now have an inkling, a taste of what I mean by the implicit element of a person. Through the path of this inner perception, also called "inner attentiveness," we can be surprised by the meaning of our character fixation.

If we experience our type, our structural dependence through this inner physical perception, at that same moment something else becomes clear: I'm not that, or you're not that, in any case that's not what makes me, it's not the essential. I can experience, I can imagine a more essential world that lies behind or beneath my structural dependency. Possibly we sense the physical impression of an inner homeland, an inner space filled with light, love, clarity and a simply self-evident being. Something like a temple where I meet God; more than that, where God waits for me with his spirit. "Don't you know that you are God's temples, and the Spirit of God dwells in you?" asks the apostle Paul (1 Cor. 3:16). Mystics have experienced this in every age. Meister Eckhart, for example, speaks of the "divine foundation of the soul" that lies behind our structural dependency. Anyone who comes into contact with it, can "grasp God in all things," and "accustom his mind to having God present at all times, in the heart, in striving, and in love."[1]

To give a name to this world of experience which lies beyond my type I like to use the words of mystics and seekers for God. Even if some of these words about the Ultimate Mystery seem too grand or too trite, the important thing about them for me is that in one form or another they aim precisely at this world of experience. Only by consciously turning toward this infinite mystery in me which, I daresay always points simultaneously to the mystery of God, will our essence be able to develop into its purest and noblest self. This unfolding will be nurtured by the sources of experiential love, of rooted being, and the free spirit. Experience is what counts, not some sort of resounding phrases.

A little story tells me what the Enneagram may be good for: A simple Oriental warrior is said to have brought back from the wars a very valuable and beautiful carpet. He himself has no use for such a splendid object, and so he sits in the bazaar to sell the carpet for a hundred dinars. A friend runs into him as he sits there and asks in astonishment why he's selling this wonderful carpet at such a cheap price. Whereupon the warrior asks in surprise: "You mean there are more than a hundred dinars?"

This is what it's all about: Is there more than my personality out there, more than my character fixation, more than my structural dependency? Is there more in my life to experience and to live than what I believed up till now? The Enneagram's answer is: We have precisely nine different possibilities of shaping our lives. Granted, that's not much. And we live out one of them — like a programmed machine. There's no mention of decision-making here. The Enneagram isn't even interested in how we got into this program: from our genes, our family background, by accident or necessity or any other way. The only really important thing is that we find ourselves described. And so we have the opportunity to recognize our structure, crack our code, and gain access to our own program.

Despite all the uncertainty about how the Enneagram came into existence and where exactly it came from, one thing is quite certain: The point is not to work so that now we can function better with our structural dependency or discover our peculiar strengths. What's at stake here is rather the essence of life — of my life. Our scientific psychology and psychotherapy are, in the final analysis, therapeutic only to the extent that they want to help us to function better. A detailed psychopathological scheme of diagnosis is concerned, on the one hand, with getting the bill paid by the health insurance companies, and, on the other, with designating the "deviations" from the standard "parameters" of psychic health. Scientific psychotherapy is employed to make us capable of functioning again.

But from the spiritual point of view this psychic apparatus is as bad as the disease. Only if we go beyond it will we find health. St. Augustine says, "Our heart is restless, till it rests in you."

THE PATH TO THE SOURCES: BIOSPIRITUALITY

We are all familiar with moments when we step out of our type number — just as we now and again step out of the social role that we play — where we are close and connected to ourselves and others in an essential way.

When we do this, we experience what it's like to really live in tune with ourselves in our own body, to sense the power of love and at the same time to be clear and level-headed both in our feelings and in our minds. In these moments we get some understanding of the tree, "planted by streams of water, that yields its fruit in its season, and its leaf does not wither" (Ps. 1). Then it's all there, all natural, all divine, nothing has to be done, everything is already contained, the tree's knowledge of its fruits and the brook's urgent path to the sea. Everything is quite simple and taken care of in these moments. "It" flows without our help and is experienced as a gift from God. Breathing becomes slower and deeper, connecting our life with the life around us. We become part of creation. In these moments change occurs: inner healing. And that's exactly what we're after.

At this point I would like to invite you to pause for a little while, to go back over your memories of such experiences. Go out of your head center and move with your attentiveness in the direction of the center of the body. Look at this specific tree by the streams of water with your inner eye . . . Do you see these leaves? Perhaps you can hear the brook rushing? Calmly take some time; the rest of this article isn't going to run away from you. Let yourself soak up the whole atmosphere of this impression, and as you do you can ask yourself — still aiming at the "gut" — "What would this image say to me, if it could talk?" Keep on waiting, so that something in you can make itself heard from within, from the vague physical chords struck by the image. Should a sentence, a word, an inner picture, a memory, present itself, stay there, track down this experience, sense the felt meaning for yourself.

In case you're still searching your memory for earlier experiences of this sort, please don't just think of "pious stories." In perfectly ordinary daily life we often fall out of our number. One particular access to this is opened up for us through sexuality. If we can throw off our inhibitions and encounter our partner in a completely free and natural way, then the two bodies will join in a single harmony. As it says in the biblical creation story: "And they will become one flesh" (Gen. 2:24). "One flesh": I can forget who or what I am. I am allowed to be, but I can forget my little ego. Now I am just existence, loving and playful in union with another existence. At this moment the head isn't called for. Past and future have ceased. I am — here and now — entirely in the present.

Perhaps you also know from your own experience what it's like suddenly to receive the gift of a meaning and goal for your life. It isn't always exactly what you would have wished. But if this meaning unexpectedly opens up to you, this can release enormous reserves of energy. Admittedly, this sort of experience seldom provides a solution for our everyday problems. Still this sensuous experience, which comes out of nowhere, can sometimes bring with it a profound solution. This also makes it possible to deal differently with our problems and the pain of our existence. So this isn't just an imaginary, cerebral meaning, but the *experience* of a meaning that pops up unexpectedly. We have this experience as if it came from outside, although we sense the meaning in us and we can also get a rational handle on it. This "outside" relates to our type: It transcends it and leaves it behind. It's as if a deeper energy and a absolutely vital message had reached us in our character-machine and thereby generated change.

Sometimes a glance, a flower, a stroke of the clock lets us look — as if for brief moments, fractions of a second — behind our type. We often take a deep breath, and this experience is always sensuous and physical.

The dimensions of experience "behind" our type are: a certain quality of bodily experience; finding ourselves in the "immediate Now"; a letting go, a dis-identification with our type and the belief system that goes along with it.

Although I have thus far taken pains not to use clear conceptual terms,[2] it may be good to explain somewhat the terms "immediate Now" and "dis-identification."

This *immediate Now,* in other words "just Now" — and now it's already "another Now": By that I mean precisely the sliver that lies between "a little while ago and already past." This is the goal of all schools of mysticism and humanistic psychology as well, the only difference being in their depth and intensity. The *immediate Now* is this entrance, this narrow chink in time that lets us experience ourselves in a more essential, harmonious way. And the more deeply we let ourselves sink into this Now (for example, through conscious breathing) the more this Now will become a path leading far beyond our fixation. Here is how Alan Watts describes this kind of spiritual experience:

> The central core of the experience seems to be the conviction, or insight, that the immediate *now,* whatever its nature, is the goal and fulfillment of all living. Surrounding and flowing from this insight is an emotional ecstasy, a sense of intense relief, freedom, and lightness, and often of almost unbearable love for the world.[3]

Dis-identification opens up a pathway to myself as if to an event in nature. I observe myself from a distance like the one in which I observe a mountain brook. I see, I gape, hear the rustling, watch the play of the water around the stones — and am happy to let things be the way they are. Scarcely anyone would start thinking that this rock really ought to look different, and the ripples around it should go in a different direction. No, we let it all be the way it is. This is what we have to do: Get a few steps closer to our own Now, without any evaluation, without any "should's" and "must's." It registers quite simply in us: So that's the way it is. This is an attitude that as a matter of course lets us be a person — man or woman — the way a tree is a tree. This is a specific attitude — curious, friendly, with no ulterior motives — toward myself, in which I sense the flow of my experience. Whether or not this makes change and growth possible, or I remain in my fixation the way I have always been, depends on *how* I experience myself in that experience. It depends on my self-perception.

Piero Ferrucci writes: "In every moment of our life we can take the position of the tranquil observer, and then the first effect we will experience is liberation: I'm afraid; I observe my fear; I recognize it quite clearly; I understand that I am not this fear, and I feel liberated from it."[4]

There are all sorts of methods available for practicing this letting-go. One simple exercise is to spend sixty minutes simply answering the question: "Who are you?" I could answer, "I'm Klaus Renn, I'm a focusing therapist, I'm a father, I'm someone who's in search of . . . , I'm . . . " Sooner or later I'll run out of labels, and that little chink will open up and reveal the implicit element of my person: I'll move from a superficial identity to an identity of myself experienced as truer and more essential.

The other dimensions of life lie folded in the *dimension of bodily experience,* not the way a piece of paper is folded, but the way a chestnut contains all the information needed for the fully grown tree. Everything connected with the tree lies encoded in the nut: growth, seasonal "behavior," up to and including its death. Of course, I mean "body" not in a purely physiological sense, but more broadly. Eugene Gendlin has described this perception of the body as the *felt sense.* If you ask, for example, how you feel at this moment, and listen (as with a stethoscope) in the direction of your chest and gut to your feeling for the present situation, the first answer you get will be a hazy totality. Another example would be the attempt to get to the bottom of your feelings about any person in your life. What is the overall feeling, for example, you have toward your father? Just try for once to grasp the whole quality of your relationship to him without concentrating on specific thoughts or representations. If you do, you'll find that this overall feeling has no definitive form, but a highly global "emotional quality."[5] For Gendlin this felt sense shows how we interact with the world. We experience the world around us in a comprehensive, inner way before we can articulate it. To take the example of the felt sense toward your father, you'll be able to determine that this all-embracing feeling contains everything that you have ever learned about him or experienced in interaction with him: all the joy, anger, disappointment, hurt. Your entire experience with him will be concentrated in this felt sense. As soon as we try to focus sharply or pick something out of the whole picture, we are already beginning to view individual aspects in an explicit — hence "unfolded" — fashion.

When Gendlin's focusing method is used in a spiritual quest, then we speak of biospirituality.[6] Both spiritual and psychotherapeutic work that use the felt-sense construct as a theoretical *and* practical tool seem to fit today's scientific paradigm better than the conceptual world of traditional psychology. Furthermore this renders the process of changing oneself much simpler and easier. On this point Welwood writes:

> However, the traditional model of the unconscious in depth-psychology makes it seem as if the unconscious had at its disposal an

unfolded structure, as though drives, wishes, repressions or archetypes existed there in a developed form, as if the unconscious were a sort of alter ego. Here I can only postulate that what is unconscious is rather the implicit ordering of experience rather than a quantity of autonomous or unfolded "contents." *What is unconscious are holistic structures that can be unfolded in different ways and on different levels of the relationship between the organism and the environment.*[7]

If we practice inner attentiveness and relate to this vague bodily background-haziness, that is, the as yet unfolded structures, then essential inner images and imaginative worlds will unfold, crucial energies will make themselves felt, concrete thoughts will develop, initiating through their appearance a process of transformation.[8]

This process of change cannot be carried out by strenuous effort, we experience it instead as a self-relinquishment. I "only" need to let myself go. Life in me or the Divine in me does the seeking all by itself. Or as Francis of Assisi put it, "What we seek is what is seeking us." Our contribution is this specific relatedness to the inner world of perception.

In the Enneagram we find developmental directions spelled out by the "arrows." It now becomes clear that such development is undoable. "FIVEs" may strain and struggle all they want, they will newer attain the power of an EIGHT. Nevertheless this will take place in the inner process as if spontaneously, if access to the implicit element is opened up, if the fixation is transcended. So the path of change doesn't run from FIVE to EIGHT, but from the FIVE to his or her inner edge of experience and beyond that into the implicit world. People who up to now have seen themselves labeled as FIVEs will now be able to have a fresh understanding of themselves in their superficial identity with the possibilities and energies of an EIGHT. And depending upon the kind of search and the next inner stage of growth, this can be interpreted as psychotherapeutic or spiritual work.

THE THREE ENNEAGRAM CENTERS: HEAD, HEART, AND GUT

The Enneagram describes three body centers — head, heart, gut — that then break down into the nine different types. These energy centers were already known to the ancient Israelites and have been of great importance in Christian mysticism. In Hinduism we find many techniques that work with these energies and open up the way to enlightenment. We are talking here not just about gut-, heart-, and head-people, which would simply describe a superficial identity, but much more about the potential energies humans experience. In implicit perception we find essential sources that foster our human and spiritual growth.

In the *heart center* we find our way to a love that can be characterized as "blessed." A love that pours out for ourselves and goes on to work far beyond us for our fellow men and women and nature. It may be like a healing immersion and incorporation in the whole environment, which we experience as connected to us.

In the *gut center* we find the experience of rootedness, as if we were fused with this earth, which itself is "sublated" into a larger planetary order; the security of an "I am" force as well as the force of aggression and sexuality, the sense of existence as something to be taken for granted, just as a tree is a tree.

In the *head center* we find many openings for vast distances and a fine sensory world that gathers information. This is a power that can leave everything the way it is, and in addition a many-sided transmitting world capable of subtle communication, a store of information that can use the available programs to translate perceptions into structures. Otherwise we would actually see everything upside down. Only through head-work does our visual perception get things right side up.

A development-oriented or biospiritual approach to the Enneagram will be able to unleash many impulses, and at the same time lead to profound insights into the way humans function, as well as to the formation of theological and mystical concepts.[9] The standpoint that I speak for here includes the notion that everything we can name, speak of, or think represents explications of the implicit — the implicit element bound up with the organism of our entire environment. In the cognition-biological research of Humberto Maturana and Francesco Varela this is formulated as follows: "The world in which we live is the world that we create together in the process of perception and knowledge."[10]

Making explicit and creative together — whole worlds lie hidden in these phrases. To explore them we need something like an experimental theology, which can give rise to a spiritual "cure of souls."

Changing One's Own Type: Simple — But Not So Easy

This growth-oriented, biospiritual work with the Enneagram might create the impression that the whole thing was a snap. My impression — and my hope — is actually that in and through this kind of spiritual care some things *will* become easier, perhaps more honest and transparent as well. Thanks to this approach texts and parables from the Bible take on for me much broader vistas and touch my life in a new way. If I hear, say, from Paul: "It is no longer I that live, but Christ who lives in me" (Gal. 2:20), he prompts me once again to search for a way out of my fixation, the way out of my imprisoned "I." I can leave behind the condition of identification with my "number" — and let Christ live instead of me.

Perhaps some biblical texts will also occur to you that can speak to us in a new way from this perspective. Perhaps the sentence, "Unless a grain of wheat falls into the earth and dies . . . " (John 12:24), or the parables about the Kingdom of Heaven; the story of the man who discovers a treasure in a field, and then sells all he has to purchase this field with its treasure: In the biblical texts we are continually being challenged to be watchful and awake. "For by the grace of God you have been saved through faith; and this is not your own doing, it is the gift of God — not because of his works, lest any man should boast" (Eph. 2:8). Doing good works, worrying about righteousness, wanting to stand morally irreproachable before our neighbors and God — all these are actions of our fixation. It has nothing to do with Jesus's message, with the reason why he cast his life into the balance. If we live with this Jesus, our fixation will be interrupted and broken up. Notwithstanding the finely calibrated belief-systems in our heads, we are directed to the rich treasure that we, as God's children, can simply find — here and now, today. It is simple, but not easy. Paul says at one point: "Not that I have already attained this or am already perfect; but I press on to make it my own, because Christ Jesus has made me his own" (Phil. 3:12).

From current research on transpersonal psychology[11] we know that spiritual experiences can only be had by, and lead to corresponding changes in, individuals who have achieved a certain degree of stability and security in their prepersonal and personal development. (The prepersonal phase refers to the period up to, perhaps, the age of six; the personal phase refers to the development from the sixth year onward.)

This means that an individual has at his or her disposal solid structures that make it possible to interact satisfactorily with himself or herself and the surrounding world. In this context traditional psychotherapy is the means to finish off development. Its goal is to support individuals in leading their own responsible lives and in overcoming crises with their own resources. Only when this is achieved is transpersonal development really possible.

Thus it's important to become a person first; then this person can again abandon himself or herself in order to turn to deeper implicit worlds. If there are injuries on the prepersonal and personal level, any spiritual development will at the very least be made more difficult, since all experiences, knowledge, and energies are needed to support and serve the structure of the self. The individual may talk religion, and perhaps identify more with his or her group. But it may take a long roundabout route before such a person will be able to love authentically or even really participate in social life. Such people will likewise have trouble in coming to a clear perception of themselves.

Often they will be religious super-achievers, without getting anything out of it. For example, if the "inner child" is still hungry for recognition and love, in grown-up life the person will do anything to get this recognition and love. Everything having to do with faith, God, etc., will be infantilized.

This applies to all of us. None of us is finished. There is only wayfaring, searching for inner healing. This means searching to learn how I became the person I have become. This is a difficult intersection and turning point, which can't be handled without an experienced advisor or therapist, and generally not without a support group. It's simply too seductive to use one's own fixation to grasp — in both senses — the spiritual world. Obviously we have a paradoxical situation here: Only if I find myself, that is, experience my fixation and thereby become healthier, can I commit myself more freely to the adventurous deeper world. So, first I have to accept myself and then let myself go again. If I accept myself and my qualities, which I find described in the Enneagram, if I accept my body and my relationships, then I can let myself go.

But I can't do any accepting without a Thou. I am accepted by you, and so I can accept myself a little more — these are our modest human possibilities. Thank God, I don't have to accept myself all at once, but only enter upon this path to me, so I can let myself go a little more. This path behind the fixation is a daily process of becoming. It means that I get in touch with myself every day on the level of my fixation, and I seek to get from this a deeper connection with the Divine that always transcends my little ego. In this way the light, the power, the love, and the depths can come through to me — to my fixation, which thereby goes on being healed. What has become healed in me can pass over into the whole context of my life. In this way many other fixations become more accessible and put new life possibilities at my disposal.

My subliminal message here is perhaps quite simply the stunned surprise of the Oriental warrior: "You mean there are more than 100 dinars?" You mean there's more than living the life that I now find myself in? It also does me good to present to the public what I think and do in groups as a trainer. I want to exchange my thoughts and feelings and work with people who, like me, are on this quest for a "full life."

Part III

Perspectives for Spirituality and the Church

The Enneagram: On Working with a Spiritual Theory of Personality[1]

Christian Wulf

The Enneagram is in. Both in the Church and in esoterically tinged circles people are talking about this theory of personality. You hear about it at parties and in conversations with colleagues: What type are you? A ONE or an EIGHT? When it comes to the Enneagram opinions are divided. Some are totally enthusiastic, while others announce epistemological reservations or resist being pigeonholed. What lies behind these numbers? Is it even worthwhile to take this new psychological fashion seriously? What's Christian about it?

In the following pages I would like to shed some light on this and attempt an evaluation of the whole phenomenon. Since I myself am a co-founder of the Ecumenical Workgroup in Munich, I speak as a sympathetic biased observer.

JUST ANOTHER PERSONALITY THEORY?

A glance into psychology textbooks will show you that there already is a whole series of typologies. Behind them all lies the experience that despite all our individuality there are certain groups of people who display common characteristics. Along with the ancient theories of the temperaments we find the physical typologies (Kretschmer, Reich, Lowen) as well as those oriented toward depth psychology (for example, Freud, Jung, Adler, Horney, Riemann). Why do we need another one?

Practically all modern typologies take images of disease for their point of departure, and they describe "is" conditions: "This is the way you *are*." As a dynamic model, the Enneagram takes a different tack. It describes the ambivalent personality structures of all individuals with special emphasis on their peculiar compulsions and possibilities for change. Its center of gravity lies in the invitation to change or, biblically speaking, the call to conversion.

The Enneagram wants to support people as they find their way to themselves and to God. This is where the new perspective comes in: Anyone who finds himself or herself on a spiritual path or is guiding others on their way will find the Enneagram very helpful. It broadens your outlook, it points up unsuspected connections and uncomfortable truths with a few quick, powerful strokes.

WHAT CAN THE ENNEAGRAM OFFER US?

Basically we can distinguish between three lines of sight here: The first is aimed at explaining which of the nine personality "Gestalten" most corresponds to one's own person. Once you have found your Gestalt type, the Enneagram turns our eyes to the paths of change or "redemption." Then through further work the connections with other personality types reveal themselves to us. In an overview it looks like this:

Diagnosis: Which Personality Type Fits Me?

The basic assumption of the Enneagram is this: On the basis of the psycho-social development specific to each person a certain psychological structure is formed in all of us, which can be discovered through certain repetitious (mostly compulsive) behavior patterns. One's own patterns become clear when, with the help of the Enneagram categories, the following questions can be answered: In which of the three fundamental areas — feelings, action, relationships — do I have most difficulties? What avoidance strategies and defense mechanisms do I use to cling to my "false" ideal of self? What root sin lies at the bottom of my attempts at self-redemption?

Change: Which Paths Lead to More Freedom? What Am I Called To?

Redemption from compulsive behavior patterns presupposes a threefold conversion: intellectual, affective, and intuitive. The goal of this phase is spiritual discernment of one's own personality development, which tends to lead either to the integration or disintegration of the person (to life or death).

Differentiations: Depth Dimensions and Relationships Between Types

What nuances can be found in the other types? How is the web of relationships formed within the Enneagram? What relationship does each type have to its neighbor? How do the individual types deal with the world and time? Is there an especially appropriate kind of prayer for each type? Can facets of the Enneagram also be found in Jesus?

In the first approach the whole map of the soul opens out in front of us. The descriptions are sober and precise. When they seriously look into it, most people at first feel a little sick: "How can anybody take my own truth, which I desperately want to hide, and call out its name so unsparingly?" This is a truth that hurts quite a bit and at the same time sets us free. The Enneagram simultaneously gives us a feeling of tranquillity: "I can commit myself to this (painful) process of self- knowledge and still be full of trust, because just as I am, I am also loved."

Recognizing one's own personality structure and beginning to act in the "preferred" ways is a first step. But in my opinion this--necessary--psychological approach falls short without a spiritual orientation. It's too easy for the individual to feel pressured to have to redeem himself or herself: "If only I work hard enough on myself, I'll succeed in becoming better."

I believe that when the Enneagram is viewed as a psychological system against a very general spiritual background (Riso, Jaxon-Bear), it lacks some essential perspectives, and the danger of self-redemption leaps too prominently into the foreground. And these very attempts at redeeming oneself lead us still deeper into the toils and fixations of our own compulsiveness. We are saved from this by looking at the face of Christ. Redemption is not one more achievement of the individual on his or her path to spiritual perfection, it is above all a gift of a loving God.

One caveat here: All the books written about the Enneagram — at least those written in German — speak from an exclusively male perspective. Women keep remarking that they often don't recognize themselves in the picture, because the masculine viewpoint is so dominant. This objection must be taken very seriously: Instead of transcending traditional role behavior and aiming at a holistic vision, sexist shortcuts are creeping in. This calls for some fundamental rethinking.

Among all the Enneagram authors there is also a widespread bad habit of fitting "famous" persons into the typology of the Enneagram. This strikes me as deriving more from a superficial need to come up with illustrations than from a wish to achieve deeper understanding. The Enneagram is above all a path of *self*-knowledge, not a system for pigeonholing other people.

All Enneagram books should have a glossary so that readers could look up "technical" terms. There is still no uniform terminology, which sometimes creates confusion. Enneagram language could also be better coordinated with standard psychological terms such as ego, I, the self, which right now are tumbling chaotically over one another.

THE IMPLICIT ANTHROPOLOGY OF THE ENNEAGRAM

The following notion may be helpful: Imagine God's "qualities" being broken down, like light passing through a prism, and shining upon human beings in a nine-band spectrum. That way the greatness and splendor of God would be re-discovered in the manifold kinds of men and women, would shine out in the relationships of people with one another, and would find their way back to their original unity. This may serve to express how important every individual person is, because there has to be completeness to display God's abundance and his kingdom.

At the same time this shows us the implicit image of the person in the Enneagram: The person, as created by God, is good. This can become an occasion for surprise, awe, and gratitude in response to our own uniqueness and our need for completion.

On this basis, which corresponds to the "Principle and Foundation" experi-ence in the *Spiritual Exercises,* a person can turn to his or her negative and wounded sides. The Enneagram presupposes that we are exposed ever since con-ception to destructive and ambivalent forces. Within the sinful structures of this world there can be no absolutely good person. Our own need for redemption is thus an existential fact of our humanness, as conceptualized in the Church's teaching on original sin.

The Enneagram starts out from the assumption that ever since a fundamen-tal sin occurred each one of us lives in the shadow of a singular compulsion. In our psychological development and maturation, beginning with childhood, each of us has stressed one ability over against the others and has overdeveloped this one side. In a very early but "free" decision each person, as a small child, chose to deal in a specific way with his or her body, with other people, and with the world. Out of this "decision" certain behavioral patterns have evolved, consti-tuting the basis of our further development to this day.

In all this the central feeling can be identified as fear. The little child is overwhelmed by fear and adopts defensive behavior to combat elementary fear and protect himself or herself. This unconscious stance then becomes a com-pulsion that marks every one of us even today. Into this compulsory obsession the Enneagram brings the profoundly biblical message: "You can be redeemed and set free to find your true form."

The descriptions of the Enneagram start out from these unredeemed com-pulsions and aim, after the manner of the discernment of spirits, to show where freedom lies for each of us. These are very much individual "messages of salvation," because one person's medicine is another's poison.

PERSONAL PRESUPPOSITION
FOR DEALING WITH THE ENNEAGRAM

The Enneagram is a very effective instrument for the journey of the spirit, but it doesn't work by itself. It presupposes the longing and readiness to get away from one's own compulsions. This will also hurt. The first step is to realize one's own truth within the whole picture and to let it stand forth undisguised.

Anyone who gets involved with the Enneagram should be psychically stable to some degree and should have an advisor, if at all possible. Reading books alone is not enough to reach the real depths.

The Enneagram does, it is true, unfold healing powers, but it's no substitute for therapy. Even after working with the Enneagram our basic structure is still in place — with the difference, however, that we can open up and freely decide for alternatives, while letting ourselves be completed by the structures of other types.

The Enneagram shows us how our "program" runs in our subconscious, and just how far the journey to those depths can go. It's a disillusioning experience to find our true self, our soul, and God. The Enneagram invites us to seek out the place where we can encounter God, where God ceases to be a mere projection of our wishes, but where we as free men and women encounter the free God. The point here is to find and maintain the balance between our own individuality and "typecasting" through the descriptions of the Enneagram.

POSSIBLE APPROACHES WITH THE ENNEAGRAM

Working with Married Couples

With increasing frequency married couples have been asking me about the Enneagram. Sometimes they disagree about it: The wife is very much taken with it, while the husband is appalled. Communication between the two, which surely wasn't that smooth before this, is now even worse. Then again there are many couples who have experienced the Enneagram as a help in seeing their partner with new eyes and understanding him or her better, from within. In such cases the Enneagram has stimulated and deepened the dialogue between them. It becomes clear which patterns were operative in the choice of partner, how and where partners are a burden or a support to each other, and where possibilities for developing the relationship can be found.

In Spiritual Advising and Counseling and Retreat Work

Anyone who wants to guide others must first of all learn to understand himself or herself better (one's own inner structure, motivational forces, defense mechanisms, preferences, blind spots). Furthermore, guiding others means being able to look away from oneself and learning to see the world with the eyes of others. Kierkegaard advises us to view ourselves objectively and others subjectively. The description provided by the nine types makes it possible to comprehend ourselves more precisely and to expand considerably our own understanding of people.

In spiritual counseling and retreat work I bring in the Enneagram very sparingly, using it at first only to orient and correct myself. In advising my primary concern is not the Enneagram, but the path of the individual. Meanwhile I can make use of the Enneagram's knowledge of the opportunities and dangers one meets on the spiritual path. But it's another story when my dialogue partner is already familiar with the Enneagram. Then it can be extremely helpful for both of us to make the cross-connections and to characterize processes with terms from the Enneagram. I leave the initiative of bringing up the Enneagram entirely to my dialogue partner. In that sense I also don't give any Enneagram retreats. At most I could imagine holding group sessions as an introduction to the Enneagram.

One basic statement of the Enneagram is that the ways to God are strewn with pitfalls and offers of redemption specific to each person. It would be worthwhile to reread the *Spiritual Exercises* with that in mind. What roles do the individual personality types play in the contemplation of one's own chief sins, the "election," and the discernment of spirits? Does everyone have a particular prayer to obtain love?

In the Formation and Continuing Education of Coworkers in the Church

In this area there are two sides to be considered, the first being seminaries, religious orders, and the formation of lay theologians, while the second is the continuing education of coworkers in the Church, training them to be retreat-givers and spiritual advisors. In this context the Enneagram cannot be recommended without reservation. The reasons for this may be found in developmental psychology.

We can assume that one's personality type takes permanent shape in the third decade of life. In childhood, adolescence, and post-adolescence changes in social and personal identity are the order of the day and therefore a positive precondition for becoming a grown-up. During this time it seems to me both pointless and dangerous to work with the Enneagram since it contains too many normative elements. There is a further danger of inscribing one's own behavior in concrete: "I'm this way because I'm an EIGHT." This temptation has to be resisted. A young person should not be thinking up his or her identity but living it out. It's more important to begin by gathering experiences and then evaluating how they differ than to confront a typology of personalities. Hence it doesn't strike me as very sensible to bring the Enneagram into action and to fire its big guns until the person is over thirty.

In formation, therefore, the Enneagram can play only a secondary role. It belongs in the hands of the novice master or mentor rather than in the hands of young people preparing for Christian ministry. In the hands of an experienced advisor, of course, it can produce a variety of good results.

A graphic example of the Enneagram's insights is the evangelical counsels. The Enneagram turns our eye away from the merely behavioral level toward the deeper level of motivation. A seminarian, for example, who distinguishes himself by a sharply defined understanding of obedience, will as a rule get plenty of approval, since this is just what his superiors have in mind. From the Enneagram's point of view this can actually be a way of strengthening his compulsive behavior. This seminarian should first of all get in touch with his primal energies (sexuality and aggression) and his feelings, to realize what sources his urge to obey is feeding on. In the same way the motivation for a life spent in virginity and poverty could be explored to find its underlying motives. What lies behind it? Is it really the call to more freedom and love, or do fear and denial of life play the leading role?

In the meantime use of the Enneagram in continuing education has most definitely proved its value. Over the longer haul of continuing education (courses given at from one- to two-year intervals) you can achieve an integration of experience and transmission of knowledge which guarantees that work with the Enneagram will be responsible and critical. These courses keep showing how helpful it is for the trainees to have books on the Enneagram at their disposal. But it takes more than mere reading to grasp and use this instrument in all its depth. An intuitive approach (for example, through focusing or inner images) and prayerful dealing with one's own experiences are a necessary prerequisite. If the Enneagram is passed on in an appropriate, holistic manner, it greatly expands the basic qualifications of an advisor. It describes the topography of the soul and possible spiritual paths as well as the dangers inhibiting spiritual growth.

In Parishes and Other Religious Communities

Up to now I may have given the impression that the Enneagram is primarily a tool for shedding light on the path of the individual person. This is a likely enough notion, given the Enneagram's origins. But practice shows that it can also be understood very well socially and politically. There are certainly some treasures yet to be uncovered here.

In summary, it can be said that the Enneagram is in itself a neutral instrument, like many other methods and devices. Only in the hands of individual people does it unfold its powers (which aren't always calculable) and point to far-reaching goals. Discreet, critical, and responsible dealing with this tool is a sine qua non condition if the Enneagram is actually to heal and liberate. You don't take medicine without first talking with the doctor and carefully reading the label. What becomes of the Enneagram depends on us.

The Nine Faces of the Soul of Christ

Dietrich Koller

PRELUDE

Two preliminary remarks. The first is by way of protest against the denial of Christ in the Church.

We were team-planning a conference on "The Enneagram and Community Development." We were asking: Does the continuum of the Enneagram also produce a continuum for the unfolding of a community? The partial results we got were interesting, but we didn't continue. We paused. Then an icon of Christ caught our eye. We knelt down and sang the Taizé hymn, "*Oculi nostri ad Dominum Jesum* — Our Eyes Are on the Lord Jesus." Then we noticed: Thinking about the Church and community without having Christ in view is after all the Church's typical temptation. But "she" is supposed to develop according to his image and to unfold his features. We take all sorts of pains over "our Church" and trudge along with "our community" instead of with His. An image occurred to us: A churchman is laboriously plodding down the street with the model of his church, a massive cathedral, in his arms, his hands grasping it like claws. Alongside him walks the barefoot, thorn-crowned Christ and holds out his hand like a beggar: "Give me my Church back!" Angry and mistrustful the churchman squints at the Lord, as the Grand Inquisitor once did in *The Brothers Karamazov*.

A woman psychotherapist, who is studying the mystery of the Church against the horizon of secular esoteric teaching, told me she had been to Boulder, Colorado, to the Naropa Institute, the American center for Buddhist psychotherapy. There she took a course that met in the Protestant community center. Almost all the participants flatly rejected Christianity. The chapel had been cleared out till it looked like a skeleton, and all sorts of Buddhist symbols and totemic images were hung up. Only one massive wooden crucifix couldn't be moved and had to left there. At that conference she learned — and wept to see it — what the "denial of Christ" is, and how many things the denied Christ can include.

Perhaps it isn't really the Church, she wrote me, that denies Christ, but Christ who denies the Church. That can't be, I spontaneously shot back. But then it occurred to me that in Matthew 25 at the end of the parable of the ten virgins Christ says to the foolish ones, "I know you not!" And this is precisely the same formula of denial that Peter uses in the court of the high priest, when he says of Jesus: "I do not know the man!" Could this church and community of "ours" no longer be what Christ wanted? Does it teach and love what he taught and loved? Do we preach only the Sermon-giver on the Mount or the Sermon he gave as well? Is our Church just a given unit in a certain religious category, with any number of borrowings from the Gospel? In that case "denial" would be the spiritual and ethical term for a process that psychoanalysis calls "repression." The individual or collective psychic repression of Christ might be equated, spiritually speaking, to the individual or collective denial of Christ in and through the Church.

But surely his Church, his Body, must be living somewhere on earth. "And we all, with unveiled face, beholding the glory of the Lord, are being changed into his likeness," says Paul in 2 Corinthians 3:18. Is that glory reflected in us? "It does not yet appear what we shall be, but we know that when he appears we shall all be like him, for we shall see him as he is" (1 John 3:2).

This Church, which mirrors the Lord, lives hidden in the Diaspora, scarcely visible because it is scattered hither and yon throughout a network of denominations and institutions and movements. It is formed from the concrete men and women who have pressed through to the unconditional love that the Sermon on the Mount speaks of. From the standpoint of developmental psychology that love is an altogether reachable height, if with the help of the Spirit of Jesus we can escape the neurotic world of egotistical claims, deceptions, and self-deceptions, and are no longer totally consumed by the objective world of mere functioning, but have arrived at Christ himself. But that calls for a long path of repentance-work, putting behind us the denials and repressions of Christ.

A second preliminary remark: By the nine faces of the soul of Christ in my title I don't mean something purely psychological. The soul of Christ as the soul of the Church is something pneumatic. You can, of course, describe the traditional portrait of Jesus of Nazareth from the standpoint of psychology and the Enneagram. (This is beautifully done in Rohr and Ebert's *Discovering the Enneagram,* pp. 213–26, and in Beesing, Nogosek, and O'Leary's *The Enneagram: A Journal of Self-Discovery.*)

But, after all, we can't come up with either a historically or psychologically exact reconstruction of the person of Christ. Hence — since the days of the evangelists — we all carry our own image of Christ within us, which undergoes a radical transformation in the course of our development. A developing community or a Church that passes through different cultures likewise keeps discovering new aspects of Christ.

In the final analysis these representations of the soul of Christ in our souls are not the pedagogic or "psychohygienic" effect of one great model: They are the incarnation, the embodiment of the eternal Logos in the shape of the Church. As we all know, the Church doesn't simply confess its faith in Jesus, the great man, but in the God-man, as he took shape in Jesus. "True God and true man." The Logos became (at Christmas) flesh in Jesus and (at Pentecost) flesh in the Church of Jesus. How should we translate "Logos"? "Word" says too little. Among the Stoics Logos was used to designate the World Soul, the divine World Reason. Judaism and the wisdom literature of the Old Testament spoke equivalently of "Wisdom," the divine *Sophia* that plays in God and in Creation (Prov. 8:30–31).

Thus the soul of Christ is not a human psyche, but the *Hagia Sophia*, the holy Pneuma. "Spirit" in Hebrew, like "wisdom" in Greek, is a feminine noun, which also provides us with a feminine term for Christ: Psychologically speaking, Jesus is the non-*animus* man who has completely integrated his *anima*.[1]

But the incarnation of the Sophia-Logos preserves both the natures, the divine and the human, "unmixed and unseparated," as the classic formula puts it. The divinity and humanity are not side by side, the way "two boards are glued together." No. "Just as in a glowing iron there are not two sorts of powers, one to illuminate and another to burn, but the power to illuminate and burn is the quality of fire. Yet because the iron is thus united with the fire, through this union the glowing iron also has the power to illuminate and to burn."[2] In this way, then, Christ's human nature is taken into his divine nature.

Thus if we now reflect on the nine images of the soul of Christ and take up the Enneagram as an aid in profiling the image of the God-man, we still have in the background the biblical image of the invisible God himself. The diagram on page 111 is an attempt to see Christological and theological statements as integrated together. Ultimately what we are talking about is the "highest consolation of Christians," namely, the "promise of the presence and indwelling of your head, king, and high priest . . . , who has promised you that not only would just his divinity be with you (which for us poor sinners is like a consuming fire turned against dry stubble), but the one — the person who has spoken with you, who has tasted every sort of distress in the human nature he took on, who therefore can have compassion with us as his fellow humans, brothers and sisters — who wishes to be with us in all our troubles, even according to the nature thanks to which he is our brother and we are flesh of his flesh."[3]

But then we also have to take seriously the fact in Christ all nine root sins lurked as pitfalls — permanently; except that while he, as the Letter to the Hebrews says, was indeed tempted in all things as we are, he remained without sin (Heb. 4:16).

This gives rise to a positive and critical view of the history of the Church, in which the faces of the soul of Christ want to be reflected.

Now I would like to begin with the Enneagram of Christ and, first of all, to describe Christ as a TWO, because we can assume that this heart-point serves the essence of Christ and the essence of Christianity as a specific point of departure.

FUGUE

Jesus Christ as a TWO

The Savior, the Helper, the Attendant, the Physician, the Friend.

I am looking at the icon of a loving friend, who feels joy in looking at me, in communicating with me, anointing me, binding my wounds, taking care of me, as the good Samaritan did. Here we have selfless love in person, which culminates in his laying down his life for his friends. The friend of men (even to Judas he says, full of warmth, "My friend!"). The friend of children. The friend of women. Jesus is the sort of person you immediately make contact with. And so to this day we keep hearing the old refrain: "The Church? — No. God? — Maybe. Jesus? — Yes!"

Is the Christian community animated by this friendly openness and intimacy of the soul of Christ? Or has everything degenerated into mere ministry?

It's amazing: The Savior is threatened by the constant temptation of TWOs — to forget himself, to pour himself out in altruism and to live in the unconscious pride of how badly he is needed. Obviously he didn't succumb to this inclination. Because Jesus could connect with himself. He had access to his integration point, FOUR.

Jesus Christ as a FOUR

The Artist, the Dramaturge, the Liturgist, the High Priest.

I look into the icon of the sensitive artist, who knows and expresses all feelings in their extremes, who lives out a dramatic destiny between fear of death and mature freedom, between mourning and perfect joy, between love and hatred. Anyone who doesn't hate his interpersonal entanglements can't be his disciple. "Who is my mother, my brother, my sisters?" he asks in the face of his worried family. I can tell that he won't let me take him over in some sort of psycho-spiritual monopoly. *Noli me tangere* — don't touch me!

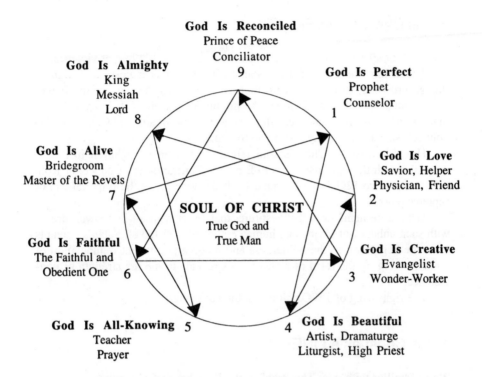

God Is Reconciled
Prince of Peace
Conciliator
9

God Is Almighty
King
Messiah
Lord
8

God Is Perfect
Prophet
Counselor
1

God Is Alive
Bridegroom
Master of the Revels
7

God Is Love
Savior, Helper
Physician, Friend
2

SOUL OF CHRIST
True God and
True Man

God Is Faithful
The Faithful and
Obedient One 6

God Is Creative
Evangelist
3 Wonder-Worker

God Is All-Knowing 5
Teacher
Prayer

4 God Is Beautiful
Artist, Dramaturge
Liturgist, High Priest

I see how he "puts on a show." How he lets himself be fêted when he rides into Jerusalem. How in his farewell session with the apostles he "stages" a mystical banquet, expressly commanding them to repeat it, so as to recall the presence of his body and blood. He demands of us a nuanced relationship balancing nearness and distance. I see the drama of his passion, his readiness for death, his double role as high priest and sacrificial lamb.

Is the Church, is my community animated by this artistic drama of the soul of Christ, or has our liturgy succumbed to lethal and museum-like boredom?

I sense the continual temptation of Jesus the mystic: to fall prey to Weltschmerz and self-pity, to feel misunderstood, secretly to yearn for heaven (there and then is better than here and now!). "Have I been with you so long, and yet you do not know me?" he sighs (John 14:9) — but he doesn't fall into the root sin of envy and false longing.

The disintegration point of TWO is EIGHT. Beware when a stressed TWO plays out his or her dark power to dominate people completely. But as a redeemed TWO, Jesus was also a redeemed EIGHT.

Jesus Christ as an EIGHT

The King of all Kings, but meek, the Lord of all Lords, but free of violence.

I look into the eyes of a messianic king who has majesty and dignity, though crowned, to be sure, with thorns. I look into the icon of the Pantocrator, but behind his head shines the nimbus of the cross. It is an authority that doesn't keep me small, but offers me a share of greatness: "Come, take on your full size at last, to my honor and to yours."

Has this form of Christ's soul left its stamp on the Church in its triumphal march through history from Emperor Constantine to Chancellor Kohl (to mention two EIGHTs)? Or have we been done in by the imperial use of supreme power?

What a tremendous self-divestiture, that Jesus with all his power, armed with such unheard-of divine and human authority, resisted all Satan's attempts from the beginning in the wilderness and made a permanent renunciation of power, taking on the form of a slave. This reveals to me the strength of non-violence.

The right wing of TWO belongs in the gut-center.

Jesus Christ as a ONE

We're familiar with this: The Prophet, the Preacher of Conversion, the Pastor with the gift of looking into hearts, the man who demands that we be perfect like God, who makes his sun shine on the just and the unjust.

I look into the eyes of an incorruptible prophet: "There is no place that does not see you: You must change your life" (Rilke). He has "eyes like flames of fire" (Rev. 1:14). Whip in hand, he storms through the courtyard of the Temple.

Does his community still have the fire of his prophetic soul? Or has it become "liberal" and limp, lukewarm to the point that he will spit it out (Rev. 3:16). Where anything goes — except for binding community rules?

The continual temptation of the angry young man is to slip into negative pharisaical criticism. Jesus became the merciful one, the man who granted absolution to people whose lives were shipwrecked, who didn't come up to the norms of the Law: "Where are they? Has no one condemned you? . . . Then neither do I" (John 8:10). Through his patience and his parables about the ripening crops he makes it possible for his disciples to grow. Despite his occasional sighs the teacher of righteousness does not fall into the trap of disappointment and impatient anger.

Now I go to the left wing of TWO.

Jesus as a THREE

The Evangelist and Wonder-worker, the Spellbinder, electrifying the masses.

We see his gifts as a preacher, the strategy by which he first wins over half of Galilee, the "land of darkness," then heads for Judea and Jerusalem, first sending his disciples to the lost sheep of the house of Israel, then on Easter charging them to take the Gospel to "all peoples" through "all the world." He skillfully mobilizes them, and they learn by doing. I look into the eyes of a master who wins me over at once, so that I drop everything, who calls me to follow him and immediately bids me to become active as a "multiplier" in his name. He insists that like a capitalist I charge usurious interest rates on my pound. He inspires me with visionary goals and raises me to a level of activity I never dreamed of.

Is my Church community infected by this visionary, energetic, and success-oriented side of Christ's soul? Or has everything drifted from one year to the next into aimless activism?

On the other hand I also think of this: The constant temptation of the missionary and wonder-worker to bring off miraculous exhibitions or in the end to come down from the cross: "Then we'll believe you" — isn't our cry a temptation to him? Now I move across to FIVE, the disintegration point of EIGHT.

Jesus Christ as a FIVE

The Teacher, Wisdom in person, in lonely prayer on the Mount of Olives.

For Jesus renouncing power does not mean retreating into untouchable inwardness. Neither overaggressive like an unredeemed EIGHT, nor self-centered like an unredeemed FIVE, Jesus Christ has become for us the quintessence of the hidden Wisdom that invites everyone in the streets and squares to come, to learn, and to find rest for their souls (Matt. 11:19b, 28).

I look into the eyes of a teacher who explains the mysteries of God's kingdom in simple parables. I hang on every word from his mouth when the Gospel is read at services in church. And he takes me aside into the loneliness of the night, as after Emmaus or the ascent of Mt. Tabor. I hear his invitation: Come, I want to talk with you, I want to listen to you, I want to teach you to pray. He leads me on the path into mysticism, into meditation, and contemplation. (As a FIVE I get along well with him.)

Does my Church have something of this kind of simple catechesis and homiletics? Does the Church teach the way he taught? Does it really teach the Sermon on the Mount as the rules for the community? In our religious formation are we taught the "science" of theology or wisdom? Morality or mysticism? The dogmatic theory of the two kingdoms or how to recognize the kingdom in the loaf of the world?

The temptation to be silent must have been very strong for him. Why not keep the knowledge of the mystery of the kingdom to himself, instead of preaching it to thick-skinned, uncomprehending ears? Not to cast the pearls of wisdom before swine, and yet sacrifice oneself completely to the world — this is in itself a kind of sublime brinkmanship.

But a highly concentrated teacher and stressed-out ascetic can easily slip into the role of an unredeemed SEVEN.

Jesus Christ as a SEVEN

Jesus Christ, no escapist monk, but a joyful SEVEN, a Bridegroom and Master of the Revels.

I look into eyes full of radiant joy. He calls us to freedom. Come and drink the wine of my love. I am life! "And they began to make merry" (Luke 15:24). That's how it was at the table of the tax collectors and prostitutes where, as at the marriage feast in Cana, the wine of joy never ran out, so that the Pharisees murmured, "Behold, a glutton and a drunkard!" (Matt. 11:9).

Does my Church have something of this liberating feature of the soul of Christ? What sort of a tone is there when we sing the Bach chorale, "Jesus, my joy! Hence, you mournful spirits, for Jesus, my master of revels, makes his entrance here"? He did come, after all, so that we might have "life" and have it "abundantly" (John 10:10).

And all this has its dark, seductive side, namely the temptation to avoid pain, suffering, and the cross, when Peter in an altogether human outburst, says: "God forbid, Lord! This shall never happen to you." To which the answer is, "Get behind me, Satan!" (Matt. 16:22–23), when Jesus the SEVEN recognized his pitfall.

Now I return again to the middle triangle of points 3, 6, and 9, the connecting points of the three heart, head, and gut centers.

Jesus Christ as a SIX

I look into the eyes of the Servant of God, the Faithful and True, the obedient Son who was nevertheless a son come of age, the Slave who was nevertheless an unafraid and voluntary slave. I think that this is a precious wonder of Christ's soul. I am especially moved by his fidelity. "If we are faithless, he remains faithful — for he cannot deny himself" (2 Tim. 2:13).

And he overcomes the fear of being abandoned by all people and having to enter of state of abandonment by God. Again I am very moved by the way he resists the double temptation of fleeing or fighting, and lets himself be arrested with the words: "If you seek me, let these men go" (John 18:8).

One great problem the Church faces is fear of human authority, the temptation to conform to the world and give in to the persecutions and seductions of the various cultures.

Jesus Christ as a NINE

Jesus the Prince of Peace, the "Reconciler of all things" (Col. 1:20), the all-integrating Word.

I look into the eyes of Buddha, sitting in tranquillity and giving his blessing. A shimmer of gold and iridescent color shines around him. Streams of living water pour from his body. His arms are open. From all sides children and people seeking justice come to him. He gives his blessing to them and helps them find justice and reconciliation.

How lazy is the soul of the Church? Has it become bourgeois and harmless? Looking at the Christian community, one thinks: The reason the world is going under isn't the wickedness of the wicked, but the laziness of the good.

This temptation to bourgeois existence is depicted with a broad brush in the famous/infamous Martin Scorsese film, *The Last Temptation of Christ.* In a feverish hallucination Jesus dreams that he can come down from the cross because he's suffered and been tested enough. Walking down from Golgotha he meets a marriage procession. The bride is Mary Magdalen, who has come to pick up her bridegroom — Jesus himself. He marries and has a family and lives to the age of seventy. The last temptation is an authentically biblical one: not sexual desire, but the wish to settle down, at long last, in a comfortable, well provided for private life. But no, Jesus doesn't die peacefully in bed, he goes back at the last minute to the cross, where he wakes from his dream.

Does the soul of Christ with its many faces live in the soul of the Church? *Alma de Cristo, sanctéficame.* Soul of Christ, sanctify me. *Cuerpo de Cristo, sálvame.* Body of Christ, save me. *Sangre de Cristo, embriágame.* Blood of Christ, intoxicate me." Ignatius Loyola places this prayer at the beginning of his *Spiritual Exercises,* which aim to bring the Church and Christians back to their original image.

I can still believe in the

presence and indwelling of your Head, King, and High Priest . . . , who has promised you that not only would just his divinity be with you (which for us poor sinners is like a consuming fire turned against dry stubble), but the one — the person who has spoken with you, who has tasted every sort of distress in the human nature he took on, who therefore can have compassion on us as his fellow humans, his brothers and sisters — who wishes to be with us in all our troubles, even according to the nature, thanks to which he is our brother and we are flesh of his flesh.[4]

The Enneagram:
Possibilities and Dangers for Pastoral Care

Dirk Meine

1. WHAT DOES THE ENNEAGRAM WANT?

Every person can be considered as both unique and as comparable to others. Both aspects relativize each other and are therefore interrelated.

The Enneagram tries to understand better the individuality of a person and to deal with it — by looking into the ways he or she is like others. People with similarly structured natures are compared with one another. The idea is to make clear the fact (and how it happens) that "out of the broad spectrum of possibilities for concretely realizing values . . . only one specific band is ever chosen and really lived out."[1] Given this situation, the Enneagram offers help for living and believing that we can observe in three major areas: knowledge, change, and relations with God.

Knowledge

The Enneagram aims at self-knowledge and knowledge of people in general. The starting point here is a negative one, namely the "illusionary ideals"[2] that everyone develops in response to his or her encounter with the outside world, and that can be summarized in nine categories. These ideals have two negative consequences: First, they make people fixate on their self-image and their personal, limited view of the world, by means of which they justify themselves and judge what is good. Second, they are the source of false guilt feelings that arise when people don't fulfill their ego-ideals[3] and that blind them to true guilt and their real shadow sides.[4] The reader is called upon to identify his or her ego-ideal, because this is "decisively important — thanks to both its concrete structure and its dynamic results — for shaping the limits and contents of possible experiences that get excluded. In addition the ego-ideal is "an essential pillar in the structure of human relationships."[5]

Knowledge, to be sure, isn't the same as redemption. But the shock of recognition can prompt a quest that becomes a transitional stage on the way to responsible repentance and change.[6] The insights that the Enneagram seeks to transmit, therefore, are not designed to solidify the type and make it permanent, but on the contrary to break its chains.

Change

But how can the old ego-fixation be changed? To put it theologically, how are penance and liberation possible? The Enneagram has two answers ready.

First, "Redemption is the work of God's grace, which takes place without our doing anything . . . even the letting go and opening of ourselves was not our achievement. We were 'seduced' by Someone."[7]

Second, the Enneagram cites concrete attitudes and ways of behaving that one "must learn."

The fact that there is no separating patience and initiative, passivity and preparedness, shows what we humans are: simultaneously dependent and responsible for our path in life.

A clear knowledge of our shadow sides and a corresponding keener awareness is the prerequisite for charting the direction of work on our own personality. The Enneagram can help me to see the doors that either block my path or lead me farther, the passageways that I have to take, but that I will unconsciously stumble into only in exceptional cases. The Enneagram aims to clear the path to a more diverse personality by combining the concentrated awareness of one wing or positive partner energy.

When we call our illusions by name, we unmask and weaken them.[8] To call them by name also means to seek self-revealing dialogue with others and thereby to work not on the "fixed" type but on our nature as it has evolved and still is evolving.

Finally to cite Jesus as an example: He was a man of permanent repentance with respect to his own pitfalls and temptations.[9] He was compassionate with people, recognizing their different needs and qualities, and treating them accordingly.[10]

Relations with God

The goal of the Enneagram is to make us "able to hear Christ's call to our life" and to have a "personal relationship with Jesus."[11] This raises the question of whether and to what extent self-knowledge (the main theme of the Enneagram) goes together with knowledge of God.

This is surely not true in the sense of an automatic or autonomous human capacity. There are mature people who are not religious, and there are religious people who have to be labeled as neurotic. Still, religious people keep discovering images and mottos in their life story that have proved crucial in forming both their personality and their notion of God. They also find that piety and images of God always develop in the context of their respective personal, social, or historical image of the world.[12]

The Sufis are supposed to have called the Enneagram the "face of God," because the nine refractions of the one divine love appear in it as in a prism. Hence each type would reflect one part of the face of God and thereby challenge people not to claim their own idea of God as the true one, but to become free to recognize and accept various ideas.

With its representation of the negative motive forces, the Enneagram spells out concretely the broad biblical formula that we "all have sinned" (Rom. 3:23). And it directs our attention to the ways that we block the divine force with our attitudes and behavior. Positively stated, this means that the longing that runs through my life is raised to a higher level and fulfilled in God.

2. WHAT DOES THE ENNEAGRAM DO?

Strengths of the Enneagram

Given the exploding pluralism of lifestyles and opinions today there is a distinct need for help in getting properly oriented. In today's confusion, competence in decision-making and reliability in diagnosing trouble, both in the private and the public sphere, have largely been lost. This need for direction has been sensed by the New Age movements, whose leaders have produced a swelling harvest of therapies, developmental schemes, and methods of guidance — and hundreds of how-to books about them. People are looking for psychological, spiritual-religious, and esoteric techniques that they expect to help them cope better with everyday problems and promote their personal transformation.

For the most part, the younger and middle-aged generations no longer look to the Church for acceptable answers about guilt and healing, although such topics are precisely the sort of thing the Church is genuinely concerned with. The Enneagram — as reader responses to books on the subject show — has landed in the middle of what is practically a meaning-vacuum. The Church is not exempt from this either, because personal counselling ranks very low on the list of needs expressed by churchgoers.

In the following pages I shall discuss the most relevant basic concerns, especially those of church-oriented people, that the proponents of the Enneagram feel bound to attend to.

The Enneagram Is Self-Critical

It claims that its function is to point the way, but only as one pointer among many, not as the answer. It expressly resists being glorified as a new absolute doctrine of salvation,[13] and thereby subjects itself to criticism in keeping with its own message that a gift can lead through fixation to the greatest weakness and sin.[14]

The Enneagram Is Oriented to Experience

Experience forms the double criterion for the Enneagram model. On the one hand, it invokes a long oral experiential tradition.[15] On the other, it invites readers to scrutinize it with their own experiences.[16] Thus in the origin, development, and use of the Enneagram the rule is that knowing means experiencing and "living out." The subject-object split into a knowing "subject" and a known "object" disregards — and often fails because of this — the persons and things outside itself, by confusing observation with participation and argumentation with insight. This is a burden that weighs on the western world, and on Protestantism too, which drove experience out of the Church this way.

This can be clearly seen in the Protestant style of dealing with sin, which is turned into generic sinfulness with no concrete content.[17] Dietrich Bonhoeffer describes the problem as follows: "People are accustomed to justify themselves with general confessions of sin. [But] I experience the full perdition and corruption of human nature — insofar as I experience it at all — in my specific sins."[18] And what holds for concrete conversion holds too for concrete liberation in "a"forgiveness of their particular sins."[19] The classic illustration of this is the confession of public guilt on Good Friday, which remains vague and undetailed and thus promotes an empty faith in justification, degenerating into empty ritual.

The Enneagram aims at this experiential background. It makes no bones about calling concrete errors in attitude and behavior by their names, so that repentance and liberation can linked to sharply defined and "testable" particulars.

The Enneagram Is Capable of Dialogue

As we have already seen in the three presentations of the Enneagram — Jaxon-Bear's esoteric version, Riso's psychological approach, and Rohr/Ebert's Christian perspective — the model can be taught in combination with the most varied world views. Rohr and Ebert's book is especially popular in Catholic and Protestant circles. Thanks to its simplicity and its capacity for expressing traditional Christian tenets in a novel way,[20] it has been notably helpful for people alienated from the Church. It encourages them to start all over with the Church, and they find in the Enneagram a substitute for a language, which they had thought lost, to talk about sin, redemption, and so on.

The Enneagram Has a Spiritual Orientation[21]

The blurb for Rohr and Ebert's book points this out: It calls the Enneagram a "spiritual psychology...that blends spiritual experience and modern anthropology" and a "handle for making changes that begin inside us."

The GCL (Communities of Christian Life, a lay organization of the Jesuits) uses it for retreat days and, in combination with the *Spiritual Exercises,* for opening up awareness of one's own way of conversion. This is not a matter of cognition, but a spiritual growth process (with the mind and will making the decisions), a directed vital evolution.

The Enneagram Is Grounded in Theology

Rohr and Ebert unfold their arguments amid frequent references to the Bible and continual allusions to the Church's doctrine of grace. The concept of sin is defined so as to avoid moral misunderstanding, and interpreted as a failure to reach relational goals, thereby cutting me off from God, my neighbor, and myself. The person is confronted with his or her guilt, there is no shifting the guilt to one's surroundings. The Enneagram is not trying to give superficial strength to the ego, but to stir up humility before God.[22] The reader is told: "You are God's beloved son, God's beloved daughter. . . . Our identity is primarily created through a relation."[23] In this way it aims to strike a balance between acceptance by God and acknowledgment of sin, between accepting oneself and challenging oneself. Another balance is maintained between liberation and redemption: Thus repentance is characterized as at once "our greatest human deed" and "a gift of God" that we cannot make.

The Enneagram Is Inviting, Unburdening, and Full of Promise

Along with its negative starting point, the Enneagram also has a double positive one. First, the longing concealed behind our sin comes into view as a gift of God — for example, behind the workaholic, know-it-all manner of ONEs lies a longing for perfection that Jesus himself enjoins (Matt. 5:48). In this way we can deal more compassionately with others and ourselves.

Second, when people get a look at the capacities inherent — but sometimes ignored — in their type, along with its wings and partner energy, it gives them a taste for working on themselves: "When I see all the things that I can become, I look to the future feeling good and confident."[24]

I can also draw support from the realization that I am not the only one of my type, that there are others with their weirdness and gifts, that, besides, *all* types are "fallen" and in need of redemption, and that no one is morally better or worse for his or her gifts.[25]

Along with all its seriousness, the Enneagram, as Rohr and Ebert present it, is shot through with a playfulness that tries to make its message more accessible through a helpful use of association. This can be seen in the non-dogmatic correlation of symbolic colors, animals, and countries with the different types. A glance into the index of names illustrates the book's spirit: just above Dostoyevsky we find Donald Duck, and above Luther the *Peanuts* character Lucy. Unfortunately humor is not yet a category of dogma, but it shows a Christian freedom that preserves the richness of the human condition and doesn't turn pale in antiseptic purposefulness.

The Enneagram Is Analytical and Synthetic

It operates in the tension created by, on the one hand, describing the features common to each type (that is, groups) and on the other encouraging people to come to know (through self-knowledge) their incomparable individuality. It analyzes modes of behavior, which are combined in specific attitudes. It also explores the source of guilt feelings, and the ego-ideal lurking behind them is brought in too. It concretizes liberation in steps that can be experienced and observed, and these are inseparably connected with the grace of God that effects them.

The Enneagram Is Dynamic

It understands the description of types not as something etched in bronze, but as the necessary recognition of our own fixation, so that we can be released from it. It brands as an abuse "fitting oneself and others, in a cheap, flat fashion, into a scheme, so as precisely not to grow, but to petrify."[26] It offers us partner energy, the wings, and the qualities of "unredeemed," "normal," and "redeemed" (internal to the type) as a threefold dynamism and goal for our own active participation.[27]

This lays out before us the variety of possibilities not just for us but for life itself. In this way self-realization doesn't have to end in rigid egotism, but gets relativized by the equally valuable abundance of other life.

The Limits of the Enneagram

Working with the Enneagram involves a number of dangers of possible misuse, which are heightened by some structural and substantive weaknesses of Rohr and Ebert's book. The model aims at being an instrument in the service of self-knowledge. But it might also seduce readers into reinforcing both old and new prejudices or lead them, through the enthusiasm it generates, to greatly over-estimate its possible applications.

The Enneagram as a Doctrine of Salvation

Insecurity and inability to get oriented make people susceptible to the appeal of systems that offer them a grand overview, solid support, and a chance to become whole in a day-to-day world that is both confusing and threatening. Then the Enneagram's function as a map is turned into that of a handy plan of salvation or an objective rule book for seeing through people. Readers forget that maps and reality aren't identical, that reality has far more nuances. Surely it's true that all systems, tools, and convictions can be perverted, and people have to be allowed their status as adults, with the right to make their own decisions.

After all our experiences in seminars and correspondence with readers, it's clear that we must be more sober, more careful, and less system-happy in pre-senting the Enneagram as a limited aid (1 Cor. 13:9). We must also lay more stress on warnings against misuse and on the fact that it's a series of snapshots, not the whole picture. Otherwise it develops its own dynamic and becomes an autonomous force.

Fixating on One's Own Type

This is the greatest danger and the most frequently voiced objection to the model. It can be seen in three forms: regressive, aggressive, and compulsive.

When someone has found his or her type, this can lead to "typecasting" and self-limitation. The Enneagram "believer" may trace every action and attitude back to the energy of his or her own type. One can then withdraw into one's shell and become blind to the wealth of other possibilities still slumbering within oneself. The support available from the wings and partner energy is overlooked, since they are experienced as alien and not a part of me.

The aggressive variant appears in the form of self-righteousness: "That's just the way I am." We deny our own responsibility and, with the help of the system, relegate it to the force of destiny or our environment. In this way the Enneagram turns into a psychoanalytical trick: The causes of our own lapses are laid at the door of our "type," and our own moral structure is treated as an external category.[28] This method of dealing with the Enneagram is thereby unmasked as an absence or denial of God's authority to judge, before which humans are personally guilty.

The third variety can be described as a self-fulfilling prophecy. This is compulsive behavior that consciously or unconsciously conforms to the pre-dicted reactions of a type. Knowledge of our type can subliminally direct our behavior and decisions so powerfully that we wind up flirting with a caricature of ourselves.

Labeling Others

The chief misunderstanding consists in taking the Enneagram for an "interesting bit of information about people to satisfy our curiosity."[29] The most oft-heard complaint is that people use it "to pigeonhole one another."[30] It is in fact tempting to "get someone's number" with the handy categories of the Enneagram. It's particularly tempting to use this knowledge as a weapon in arguments: "How typical, you with your ONE energies!"

The Enneagram itself offers an unfortunate example of this by naming certain nations as symbols, thereby cementing cliché-ridden prejudices. If SIX is associated with Germany as a symbolic country, does this mean that Berliners, Bavarians, and Rheinlanders are all bursting with SIX-energy?[31]

The Practicability of Redemption

The formula, "just try a little harder, you can do it," fails both theologically (Rom. 9:16) and psychologically.[32] People are not merely passive objects as far as their psychic development is concerned. Failure to recognize this has let a large number of phrases slip into Discovering the Enneagram that suggest we can redeem ourselves. We supposedly can "cut our way through" our pitfalls; for every sin "there is a cure . . . the medicine for anger is called patience"; moving to the wings "can be . . . done with relative ease."

Moralizing Redemption

When sin is concretized the basic idea of the relational level or at least its decisive importance can drop out of sight. Of course we can experience our sin and the brokenness of a relationship only in our concrete attitudes and actions. Still sin remains a theological category. And I need the divine Thou, which takes me back into relationship with itself.

Theological Foundation and Terminology

For reasons of strict internal coherence the theological foundation of the book is emphatically worked out in the first and third part of the book, as well as in the concluding meditation by Dietrich Koller (see Appendix A). But, in comparison with this, the presentation of God as the "Totally Other" in the concrete description of the types in Part Two is inadequate. At this point it should have been linked to a concrete discussion of divine grace. In my opinion the authors missed a chance here to get rid of an overly spiritualized, abstract conception of grace.

Another problematic element, it seems to me, is the conceptual mixture of psychological and theological redemption, sanctification and maturity. This leads to the unavoidable impression that the maturing and growing person gets more redeemed. But then the holistic and paradoxical character of justification must inevitably suffer, obscuring the fact that our redemption comes entirely from God, although we are sinners.

A similar problem arises with the "creative power of forgiveness," which is unfortunately given only isolated treatment (in the final meditation). But this is precisely what serves as the bulwark against grace being turned into "a refined culture of vanity," into cheap grace.[33]

The center of the Enneagram should be conversion, which humbles and mortifies us. But without personal confession and absolution (in whatever form) this goal cannot be reached.[34]

Analytical Weaknesses

Tracing the types back to a specific kind of childhood is dubious. "How did I turn into what I am today, what personal experiences lie behind this?" This line of questioning is not of immediate concern to the Enneagram, but it gets touched upon in conjectures and generalizations.

Nevertheless, the question of the concrete sources of character remains one of the responsibilities of people who have been prodded by the Enneagram into working on themselves. In this process our own dreams and childhood memories are particularly important for gaining access to the unconscious.

Individualistic Extrapolations

The origins of the Enneagram are for the most part shrouded in darkness. If we compare the various presentations, we find many divergencies and not just as regards the goal and form of the Enneagram. There are also some clear and substantial differences in the descriptions of the types. The authors handing down on the tradition, whether directly or indirectly, approach it in ways that reflect their conflicting personal preferences and models of thinking and perception. Once again this makes it clear that the Enneagram has to be used with caution, because though the message seems legitimized by its long history, its tradition, under certain circumstances, turns out to be short and highly subjective.

Likelihood of Misreadings

There is no denying that because of the associative nature of the system "something always adds up." But this is like horoscope typologies, where you can recognize elements of your own personality in almost every type.[35]

One is struck by the uncertainty of self-identification that people display at Enneagram seminars, the vacillation between two or more types. I myself initially located myself in the wrong type, and even later on had doubts about where I belonged. Andreas Ebert had a similar experience.

Faults Due to Arbitrary Use

The recipients of Enneagram training can distort the statements and goals of the model into rapid-fire, facile information, into cool, objective psychological self-help, into cognitive data about a person, with no need for emotional involvement or penance.

A further variant of this approach is falling in love with one's favorite type: "That's how I'd like to see myself," or "These are precisely the positive qualities that distinguish me," thereby overlooking the dark, negative sides.

A third kind of personal error in using the model is seen in our type-specific ego-ideals: The system is harnessed to the energies of our own type. Thus EIGHTs use it as an instrument of power, FIVEs as a instrument of knowledge, ONEs as a instrument of self-perfection, etc.

Book Form

The Enneagram used to be passed along in an oral tradition from master to disciple, which guaranteed that there would be spiritual counselling. But this is eliminated by the book form. The Ecumenical Enneagram Workgroup is trying to address this problem and come up with enough counselling opportunities to meet the need. The program is still in its initial stage and accordingly overburdened. Still, to be redeemed I must have the Thou, as a challenge and complement to my own limited perception.

Social-Political Context

The Enneagram points a way from within to without. The handful of social and political observations are embedded in considerations on a personal path of redemption.[36] The reflections needed to apply the Enneagram as a tool to shape the community's thinking are still in the testing phase.[37]

People who have been positively changed can effect positive changes. Conversely, however, practicing psychoanalysts have learned that persons whose mental health has been restored aren't strong enough to stand up to their environment, which has, to some extent, made them what they are. Thus the Enneagram contains a twofold danger: first, of too much turning inward and second, of underestimating the power of social and political structures. By contrast, redemption through Christ aims at transforming both the individual and the community (1 Cor. 12).

Non-Christian Origins

The psychological approach, the kinship with esotericism, and the non-Christian source of the Enneagram frighten many conservative Christians who see it as endangering the "essence" of Christianity. But those who are prompted by their aggressive fear of the Enneagram to give it such labels as "unmistakably sophistical thinking," "pseudo-religion," "ideology," "super-stition," "numerology," or "neo-occultism," are openly and embarrassingly showing how ill-informed they are.

One might ask whether the first Christians were actually so original and independent of Hellenistic or otherwise pagan ideas, terms, and language that those things didn't make their way into the "essence" of Christian faith and piety.[38] Nowadays no one would apply this standard so as to strike the notion of the Logos from John's Gospel or to abolish the feast of Christmas. The question is whether the new material has been adequately baptized, that is, made serviceable for Christ. Hitherto the Gospel has always found its way into the world, been adopted, combined with other elements, and reinterpreted, thereby changing its form. But the goal of reasonable criticism is to keep form and content separate or to indicate that there has been mutual penetration.

In the case of the Enneagram, the most basic danger lies in the fact that only with difficulty can it be separated from the context of esoteric and self-help movements (look at the cover of *Das Enneagram*!): But the upsurge of such movements is predicated on the fiction that personal wholeness can be taught and learned,[39] often without any personal God as an "opposite number." The influence of such unconscious prejudices can impair the reader's perception so that the theological passages in the book get overlooked or even, in some cases, deliberately omitted.

In all this we should have sufficient confidence in the the Church's power to regulate itself (cf. Rev. 5:38–39); we should wait and see what will be left of the Enneagram after ten years of practical experience.

The Enneagram Is Not Empirically Provable

We are looking here at a confrontation between two "hostile brothers," science and intuition, who cannot be harmonized. There is no scientific proof underlying the Enneagram; it cannot be rationally substantiated, and the types are neither empirically detectable nor sharply distinguishable from one another.[40]

The Enneagram locates its strength not in scientific verifiability but in experiential intuition, and lays its claim to usefulness in the latter domain not the former. It's dangerous to mingle the two, for example when supporters of the Enneagram defend themselves against questions from science by retreating to the high ground of experiential intuition — where they become dogmatic themselves.[41] The basis of the model — the fact that humans exhibit different and comparable behavior patterns and driving forces — needs to be given a lot of latitude so that its doesn't become too rigid. Then it's likely to shatter on the manifold richness of life and our experience with it.

3. THEOLOGICAL FOUNDATIONS

I would now like to examine the Enneagram's fundamental biblical and theological position with respect to three crucial areas. In the fourth and final section I will turn to the practical field of spiritual guidance.

Anthropology and Concept of Sin

The question theology asks about the human person is a relationship question. The person is God's creation, but fallen and separated from him because of sin. But the person has been loved by God, not abandoned. Thus theology can never talk about humans while ignoring their relationship with God, be it sound, broken, or healed.

The disclosure of what is concretely blocking us and preventing us from having a deeper and more authentic relationship with God is the main purpose of the Enneagram. In taking this approach it ignores the issues of the "guilt of a social group" and "sin as personal power." But doing so might have underlined how threatening these things are and made it clear just how little room for movement there is in the human condition.

Sin has two principle manifestations: unbelief and self-exaltation. Unbelief is the act that separates the whole person from God. Along with this goes the self-exaltation by which the person makes himself or herself the center of the world. The Enneagram describes how with an inflated ego-ideal even the justice, help, or perfection that God demands can be perverted and turned into a temptation.[42] Thus when limited goodness absolutizes itself and ceases to be related to God, human greatness becomes a temptation, and our sin manifests itself not just in acts of pride but even in acts of modesty.[43]

The Enneagram points out such temptations, which we consider innocent, because they correspond to our ideals. Still more, it calls our attention to the psychological mechanism by which we bury ourselves ever more deeply in our temptation: We get guilt feelings in our conscience at the exact moment when we fail to live up to our ego-ideal. That's why we strive to allay our conscience by "good behavior" (in line with our ego-ideal), and we obstruct the view — ours and other people's — of our actual weaknesses and errors, of our ignorance and imprisonment.

In this way the Enneagram submits a silent critique of the judging authority of conscience. Because we bear within us not an objective, universally valid touchstone for "good" and "evil," but a subjective, developed voice that condemns and exonerates. When it does so, its normative "that" (the binding force) holds true, even when on the "what" (the substance of the case) it is in error (cf. 1 Cor. 8).[44] This means that everything becomes a sin when we act against our conscience. We can't dispense ourselves from it or bribe it with rationalizations. To use the language of the Enneagram: We remain a specific type till our dying day, and our conscience will take up a specific standpoint in accordance with our type. It will deviate more in a situation that is typical for us, and deviate less in others. Liberating a conscience in bondage or awakening an anesthetized one can be done with the help of (self-)knowledge (once again, see 1 Cor. 8), but only case by case and through an ongoing process.

The Enneagram is supposed to strengthen freedom and responsibility, which reciprocally condition one another. Responsibility arises with respect to the actions and attitudes that have been chosen in a personal decision. Both existential mentality and individual act go together in a practically inseparable combination. Theology distinguishes here between sin in general and sins in particular.

In our sin we turn away, personally and actively, from the one whom we belong to. But, thanks to God's fidelity, "There is no place to which humans can retreat from the divine THOU, because he overarches the ego, wraps it round and is closer to it than the ego is to itself."[45] We also find the following grace-ful and consoling encouragement in the Enneagram, which has a sense of obligation to the Gospel, understood as good news: "God loves us even when we don't take this path (that is, of penitential love); but then we are depriving ourselves of many fruits of God's love."[46]

Finally, neither the types, nor the number nine, nor the binding of every person to one type can be verified either by science or the Bible and systematic theology. The concrete person is more of a mystery (2 Cor. 2:11) that cannot be defined. But as an undogmatically applied device for self-knowledge, as a guide for confession that can also lead to repentance before God and to a lovingly changed intercourse with ourselves and the world around us, the Enneagram seems psychologically appropriate and theologically sound.

Image of God

Humans experience God not immediately (objectively), but only indirectly (subjectively). He can never be the object of our knowledge. The Enneagram expresses this idea by saying that God is the Totally Other, the Holy One, the Not-I. Nevertheless people ask about God, they seek to experience him.

The Enneagram accedes to this desire for concrete experience by interpreting the religious concern that lies behind it. This brings out the inner tension in the idea of God as a conflict between concrete specificity and unconditional being. The answer to this conflict lies revealed-yet-hidden in Jesus Christ. As mediator he represents God in dialogue with human beings, the image of God in concrete, personal, experiential reality. This shows the world "what God is and what he wants man to be." Christ is the exemplar of God and of the new, liberated human person.

After spreading the gifts of all nine types around its circle, the Enneagram discusses them as qualities of Christ and illustrates them with biblical references. Christ did not just hear God's invitations, but answered them, translating them into reality. Here we are met by the vision of our promised liberation in person: In Jesus Christ we see God's participation in the human condition and its redemption. From this standpoint it is possible to approach God in his holiness. But now that religious concerns arise, we enter a region of the Enneagram in which the transparent clarity that marked its treatment of nonreligious experience turns pale and fuzzy.

Because with only a few exceptions God is presented here as forgiving, granting grace, inviting, giving — as the God of "love." What he calls us to here is apparently nothing more than the "highest form of spiritual consciousness." What's missing is the side of God that accuses, takes to task, lays claims, is felt as a demand from the outside. The holy and just God does more than just constantly affirm with eternal forbearance: He resists, condemns, and takes a partisan stance on the side of love.

I know that the image of the punishing God has not only paved the way for a wrongheaded moralism in the Church ("One doesn't do that sort of thing"), but has also led to an astonishing variety of religious neuroses ("The good Lord sees everything"). Still, I consider it theologically and psychologically false to react to such excesses by completely concealing the insistent will of God as the Enneagram does.

We should have learned at least this much from ecumenical dialogue: You can't side simultaneously with both the oppressed and their oppressors, with the despised and their despisers. Latin American liberation theology, Africa's black theology, the Minyung theology of South Korea, or feminist theology know a thing or two about this, because they have experienced it in their own skin. Secure Christians in Europe and America, on the other hand, prefer to hear about the universal love of God, not about his demands (James 2:16).

This can also be seen in the missing theology of creation. There ought to be an appropriate, foundational statement in the Enneagram about the relationship between God and the world: It should be stressed that humanity as creation is dependent on the original, preserving, and guiding creative action of God. This would also put more solid ground underneath discourse about the grace of God, which we must await for wholeness, integration, and redemption, because we can't make it ourselves. Failure to offer a doctrine of creation squanders a double opportunity: to make plain and emphatic, on the one hand, the demands made on the creature and, on the other, the knowledge that we are borne by the grace and power of the Creator, "who gives life to the dead and calls into existence the things that do not exist" (Rom. 4:17).

Redemption

Redemption is God's work alone. He cannot become a partner in human action, his Thou embraces our I and with it the whole relationship. This is the objective side of redemption; subordinate to it is the subjective side: the things humans do in response to God's action. The Enneagram tries to do justice to both sides, and seeks to "understand the call to freedom primarily as an offer from God and not our own doing."[47]

But the central crystallization point for redemption is Christ and his cross. In it we meet the effective sign of God's redemptive action, and here too lies one of the theological weaknesses of the Enneagram. Along with several references to God's grace, reminding us that we have to wait for our integration or redemption, we find a strange, almost embarrassed speechlessness when it comes to naming and concretizing the "means" of redemption. Thus we are left in suspense about what divine grace means, which might give rise to caricatures of the "good Lord," who does nothing but support, affirm, and pass on his cheap grace, but never says a critical word of his own.

When the subject turns to the experiences and concrete events of everyday life, Christ is sometimes marginalized, shunted to a gray area, where he ceases to be the mediator between God and man, and is downgraded to a mere model. Now the primary intention of the Enneagram is not to describe a one-time-only rebirth but to prompt us to seek out a process of redemption. This process includes all the unredeemed circumstances of earthly existence, and there are many different facets or degrees in redemption/sanctification: No one is fully redeemed, because this is an eschatological category (Rom. 8:19 ff.) And only humans have the power to break the chain of stimulus and response by reflecting and deciding. Here we see the subjective element of redemption: the experience of the inner power of Christ, without which liberation would be impossible. Thus the work of the Holy Spirit in the human soul is indeed a gift, but the individual must not remain passive in the face of it.[48]

Philippians 2:12–13 (Christ's "emptying" himself) has a central importance in the Enneagram as an example of the tension between human action and divine grace. God demands human work, which he makes possible by healing the split between desire and accomplishment (Rom. 7:15 ff.) A person should act as though everything depended on him or her. Afterwards he or she will understand that it was God's grace — and not any individual — that was in charge.[49]

In this sense the "old man" should renew himself on the model of his Creator and in honor of him (Col. 3:9–10,17), in other words not just morally, but with his entire vision of life (including moral behavior). We often experience morality not as the healing of a separation, but rather as its cause, since it often seems as if the person was made for morality, and not morality for the person. Likewise redemption must not be privatized, every idea about redemption must become political, in the sense of building community.

4. OUTLOOK FOR PASTORAL CARE

Pastoral situations are redemptive situations. And the concept of redemption has as many implications as there are negative, painful conditions in need of redemption, whether this be a matter of personal guilt or a universal destiny. Accordingly, pastoral care in the Church cannot be limited to the minor, out-of-the-way domain of the rector's office or the confession box. Pastoral care covers a much broader area, it is a participatory act between individuals and groups; it concerns the whole community and not just the pastor. Its goal is "reciprocal responsibility for the faith and the inner and outer well-being of the other."[50]

Conversation is perhaps the most important form of pastoral care,[51] because here advisor and advisee can seek out common paths of redemption. But this generally requires preparation, that is, an inner openness and readiness to commit oneself to a deeper dialogue. In the sense of a gradual path even a casual chat offers a starting point in this direction, and hence should not be disdained as a pastoral opportunity.[52] The Enneagram makes a start in such "human, all-too-human" situations and experiences, but it doesn't remain at a standstill there. It also lends structural help for complex contexts.

The question of pastoral care in the Church also raises questions about the pastoral care-giver. It is obvious, "that every psychoanalyst can only get as far as his own complex and internal resistances allow."[53] The same holds true for the person providing pastoral care, with his or her projections and counter-transferences, all of which he or she could become more aware of with the help of the Enneagram. Thus the model should first of all be an aid in the process of getting to know oneself, which the care-provider knows how to handle responsibly before he or she puts it to use. And here too it would be a total misconception to try to classify every client in every conversation by his or her

Enneagram number. This would be giving answers to questions that our inter-locutor hadn't even asked, and offering diagnoses and therapy for problems that we only conjecture others have.

This would be blocking off the possibility of giving unbiased attention to the concrete persons in our care, of leaving them time to tell their story, to listen to them and take them seriously.

The Enneagram has nine categories in hand, but these are not meant to be used prematurely, which would lead to "typecasting." Under favorable circumstances the pastoral care-provider will succeed, whether in the course of a casual chat, an ordinary conversation, or an explicit plea for help, in gathering information and turning the spotlight of the Enneagram on the case. The point is to inquire into what he or she has heard and analyzed, to offer it to one's partner in dialogue, and await a response.

The Enneagram is the account of a journey that offers possibilities, but does not compel and issues no directives. Ideally it aims to observe and describe structures of human behavior. The client is not given the "right" or "better" answer to a question; instead he or she must set out to find possible answers. It takes into account the findings of depth psychology and sociology that the driving forces behind our actions are not governed primarily by thought but by the unconscious, and are likewise to be explained by the way individuals are imprisoned in groups. Resistance and aversive responses from the client are stubborn defense mechanisms that determine the level of personal possibilities for working on oneself. For this reason they are also often good survival techniques that the person has developed in the course of his or her life. Insight into these points should help to prevent the care-provider from making an idol of knowledge.

But conversely it's true that without awareness a desired change becomes difficult or downright impossible, and the spiritual advisor can deal only with personalities that have become self-conscious. This is the reason why at some point or other the client must be led either by the advisor or by his or her own insight to confront the truth: At this point in my life guilt is cutting me off in my relationships with my fellow men and women, with myself, and with God. This guilt is concrete and can be named.

The Enneagram can be a support and guide at the beginning of such a path, but it's no substitute for the client's own work. Clients must accept the challenge of spelling out and analyzing their oldest and most typical defense mechanisms. The descriptions provided by the Enneagram types are rough sketches and sometimes exaggerated caricatures, but not detailed "wanted posters" that cover each and every person. The Enneagram has no interest at all in demolishing the unique individuality and originality of a person or in making everyone equal by flattening him or her under one of the nine categories. Rather it wants to help structure the enormous quantity of human experiences, so that they can be meaningfully clustered in the mirror of one's own personal biography.

Beyond that, the Enneagram would like to offer people support for dealing with the Church's traditional complex of questions concerning guilt and redemption. These questions, in fact, can rarely be given powerful answers by a Church that has become poor in experience and therefore speechless. This is especially the case since increasingly fewer people make the Church their first choice to turn to with their questions. With its special vocabulary the Enneagram offers its readers new access to the Church's traditional teachings.

This is of particular importance in pastoral care where I can address the experiences of alienation that I have every day vis-à-vis myself and others, and where my shadow side can be given a concrete name, lovingly,[54] but without embellishing or dumping guilt on the world around me. This then is the place where one can describe those experiences as the result of separation from God and can acknowledge them as personal guilt.

The Enneagram tries to make daily experiences show their true moral colors with regard to the relationship with God. The message of the Enneagram is grounded in Christian faith. With it readers can, if they wish, betake themselves on their own path to ask searching questions about their own individuality. This is an attempt to take seriously both man's question and God's answer.

The Enneagram deserves credit for opening up this path in an inviting fashion. It speaks to a basic feature and a basic longing of developing human beings: the need for both individuation and participation.

Readers can discover their own very personal fallenness. The Enneagram model has continually served to stir up, on the one hand, feelings of recognition, shame, and dismay, but, on the other, a sense of being at home. The revelation and assessment of their own strengths and capabilities by the Enneagram has motivated readers to perceive and address their own shadow sides with hope and courage.

Another point has become clear: There are still many other people who have a structure like mine. Basically all men and women have to fight their own strengths and weaknesses. In that sense they are all ultimately "numbers," they all struggle with their self-erected barriers, they are all "broken" in their existence.

Starting out from this critical but affirmative foundation makes it easier to move toward personal development or change, thereby instituting a process that should be the key to pastoral care: critical analysis and recognition, a sense of security and acceptance, development (that is, solidification and expansion) of positive natural tendencies, change (that is, humbly letting go) of hardened attitudes and behaviors. The traditional terms for this process are (acknowledgment of) sin, (experience of) grace, sanctification, and penance.

They have a fourfold horizon, framed by my relationship with God, my neighbor, myself, and the environment, whether animate or inanimate.

At the same time the Enneagram also runs up against the limits of its applicability to pastoral care in the Church. Transmitting traditional doctrinal concepts in readily understandable and acceptable explanations conceals certain dangers: When the terms are changed the meaning behind them can be thinned out or even abandoned.

I have sought to make this clear in discussing the Enneagram's vacillating use of the term "grace," as well as the (almost) non-existent references to creation, the cross, a just and demanding God, Christ as mediator, justification, and forgiveness. The cross must not be reduced to the client's shame and pain. God must not be reduced to a comprehensive insurance policy. Christ must not be reduced to a human model.

Yet another obstacle might be the skepticism felt by advisees because of the non-Christian origins of the Enneagram. In this case it would be unwise to use it openly: The "foreign language" of the system would have a blocking effect, and its quality of being a free offer would be betrayed.

But even when the Enneagram is used as a "tool in the back of one's head" some dangers can arise. Special warnings have to be issued against speculative applications and a conscious or unconscious pinning down and/or rating of clients. Advising and interpersonal relationships are sensitive processes that can stand up only through continual and reciprocal listening, which requires time for self-perception and realization. An overhasty "numbering" denies one's conversation partner any chance of being taken seriously as an individual person. In a favorable case the counselor will be admired for being clairvoyant, in an unfavorable case the relationship of trust will be badly handicapped or rendered impossible by irritating prejudices.

I suspect that the gravest threat lies here, in the realm of the unconscious. Sentences like "Nobody else [but Daniel Berrigan, a FOUR] would have had the idea of articulating protest in this drastic and creative way,"[55] or "Anyone who wants to celebrate a liturgy that makes people cheerful should have a SEVEN work it out,"[56] show that the authors can occasionally slip into clichés out of infatuation with the system.

There must also be warnings against statements like, "I am a FOUR," if I forget that along with many elements of FOUR, I also have within myself other elements of FIVE and THREE (as wings) and ONE and TWO (as partner energies). My being cannot be wrapped up and defined by a number — I am more than that and I should learn to recognize and gradually discard my fixation on "my" type. There is no prototypical FOUR, but just as a circle consists of "infinitely" many points, every person is different from everyone else. The numbers simply provide a device for orientation and a cumulative point for similarly structured types. The theoretical openness of a person to all nine types should not seduce us into making an indiscriminate game of wandering around in search of a number — although this might prompt me to have a serious confrontation with all nine different pitfalls and temptations that have appeared and continue to appear in my life.

In any event the strength of the Enneagram lies in concentrating on the main wrong-headed attitude of each type and on its relationship to certain wings and partner energies.

Beyond that, one crucial feature of the Enneagram is that each type finds a specific image of God convincing, in keeping with the internalized voice that tells us, "I am good when I . . . " This could lead to a fresh encounter with our particular image of God and teach us how much I have created God in my own image and likeness. By disengaging somewhat from my narrow notion of God, which lies deep within in me and forms part of myself, I engage in a healthy form of self-denial.

Furthermore, the model can help us to raise our sights so we can take in a broad "ecumenical" horizon and see on it the many different images of God in the lives of other people: the combative (EIGHT) alongside the serving (TWO), the demanding (ONE) alongside the celebrating (SEVEN) and peacefully resting (NINE), the wise (FIVE) alongside the victorious (THREE), and the faithful (SIX) alongside the totally other (FOUR).

On the path of redemption the New Testament refers us to divine grace and to the fact that we ourselves are to strive for this grace (1 Cor. 12:31). One particular expression of this striving within the framework of pastoral care is the kind of prayer in which we listen, wait, and lay our brokenness before God, let it go and leave it with him. This sort of prayer "is a mature sign of the readiness of the psyche to receive the truth." Along with this goes petitionary prayer. Prayer lends an especially appropriate form to the Enneagram's double concern: In petition, thanks, and penance I become aware of the concrete shapes of both my wrong behavior and my gifts, and I lay them in God's hands. Moreover as my life goes on, I try to find solid ground and change, both of which I receptively wait for from God.

The structural limits of the Enneagram as a typology derive from the enormous area it has to cover. It says nothing, for example, about ego-consciousness, intelligence, or personal magnetism,[57] even though these things are part of being human and essential features of men and women. In this area the model has nothing to offer pastoral care in the Church.

Nor is the Enneagram a substitute for therapy, that is, in severe pathological cases it can give minimal help or none at all. It demands from the user a certain degree of ego-strength and is not appropriate for replacing careful self-analysis or personal conversion. One of its unspoken assumptions is that only a healthy person is capable of "achieving an expansion or transformation of his subjective value-blueprint, or of revising his ego-ideal."[58]

The Enneagram belongs to the domain that the New Testament calls "law." It is not freedom itself (see Rom. 3:20). But in this domain experience shows that it has helped many people by setting in motion a healthy dynamism. Personal and religious maladies can become the goal of redemptive change, because the Enneagram encourages people to get a firm psychological and theological grounding and to go forth on the path to freedom (Gal. 5:13–14). The Enneagram must be used with extreme care and within sober limits. But if this is done, it can be considered an instrument and signpost helping us to come a little closer to our neighbors and to God. It has already proved its capacity to do so.

The Enneagram and the Church: Impulses for Building Community

Andreas Ebert

The best known New Testament image of the Church is the one Paul sketches out in 1 Corinthians 12–14 (and in additional passages): For him "church" means first of all the individual community, in which a variety of different gifts and tendencies coexist. This variety led to conflict and partisanship in Corinth, when individual groups began to absolutize their special gifts and knowledge while looking down on those of others. In addition there were tensions between rich and poor. The better-off members of the community were inclined to spiritualize faith, to reduce it to an inner experience of the Spirit, which supposedly left untouched the social differences in the real material world. The poor, most of whom were slaves, suffered because the social contrasts had not been overcome even in the Christian community. At the Eucharist, for example, the rich might hold a lavish "love feast," before the poor, who often had to work until late in the evening, could make it to the community gathering. They were left with the "essentials" the sacramental meal in the shape of a little bit of bread and a mouthful of wine. But their hungry bodies went unsatisfied.

Paul unequivocally takes his stand on the side of the poor. He sees a eucharist that goes no further than non-binding "spirituality" as a betrayal of the sacrament. If the spiritual community doesn't also become a community of social equals then it's worth nothing. Anyone who conducts a eucharist where the social and spiritual reality clash so violently, "eats and drinks judgment upon himself" (1 Cor. 11:29). Nevertheless at no point does Paul thunder against the variety or "pluralism" evident in the community. On the contrary, he considers variety a reflection of the richness of God, a gift that the community can celebrate with gratitude. The image of the community as the "body of Christ" (1 Cor. 12:12–26) illustrates this:

> For just as the body is one and has many members, and all the members of the body, though many, are one body, so it is with Christ. For by baptism we were all baptized into one body Jews or Greeks, slaves or free and all were made to drink of one Spirit. For the body does not consist of one member but of many. If the foot should say,

"Because I am not a hand, I do not belong to the body," that would not make it any less a part of the body. And if the ear should say, "Because I am not an eye, I do not belong to the body," that would not make it any less a part of the body. If the whole body were an ear, where would be the sense of smell? But as it is, God arranged the organs in the body, each one of them, as he chose. If all were a single organ, where would the body be? As it is, there are many parts, yet one body. The eye cannot say to the hand, "I have no need of you," nor again the head to the feet, "I have no need of you." On the contrary, the parts of the body which seem to be weaker are indispensable, and those parts of the body which we think less honorable we invest with the greater honor, and our unpresentable parts are treated with greater modesty, which our more presentable parts do not require. But God has so composed the body, giving the greater honor to the inferior part, that there may be no discord in the body, but that the members may have the same care for one another. If one member suffers, all suffer together; if one member is honored, all rejoice together.

Paul isn't always a master of metaphor, but this image worked. He probably borrowed it from Greco-Roman popular philosophy and then "baptized" it by interpreting it from the standpoint of Christian faith, carried it one step further and thus made it fruitful for the life of the community. The symbol of the body and its organs frequently appears in classical antiquity. For example, in the year 494 B.C. when the underclass of Rome (the "plebeians") abandoned the city to protest their exploitation by the rich, Agrippa Menenius Lanatus is supposed to have gone out to them in front of the city gates and told them the fable of the belly and the other body parts: The limbs of the body rise up against the belly, which they accuse of leading a parasitical life, sponging off the rest of them. Thereupon the belly goes on strike, and the members realize that they will go under unless the belly nourishes them (Livy, *Ab urbe condita*).

Paul makes a significant change in his use of the image, in fact he stands it on its head. He is *not* interested in stabilizing the status quo by having the weaker parts first work for the stronger, so as to be "nurtured" by them. Rather Paul wants to see a reciprocal dependency within the body, with a clear-cut "option for the poor": The "less honorable" members are "upgraded," so that no split develops. It's also striking that in this early stage of Pauline theology Christ is not yet the "head" of the body (as later in the Letter to the Ephesians), but stands for the *totality* of the body.

In the tense situation in Corinth Paul didn't institute or recommend any sort of authoritarian leadership. He addresses the members of the community including his own opponents as mature Christians, and renounces any claim to purely formal authority for himself. With the metaphor of the body of Christ he offers the community a model for spiritual self-regulation. This image is more than a democratic model of decision-making for the purpose of finding consensus. It is rather set up in such a way that it can function only in a spiritual way, that is, in *common devotion to Christ*, who is present in his body, and in *mutual trust*, which has no need of everyone watching over and checking everyone else.

THE ENNEAGRAM AS AN INTERPRETATION OF THE BODY OF CHRIST

As with the origin of the image of the body and the members, the source of the Enneagram lies shrouded in darkness. The way Paul handles an image that comes from a non-Christian source encourages us to takes up the originally non-Christian Enneagram and "baptize" it. The reason, of course, is that it's an excellent device for understanding the dynamics of both human behavior and interpersonal relationships, not just psychologically, but spiritually too. Both images or reality-models, the body of Christ and the Enneagram, interpret and shed light on one another. Both images speak of the uniqueness and special qualities of the part and at the same time of its need for completion and its limitation by the other parts and the whole. Paul gives a drastic demonstration of what a surrealistic monster comes into being when individual parts either overestimate and absolutize themselves ("If the whole body were an ear . . . ") or when they underestimate themselves and thereby deny their own contribution to the whole ("Because I am not an eye, I do not belong to the body . . . ") Both the superiority complex and the inferiority complex are expressions of a sick ego. They not only destroy the person who has them, but harm all of society. The Enneagram is, among other things, an instrument for discovering and healing such egocentric disturbances.

In our earlier book *Discovering the Enneagram* Richard Rohr and I pointed out that the nine "redeemed" energies of the Enneagram roughly correspond to the nine "fruits of the Spirit" that Paul describes in Galatians 5:22, while most of the pitfalls and fixations of the unredeemed psyche can be found in the earlier "catalogue of vices" in Galatians 5:20–21. Awareness of which behavioral modes destroy human life, both individual and social, and which modes serve it, turns up in all "high" religions as well as in ancient philosophy. Beyond that, such awareness contains an astonishingly large amount of material that is not unique to the Enneagram, but continually recurs in the most varied religious and philosophical systems including the New Testament. Thus Paul can recommend to a Christian community: "Whatever is true, whatever is honorable, whatever is just, whatever is pure, whatever is lovely, whatever is gracious, if there is any excellence, if there is anything worthy of praise, think of these things" (Phil. 4:8).

The fruits of the spirit are matched by the gifts of the Spirit, which take effect in the life of Jesus. The pouring out of the Holy Spirit on Pentecost means that the fullness of the gifts of Christ are now at the disposal of the community. According to Paul, Christ exists in his body, the community, and works through the gifts of his Spirit that are given to the members of the community. The experience of Christ is inseparably linked to the experience of being a part of the network of Christians that the Bible calls the "church" or the "community" (in the Greek of the New testament there is only the single term *ekklesia* for these two words).

For this reason the New Testament has no individualistic path of salvation bypassing the social reality of the community, even if this community happens to be an extremely unattractive "field," where weeds and grain grow alongside and mixed in with one another (cf. Matt. 13:24–30). Not the least difficult thing about being a Christian is Scripture's insistence that the Church is no Isle of the Blest, nor a club for the thoroughly converted, but a place where change and conversion can constantly take place. Nor is the Church an end in itself, but a model of the new kind of community to which God calls all men and women; and as such it has meaning and importance for the whole human race.

The "incorporation" of the individual person into the community doesn't mean that individuality is abolished. On the contrary, just as the individual part of the body has its own specific function and significance, the individual is likewise precious, unique, and irreplaceable within the network of the community. The respect shown the individual is in itself a touchstone for determining whether the Church is motivated and impelled by the spirit of Jesus, which is a spirit of freedom. Variety is the opposite of uniformity. But just as every part of the body is dependent on all the others, the Church too lives on the interplay of different and partially contrary forces. Both images, the body of Christ and the Enneagram, point simultaneously to to the uniqueness and indispensability of the individual, as well as to his or her limitedness and need for completion.

In the image of the body of Christ, Christ himself signifies the whole that is more than the sum of its parts. This "more" implies that Christ *is* the community and nonetheless remains its "opposite number." This is one of the basic paradoxes of Christian faith. The community always mirrors the "face of the Lord," but only in a broken and imperfect way. And yet it is en route to ever greater similarity to Christ: "And we all, with unveiled face, beholding the glory of the Lord, are being changed into his likeness from one degree of glory to another; for this comes from the Lord . . . " (2 Cor. 3:18).

THE "CONFUSION OF TONGUES"
AND THE MIRACLE OF PENTECOST:
GETTING RID OF THE STATIC

Anyone who wants to help community rise and flourish needs a basic image of community. The body of Christ and the Enneagram are two such images. The Enneagram names the energies and gifts necessary for sustainable community to exist. In this way it imparts a vision through which a community can develop. At the same time it names the destructive forces that make community impossible and thereby presents the actual community and each individual in it with an unsparing, mirrorlike guide that calls for repentance.

Community becomes impossible any time people posit themselves and their gifts as absolute. This holds for individuals as well as for groups. You can have neither dialogue nor community with a group that claims absolute status and infallibility. Whenever people absolutize themselves, this results in the breakdown of interpersonal communication.

The biblical story of the Tower of Babel (Gen. 11) illustrates this: The people build the tower that reaches to heaven because they want to "make a name for themselves." But they isolate themselves so thoroughly in their "God complex" that in the end no one understands the language of anybody else.

I experienced an instance of the Babel story at two Enneagram conferences during a role-playing exercise that we called the "Church's Board of Directors." We asked nine participants, each of whom matched one of the nine Enneagram types, to slip into the role of a "director" of the Church (member of the parish council). Then we submitted a problem to them to be resolved collectively. On both occasions the assignment produced a hopeless breakdown in communications: The players automatically stumbled into the pitfalls of their type and were incapable of understanding one another, much less solving any conflicts together.

The New Testament story of Pentecost (Acts 2) contains what might be called the about-face of the tale of the Tower: The Holy Spirit fills the disciples so completely that the people present, who hail from all over the world, hear the apostles praising God in their own language. The Spirit of God enables men and women to relativize themselves and hence to communicate. The person who praises, absolutizes, and divinizes only himself can no longer communicate with his neighbor. The person who praises God, who lets God be God, is bound up with all men and women, and finds the language of the heart, which can find an echo in the hearts of others. When that happens it's always a miracle that we cannot perform with our own strength and that nevertheless will not take place without our longing, praying, and wanting.

At the second of the above-mentioned conferences we continued with the role-playing game of the "Church's Board of Directors" after a pause for evaluation. This time I asked the participants to activate their "best self," to "drop out of their role," to betake themselves to their "consolation point" and work out of it. The result surprised and shocked everybody, including me. In a way everything got even worse. I had expected that they would now be able to solve the problem. But by bidding everyone to be "good," I had put most of them on the spot. Instead of moving to their "consolation point," a number of the players became really stressed out. For instance, the ONEs, morally rigorous at first, did not become looser and more relaxed (SEVEN), but fell into melancholy and depression (FOUR). Afterwards several of the players announced that the constraint to "be good" had cost them an enormous amount of energy.

This result illustrates once again that the Enneagram is neither an individual nor a collective mechanism for self-redemption. Even if we keep forgetting this, the Enneagram itself corrects our dreams of self-redemption. Neither an appeal to be good nor self-produced "consolation" will free us from the pitfall, and under certain circumstances they can drive us even deeper into misery. At the end of the game we reflected on what had been missing, what would have untied the knot. Perhaps a group prayer for the Holy Spirit might have done it. This, of course, isn't something you play at.

HOW COMMUNITY IS BUILT UP — OR DESTROYED

The fruits of the Spirit that the Enneagram names are in my opinion precisely the "ingredients" that every community needs in order to stay alive and grow. *Every Enneagram type* has an unmistakable contribution to make to the whole. If even one of these "energies" is missing, the whole will lack something essential.

Likewise in the unredeemed condition *all types* hinder, check, or actually destroy growth and community. What does the contribution of the individual types to the building up of the community look like, if they serve the whole with all their gifts? And to what extent can they become an impediment to the life of the community if they remain in their fixation? Here I can only give a few subjective suggestions, a handful of catchwords. The list can be expanded as much as one likes.

ONE: ONEs immediately see what's wrong and has to be changed. They push for overcoming the status quo and promoting growth. In the Bible this corresponds to the gift of *prophecy*. The prophets of the Bible put their finger on defects and flaws, because they have a vision of the whole and they're zealous for the honor of God and justice on earth. Jesus's first sermon was: "Convert!

Change your ways!" The prophetic gift of redeemed ONEs is necessary for every community, if it is not to stagnate and if the process of change is to continue. "*Ecclesia semper est reformanda* — the Church must constantly be reformed" (Martin Luther, a ONE). But the addiction to criticism, nagging, and moralizing of unredeemed ONEs can involuntarily lead to just the kind of stagnation that ONEs want to prevent. In the atmosphere of perfectionism and continual judgment-passing others can't breathe or change themselves organically. This is exactly how the loveless demand for change can make people stiffen and retreat. Biblical prophets have labelled this state "hardness of heart." Perhaps they themselves shared some of the responsibility for this hardness of heart on account of the rigorous style of their performances. Like all unredeemed types, unredeemed ONEs bring about exactly what they want to prevent. Only when they let go will they create for other people and for God the space in which life can grow.

TWO: The gift of TWOs is service, devotion, and attention to the needy. In the Bible this corresponds to the gift of *ministry* (*diakonia*). The core commandment of the Bible is the mandate to love one's neighbor. Jesus himself toiled indefatigably for needy persons; he identified himself with the sick, the weak, and prisoners — people in need of attention: "As you did it to the least of these my brethren, you did it to me" (Matt. 25:40). In the poor we meet Jesus. Without the service of TWOs many communities would collapse, and many social and ministerial responsibilities and even such unattractive tasks as cleaning and mopping would never be taken care of.

The danger of unredeemed TWOs is the Messiah complex and the delusion of being indispensable. People who lord it over others by serving them destroy community and create unhealthy, symbiotic dependencies that are the opposite of real love. The unredeemed TWOs hide their egotism behind apparent altruism. Much as a community needs the service and energy of TWOs, in order to be a place of security with a sustainable group life, it must keep a sharp lookout for the backbiting and gossip, the lust for power, the constant longing for exclusivity that characterize the unredeemed TWO. Jesus did not just charge us to love the poor; he wants us to become poor ourselves: Blessed are the poor in spirit. The notion "spiritual poverty" includes the conversion of TWOs from their pride.

THREE: Every community needs a vision strong in hope, clearly defined goals, people who want something, creative ideas and infectious enthusiasm for the cause. Unfortunately the redeemed energy of THREEs is seldom to be found in the Church today. Sometimes it looks as if efficiency and pleasure in success were positively taboo. The genuine team spirit is hard to find. The Church's publications repel instead of appeal. But lack of success is not necessarily a sign that the Church is sharing the shame and cross of Christ. Jesus definitely took pleasure in succeeding. For example, he thought up an ingenious "advertising strategy" for spreading his message: He had his disciples fan out in pairs to cover the villages and cities of Galilee, "multiplying" the Gospel.

Still the Church is always in danger of stumbling into the pitfall of the unredeemed THREE, where there's always "more show than go."[1] And the active Christian groups more inclined to be THREE (missionary organizations, say) are constantly threatened by the temptation to chase external success by reducing the Church to an enterprise that is merely selling a somewhat different product from its secular competition.

FOUR: FOURs have some understanding of symbolic actions and dramatic effects. Jesus illustrated his message with poetic parables and creative symbolic acts and miracles. Unfortunately creativity and art have largely departed from the Church. How lively services could be, how creatively Christ's message could be shaped through street theater, film, painting, music, and architecture! To renew its creativity the Church needs the energy of FOURs, so that "God may become beautiful" (Rudolf Bohren). FOURs can shake up a boring routine, they can use shock tactics to get unrest and change in motion. They can keep on finding new images and symbols to give faith a local habitation and a name. For their part FOURs can learn by attaching themselves to the faith and the community to make an enduring commitment, to resist their own narcissism and subjectivism, and to put their gifts to work in the service of others instead of abusing them by self-centered theatrics.

Needless to say, unredeemed FOURs are an obstacle in the Church because of their affected demeanor and their need to hog the spotlight to make sure they will be really accepted and heard. People who always want to be at the center of things are misusing the community to soak up adulation, and often enough they wind up outside it. The hypersensitivity and envy of unredeemed FOURs can likewise prove stressful and repellent to others.

FIVE: FIVEs enrich the community by keeping its spiritual legacy alive though their intellectual clarity, integrity and objectivity. Jesus was not least of all a razor-sharp thinker who couldn't be bested in an argument. The Church needs this capacity for theological reflection to prevent it from falling into either ideology or foggy-minded emotionalism.

But the distance that FIVEs maintain can also become a pitfall in the Church: A purely intellectual theology is bloodless and doesn't reach people's hearts. Truth without warmth and compassion can be destructive. Penetrating insight without commitment and hard work will not change the world. Only when FIVEs release their knowledge so that others can profit from it will it contribute to the building up of community. Redeemed FIVEs are urgently needed so that good will isn't the only governing force in the Church, so that expertise and the gift of precise thinking can have a voice. The questions about the future of the human race demand enormous intellectual efforts. The "baptized" thought and wisdom of redeemed FIVEs are indispensable for this.

SIX: The Church's "core communities" are characterized above all by commitment, fidelity, and attachment to mature traditions. They look upon novelties with skepticism, they want to keep the status quo because they feel at home in it. It's important to have people who won't get on every foolish bandwagon, but slowly weigh things and can "sniff out" the dangers in a plan that are imperceptible to others. In the Bible this is the gift of the *discernment of spirits*. People who are not so self-important, but who listen to God, place their lives under God's command, and can faithfully serve a good cause, deserve respect even if these virtues aren't in vogue today. SIXes remain loyal to their faith even when being a Christian isn't considered modern. These gifts are urgently needed even in a renewed Church. The courage of the redeemed SIX leads to readiness to obey God more than man and to do the right thing bravely in the teeth of all sorts of resistance.

Of course in the bureaucracies and hierarchies of the churches, as in all bureaucracies, we find a mass of unredeemed SIX energy. In my experience it gets more concentrated the higher up one goes. Unredeemed SIX energy is probably the biggest single obstacle to real movement and change in the Church. Where fundamentalism and traditionalism are in control, people who think differently can only be warred upon. Then honest dialogue with the "world," in which both sides could wind up changing, is no longer possible. Unredeemed SIXes like all the types trigger the emotion that dominates them: fear. A community or church in which this energy prevails is a community of fear: It's sick and makes others sick.

SEVEN: Cheerfulness and affirmation of life are hardly qualities that occur to people when they hear the word "Church." In Christianity as it actually exists humor is a scarce commodity, although the Church proclaims "good news," because the Easter victory over death and the devil is a "divine comedy." Thus SEVENs have a lot to give the Church: festiveness and ideas about how community can be turned into a place for well-being; imagination for childlike happiness and joy. Perhaps the biblical gift of *consolation* is in hiding among the SEVENs. The charismatic movement in the Church rightly reminds the Church that joy in God and *adoration* (for its own sake) are sources of strength, and that God can work miracles even today. People who can rejoice in God are the lucky ones.

The only caveat is that when this movement posits itself as absolute, it becomes cramped and its gift turns into a curse: Everything that disturbs a positive self-image gets repressed. In the end where joy in the Lord once prevailed a bitter struggle breaks out against everyone who can't match the high spirits of SEVENs.

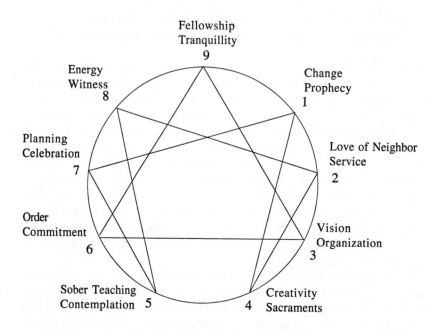

Fellowship
Tranquillity
9

Energy
Witness
8

Change
Prophecy
1

Planning
Celebration
7

Love of Neighbor
Service
2

Order
Commitment
6

Vision
Organization
3

Sober Teaching
Contemplation   5

Creativity
4   Sacraments

The Gifts for Building Community

EIGHT: The power of EIGHTs is likewise rarely met with in our churches: People with whom you know where you stand, because they have a clear standpoint, who say yes when they mean yes and no when they mean no; who enjoy confrontation and conflict, and stoutly defend their convictions. Jesus saw his mission as a power struggle between God and the "adversary" (Satan). EIGHTs are important for the community because they call a spade a spade and won't put up with lazy compromises. They commit themselves to help the oppressed and the underdogs. They're not afraid to take charge and use power. And when their convictions are at stake they are ready to stand their ground till the bitter end. This is the biblical gift of *exousia*, or bearing frank testimony.

EIGHTs' energy becomes a curse when the lust for power turns oppressive, when disputes become aggressive, arrogant, and cutting, when one ruling figure crushes another. EIGHTs have a tendency to be too loud and thereby drown out any quiet voices. Unredeemed power people can plunge others into the deepest misery without noticing it. Unredeemed EIGHT energy manifests itself in the attempt to be invulnerable while constantly exposing or unmasking others.

NINE: The serenity and peaceableness of redeemed NINEs are needed if we want to affirm plurality and seek dialogue with a variety of people. In their own person NINEs can endure and harmonize tensions that would otherwise tear a community apart. Jesus preached a holy carefree spirit born of the awareness that God knows what we need. The Sabbath is the symbol that even God "treats himself" to a rest from his constant work. This tranquillity is found in redeemed NINEs. Because they have a big heart and are open to everyone and everything, community grows up around them all by itself. The New Testament's word for this is *koinonia*.

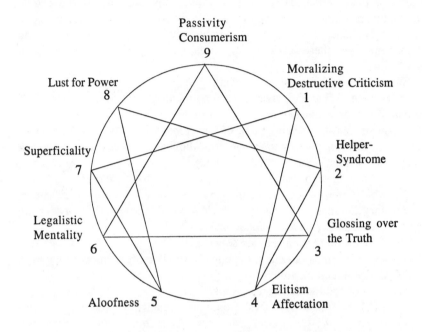

The Dangers Threatening Community

The energy of unredeemed NINEs can block necessary change, because they avoid all conflicts, want to be served and stimulated all the time, and never get around to actively shaping the world. Unredeemed NINEs resist all efforts to get them to bestir themselves. When this energy gets the upper hand in a community, the life of the Church degenerates into inconsequential *Gemütlichkeit* over coffee and cake.

IMPULSES FOR COMMUNITY ANALYSIS

The Enneagram is a device for analyzing community. The leadership council of a church community or parish can draw upon the Enneagram for critical scrutiny of their own situation. It isn't necessary for everyone involved to be familiar with the whole system. The point is not to compare numbers but to take a self-critical look at the community's dynamics and the collective pattern that it follows. It makes sense here to ask questions that allow for more than one answer, but that start processes going. Obviously the whole catalogue of questions listed below cannot be mastered all at once, but it offers help for an ongoing process.

The catalogue is meant to serve as a stimulus. It can be shortened or expanded or even replaced by particular questions, so long as the people formulating the questions are open to surprising answers and don't simply want to quiz others about what they think they already know. I recommend leaving the participants in these sessions alone to take notes, before the exchange of ideas begins.

What is the basic atmosphere prevailing in our community?

If we were to find an image for our community, what would occur to us? (Perhaps draw something here.)

Flight of fantasy: When I think of our community, what do I *see, hear, smell, taste,* and *touch* in my imagination? (Allow about three minutes for each of the "inner senses," then start a discussion.)

What do we have too much of? What do we have too little of?

To what extent does the character structure of the full-time leadership (pastor) dominate community life? How could the type of the leadership (pastor) be described with a handful of qualities?

What atmosphere prevails in our services?[2]

What special gifts does our community have? What reputation does it have in other Christian communities?

What is our community's greatest mistake?

Which of the following "vices" would most readily characterize our community: *anger, pride, lying, envy, stinginess, fear, superficiality, shamelessness, laziness*?

If Jesus were among us, what would he be happy about? On what points would he call us to conversion? (Let the community silently address Jesus, perhaps reflecting on the "letters" in Revelation.)

What is our community's biggest *external* problem? Can it be solved? What is our biggest *internal* problem? How might we deal with it?

Where do we see special opportunities in our situation at this moment?

Where do we hear a special call from God to our community?

ONE

Is a judgmental spirit, nagging or an addiction to criticism predominant among us? Can anger and aggression be openly expressed? Are we ready for change? Do we moralize? Is there preaching about concrete conversion, which embraces all of life? Can people sense in our community something of the unconditional love of God? How do we deal with criticism in the community — and of it? Are there prophets among us? What do they say? Are we capable of hearing them? What do young people learn in religious instruction and confirmation class? How do we pass the faith on to people who are in search of it?

TWO

Who are the people among us who always do the dirty work? Whom do we exploit? Do we say "thank you" often enough? Is there unhealthy, sticky intimacy among us? People with delusions of being indispensable? How do we deal with them? Who are the "poor" in our community? How do we meet them: the homeless, the sick, the handicapped, the refugees, the suffering and dying? Do we have genuine contact *with* these groups? Do we live with them or are they only looked after — or not even that? Is there a compulsive intimacy among us, or do we respect the limits of people who need distance? Do we have needs that we don't admit to ourselves? What are they?

THREE

Is mere outward appearance the rule in some areas of our life? Are there "life lies' in our community that have to be covered up? Where are we deceiving ourselves? Where are we failing? Do we invest energy, enthusiasm, and ideas into winning new people for the community? What are we hoping for? What concrete goals and visions do we have for our community in the coming year, in the next five or ten years? Do we have joy in success? Who are the visionaries among us? Is there something in the community that could attract people? In what areas have we had success that we can point to with a good conscience?

FOUR

Are there elitist cliques among us? Are we hypersensitive? Are there people who always have to be in the spotlight? Do we look with envy at other churches and communities — or at the "world"? Do we accept being a perfectly ordinary community with perfectly ordinary people? Where is there room among us for creative development, theater, dance, art, and music? Who are the artists among us? Are their gifts in demand? What sort of esthetic shape are our buildings in? Are our services beautiful? How do we deal with the sacraments? Are there any "fine-feathered birds" in our community? Do we put up with them? Do we confront them? Is it all right to be sad among us? How do we deal with mourners? How do we observe Holy Week?

FIVE

Are there cold and distant people among us? Is there intellectual arrogance or a know-it-all attitude? Are the services too impersonal or cerebral? Are we a stingy or a generous community? Do we cling to something that binds us together? What should we really let go? Do we permit real intimacy? Are we forever just talking, or does something really happen? Is there room for information about the faith? Are intellectuals and their gifts in demand among us? Are we capable of objectivity? Where is there room for silence and meditation? How do we fill our emptiness? Where are the wise old men and women among us, from whose experience we could profit? Are *they* in demand?

SIX

Where are moral narrowness and legalism prevalent among us? Are we ready to change something, even if "we've always done it *this way* before"? What do we have to get rid of? Is there a hierarchy in our community? Who's on top, who's on the bottom? Who's afraid of whom? What are we collectively afraid of? Which written and unwritten laws and norms control us? How strong is our commitment? Who are the "faithful" ones? Do we honor them? Do we listen to warning voices, do we let our plans be scrutinized? Are there traditions in our community that we fill with life? Do we respect fidelity and simple faith?

SEVEN

Do we sweep painful facts under the carpet? What pain do we avoid? Is there a tendency to linger over aimless small-talk, so as not to get too close to one another and not to touch any sore points? Who is the the cut-up, the community clown? How does this person get along with his or her role? Do our plans tend to go awry? Who looks after humor and good feelings? Is there any laughter at our services? Where do we laugh? Can we laugh at ourselves? When did we last celebrate a meal? What do we celebrate? How important is Easter to us, and how do we observe it? How do children and young people feel in our midst?

EIGHT

How is power apportioned among us? Does one person dominate our whole community life full-time? Does any other member of the community overwhelm or oppress the community or parts of it? Does any one dare to stand up to such "power-people"? Who are the strong among us? Who are the weak? Are we allowed to be weak? To be strong? Can we fight fairly? Who stands up for the oppressed and the losers? Who among us gets things moving? Who gets things done? Is our community known for supporting social justice? Do we handle our own and others' feelings carefully? Is there open discussion among us of sexuality, money, power, and politics? Are there taboo themes? What are they?

NINE

Are weariness and lethargy prevalent among us? What tires us out? What are our greatest sins of omission? Do we avoid certain conflicts? What does our avoidance strategy look like? Do we have phases of creative rest? Where are the places for this? Can people relax at our services? Where is there room for non-directed fellowship and mellow good humor? Who are the peacemakers and mediators among us? Do we call upon their gift in time of conflict? Do we take ourselves too seriously? Who is the source of rest and serenity? How do we hallow Sunday?

The strength of the Enneagram in this context is that, first, it's an analytical instrument for getting a clearer view of the community's situation; second, that it can help us to judge our situation and develop a new vision; and, third, it contains support for the possible steps we might want to take (for example, through what we called in our first book "invitations").

Latin American liberation theology and the pedagogy of liberation linked to it has discovered how positively the continual use of the three steps *Seeing-Judging-Acting* has affected group processes. In my opinion a fourth step, *Evaluating*, should be added; and of course this already constitutes a transition to yet another act of seeing. In this way we get a "power circle," an idea developed by American management experts, and whose functioning is a life-and-death matter for the stability and continual renewal of any community.

THE POWER CIRCLE

When people join forces, there is power, there are leaders and the led, the strong and the weak, etc. The point is not to avoid power and to ignore it, but to distribute power in such a way that the entire group participates in the process of exercising it and so reciprocally "balances out." As I see it, 90% of all community conflicts have their roots not in theology but in bad leadership, that is, in a dilettantish mode of dealing with power. Unfortunately this subject practically never comes up in the course of theological formation, although handling power can certainly be practiced and optimized in a controlled learning process. Above all there is a shortage of acceptable images and models of how leadership can function. The alternative to an authoritarian style of leadership can't be simply renouncing leadership. When the areas of jurisdiction are unclear, there will always be secret leaders who exercise power by their personal magnetism and who are not subject to any democratic control.

Most people think that the person who makes the decisions has the power. In reality the right to make decisions is only a part of power. The one who gives orders is powerless if nobody carries them out. The particular way in which an assignment is taken care of lies entirely in the hands of the person carrying it out. Other forces operating here are the power of good ideas and the power of criticism (evaluation). These four factors produce the following image:

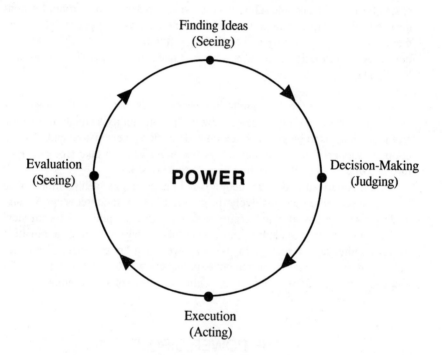

The Power Circle

The circle: idea-decision-execution-evaluation-idea, etc., allows all the participants in a group or community to share in the power. At the four points of the circle various gifts and charisms take effect. In this process not everyone has to do something — but it has to be clear *who* is doing *what*.

Idea: There is no inspiration without community life. A good idea has the power to prevail, even if it has to make its way through a fire-storm of contradiction and misgivings. Anyone who has inspiring ideas has power. In a community that can be the rank-and-file, the group leaders, the church elders, or the pastor — sometimes even outsiders. A community is unbalanced when the ideas come mostly from the pastor, and the community does nothing more than execute the ideas of the leader. A good idea presupposes a clear view of the situation (context). The Enneagram too can contribute to this analysis. And a community needs a place where the context is analyzed and ideas are developed.

Decision: Ideas have to be evaluated and judged. For this you need standards. Once again the Enneagram can be one device among others for decision-making. It's important that at some point clear decisions are reached. To insure that the decision is bearable, the leadership should consult, as far as possible, the people who will have to carry it out. If church services are to be altered, both those who attend them and the critics of the present liturgy have to be asked about it. If a celebration is planned, one should talk ahead of time with the ones who will do the dirty work, etc. Decisions made without the participation of those affected by them will either not work at all or only with pain and trouble.

Execution: Those carrying out a project have the power to make it succeed or fail. The more they take part in the planning and decision-making, the more motivated they will be on the job itself. The executors even have the power to refuse when the assignment doesn't make sense to them — at least as long as they are unpaid volunteers. But even salaried persons can either do their work gladly or "work to rule." The latter will have a serious effect on the quality of the performance.

Evaluation: One flaw of many communities is that nothing gets evaluated. There are services to which hardly anyone comes, there are groups withering on the vine, sermons that reach no one. But none of this is ever openly discussed. Without evaluation — that is, without criticism — there will be no change. Particularly in Christian circles people often have a hard time airing criticism, since they "don't want to hurt one another." But just as strong as — or stronger than — this laudable intention will likely be the fear of how the criticized person may react, and the common need for "harmony." But only where criticism is invited and accepted, can anything be changed. Criteria for objective criticism can be found, among other places, in the Enneagram.

Self-critical questions for the community leaders could be: Is this power circle functioning with us? Which people are dominant at which point of the circle? Who is dominant everywhere? Nowhere? Where and when do we evaluate?

WHAT IS A LIVING COMMUNITY?
A FIVE-POINT PROGRAM

What has to happen for a parish that merely provides "custodial care" to become a living community? This is the crucial question facing all programs and models for building up community. Some years ago Richard Rohr listed five criteria that constitute a living community (in *Warum katholisch?* [Why Catholic?] Herder, 1991, pp. 137 ff.) I shall paraphrase his five points and relate them to the Enneagram:

1. The assumption that we can believe all by ourselves is illusory. Like Judaism, which it grew out of, Christianity is thoroughly oriented to *community life*. Individualistic Christianity is a contradiction in terms. Among the questions that a Christian should regularly ask of himself or herself is: Where and how do I share my life with others? Perhaps there two or three people with whom I am "networked" in the deepest sense. But around these two or three individuals lie concentric circles of solidarity, for instance, a *fellowship group*, a *parish*, a *diocese*, a *national church*, the *Church universal*. The Enneagram offers a foundational image of comprehensive, inclusive community and reconciled multiplicity.

2. Community is the place where Jesus's call for conversion rings out and where we are challenged to hear this call and heed it. Community is found in a process of conversion, and asks itself what it means to follow Jesus here and now. Here the Enneagram is a mirror for a collective examination of conscience, continually urging us, singly and together, to concrete conversion.

3. The path of faith is a *process of growth*. Not everyone who takes the first steps in faith has the capacity and obligation to live out immediately all the consequences of faith, including political involvement, or to enter a religious order. A living community is a milieu where people can "climb on board" at the level of faith appropriate to them so they can proceed to grow. For this reason there have to be different groups in the community for initiation,[3] growth,[4] and discipleship[5] that can exist side by side and that need one another. Ideally the concerns of all the groups can regularly be voiced in the liturgy. The Enneagram helps with this process, since it too aims for growth, calls individuals' and groups' attention to deficiencies, and points out the direction that the process might take.

4. Living communities have *goals*. Part of growth is being oriented, and this holds for the community as a whole as well as for every group in it. Alongside the continually recurring *cycle* of the church year a community also needs goals, which implies a path and *forward movement*. In this context Richard Rohr uses the image of a covered wagon train crossing the plains: At night the wagons are set up in a circle, and the group gathers to rest, to take nourishment, to experience security, protection, and intimacy. This time of

gathering could also be labeled the phase of "motherly" or "feminine" energy. In the daytime the wagon train heads out and moves toward its goal. This corresponds to the Old Testament experience of the Exodus, the breaking-camp and pathfinding aspect of faith. It could also be described as "masculine-linear" energy. Both energies need each other and should not be played off against each other. The path that both are taking together might also be visualized as an upward spiral. One of the reasons why so few men find access to the Christian faith might well be that in our churches the gathering, cyclical energy has the upper hand, while clear goals are often lacking. Goals emerge, for example, from the "invitations" of the Enneagram (serenity, freedom, hope, naturalness, commitment, justice, and love).

5. A living community is simultaneously oriented toward the *inside* and the *outside*. "Opening" and "concentrating"[6] condition and nourish each other. *Inward* movement occurs in the deepening of faith through fellowship, meditation, and prayer, the return to the spiritual sources of power, reflection, and refueling. *Outward* movement is found in the Church's mandate to work to shape the world through missions, service, and politics. The ecumenical community of Taizé talks about the way contemplation and struggle go hand in hand. Richard Rohr's training center for lay people in Albuquerque is called the "Center for Contemplation and Action." Rohr rightly complains that "many groups in the Church [develop] a preference for one or the other type, instead of joining them together. Either they concentrate on feminine power and establish relationships or on masculine power and pursue goals." It's not enough that there are Christian groups exclusively cultivating the inwardness of faith, and others that are constantly in action. Rather we need a spirituality in which action and contemplation complement, enrich, and correct one another. The Enneagram can make a contribution by showing us where one or the other energy is being over-stressed and by "reminding" us of the proper balance.

The Enneagram and the Bible

Wolfgang Müller

BASIC APPROACH TO THE RELATION
BETWEEN THE ENNEAGRAM AND THE BIBLE

Some years ago I had an idea that I found elaborated in a recently published book by Mary Helen Kelly, *Skin Deep: Designer Clothes by God.*[1] In the biblical story of the Fall we are told: "And the Lord God made for Adam and his wife garments of skins, and clothed them" (Gen. 3:21). The expulsion from the Garden of Eden takes place, but God himself protects Adam and Eve from complete nakedness, that is, from a state of helpless abandonment and defenselessness. He makes the garments. When it says in Genesis 1:31, "And God saw everything that he had made, and behold, it was very good," that judgment also holds for this creative attention to fallen man. (We know from psychology that in early childhood everyone develops his or her distinctive personality by means of a "custom-made" defense against the superior force of anxiety.)

These garments of skins (defense mechanisms) might be considered an instance of God's loving care for human beings, whom he wants to survive, even if they have lost the fullness of life: a divine safeguard against annihilation. Mary Helen Kelly calls these garments designer clothes that God has, so to speak, tailored to fit the individual man or woman and that therefore have a brilliance and elegance we may well admire. On the one hand, they are merely protective suits, on the other they have a divine cut; and so they perform their protective function in splendid style. Of course, Scripture gives no indication that there were nine different garments. But if we connect this passage with the Enneagram, it sheds an entirely new light on the Fall. If we start off from the assumption that every human being wears such a garment to survive, but that each one has his or her own peculiar "suit," then it stands to reason that everybody behaves altogether "typically" in his or her survival reactions.

If this reading is valid, it means that behind each of the nine Enneagram types stands the Creator, and that none of these "garments" is better or worse than the others. At most some could be called "flashier" (2-3-4), "simpler" (5-6-7), or "coarser" (8-9-1). But for each "wearer" they are all "very good," insofar as they help in survival. Since we are defenseless without "garments," nobody can "jump out of his skin," even though sometimes we might like to. But since they are only "clothes," they aren't identical with our person. They have a quality about them that Mary Helen Kelly calls "skin deep": Without our skin we can't survive, but that's not all there is to us. The same viewpoint is expressed in the "mark" that God puts on Cain (Gen. 4:15): Separation from God is bound up with the protection that God gives humans for their survival. "And the Lord put a mark on Cain, lest any who came upon him should kill him. Then Cain went away from the Presence of the Lord, and dwelt . . . east of Eden" (Gen. 4:15–16). He survived, but far from God.

THE THREE CENTERS

Before I began searching more closely for the individual Enneagram types in the Bible, the discovery of the three different basic pathways to the reality of life was quite important to me. I kept running up against the triad that is described in Enneagram literature as the middle of the body (gut), head, and heart. In Mary's Magnificat (Luke 1:51-53) we hear of the proud (heart), the mighty (middle of the body), and the rich (head). And 2 Timothy 1:7 mentions the spirit of power (middle of the body), love (heart), and prudence (head). In 1 Cor. 1:27–28 Paul speaks of the foolish (head), the weak (middle of the body), and despised (heart), which God has chosen in contrast to what is wise, strong, and respected in the eyes of men. In the parable of the sower (Matt. 13:1–9; Mark 4:1–9; Luke 8:4–8), I can also recognize these three elemental approaches: The seed that falls on the path (head), the rocky ground (middle of the body), and the thorns (heart); or in the temptations of Jesus (Matt. 4:1–11; Luke 4:1–13) that take place in the wilderness far away from people (head), in the city amidst all the people (heart), and on a "very high mountain" above the people (middle of the body), at those points of departure that are typical of the three centers. It's also interesting that the scribe's answer to Jesus about the first of the commandments says, "to love him [God] with all the heart, and all the understanding, and with all the strength, and to love one's neighbor as oneself." When I read in Revelation 5:12, "Worthy is the Lamb who was slain, to receive power and wealth and wisdom and might and honor and glory and blessing," I am likewise reminded of the three centers. The triad appears most clearly in the three figures of Peter, Thomas, and Mary Magdalen, who when they meet the resurrected Lord reveal their character by their typical ways of reacting and responding: jumping the gun/facing the crucial question (Peter, in John 21:15–18, "Do you love me?"), running away/accepting the invitation (Thomas in John 20:24–29, "Put your finger here"), clinging to others/freeing oneself and turning to others (Mary Magdalen, in John 20:17, "Do not hold me, but go to my brethren and say . . . ").

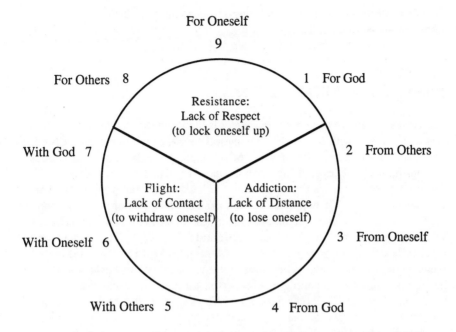

For Oneself

9

For Others 8

1 For God

Resistance:
Lack of Respect
(to lock oneself up)

With God 7

2 From Others

Flight:
Lack of Contact
(to withdraw oneself)

Addiction:
Lack of Distance
(to lose oneself)

With Oneself 6

3 From Oneself

With Others 5

4 From God

Defensive Posture and Tendency in the Three Centers

Middle of the Body (Gut): EIGHT — NINE — ONE

For this center the characteristic defensive posture is the resistance that can be expressed in a lack of respect for others (EIGHT), oneself (NINE), or God (ONE). These types tend to become locked up inside themselves. This defensive attitude fits into the realm of survival, where it shows its full effectiveness. But when it comes to the encounter with the redeeming God who offers life in abundance (John 10:10), this self-willed attitude manifests itself as stiff resistance. All of Jesus's disputes with his opponents reflect this battle, in which the body center of the person putting up the resistance is laid open and the armor is shattered, so that reverence becomes possible. But Jesus doesn't wage this battle on the level of his adversaries, with the "sword," as Peter does when Jesus is taken prisoner (John 18:10), or as the men do who wish to kill him (John 8:37), but with the Word, which has, of course, the impact of the sword (cf. John 12:48, Heb. 4:12–13). In the meeting with Simon Peter after the resurrection Jesus shows how this defensiveness is overcome, this stiff resistance broken, and the energy stored up in this protective posture set free. This is the question, "Do you love me [more]?" In this way the instinctive reaction that "kills" or "destroys" — that is, weakens or breaks off communication and relationships — is undone. This makes it possible to respond to others, oneself, and God, and thus (re)creates relationship and communication.

Head: FIVE — SIX — SEVEN

The typical defensive posture of this center is the flight that can lead to a breakdown of contact: with others (FIVE), oneself (SIX), or with God (SEVEN). It has a tendency to retreat. But this sort of survival attitude becomes superfluous and hurtful once the level of life-in-abundance is reached in the encounter with Jesus. The defensiveness that appears in the head center can perhaps be characterized as "cool." It manifests itself in the posture of retreat, doubt, and superficiality. Such individuals also meet Jesus and have good experiences when they face him instead of backing off and taking flight. The woman who touches Jesus's garment (Matt. 9:20–22; Mark 5:25–34; Luke 8:43–48) immediately experiences a cure. When Jesus comes up against this hesitant attitude, he makes a point of encouraging the person through an urgent invitation to touch and to confess their own experience. The key is not that he touches them, but that he encourages the person to dare touching on their own. At the meeting with Thomas (John 20:24–29) Jesus shows how the reaction of flight and cool resistance is overcome and how the energy contained in this self-protective posture can be set free: by accepting the invitation to find the sought-for security through contact. Convincing oneself by touching: This is the response that makes real relationships and communication possible.

Heart: TWO — THREE — FOUR

I see the defensive posture of the heart center in the quest that can manifest itself in a lack of distance from others (TWO), oneself (THREE), or God (FOUR). It has a tendency to lose itself. When the level of life-in-abundance comes into play, the survival level of compulsively wanting-to-shine-in-front-of-others — whether by giving them help (TWO), displaying one's achievements (THREE), or uniqueness (FOUR) — no longer makes any sense or has any justification. Here too we find resistance, but of a kind I would call "soft." There are people in Jesus's milieu who would like to put him in their back pocket. John 6:15 speaks of those who would make him king "by force," so that Jesus has to slip away. This habit of drawing others to our side, getting close to them, making others co-dependent on us or us on others, endangers the freedom of others or surrenders our own. Mary Magdalen's encounter with the resurrected Jesus dramatizes the way the "addictive" reaction or "soft" resistance can be overcome and the energy hidden in this defensive posture of compulsive orientation to others can be set free: This is the acceptance of the mission to others while bearing witness to one's own experience, by which the necessary and salutary distance from others, and thereby authentic communication and relationships, are made possible.

THE NINE ENNEAGRAM TYPES

As we have seen, the three centers can clearly be found in Sacred Scripture. But, beyond that, the three types corresponding to each of the three centers, which are traditionally assigned numbers, are also in evidence. Depending on their taste, the various Enneagram authors also assign striking labels to point out the characteristic features of each type. Mary Helen Kelly voices the discomfort that many people feel upon being classified as a number. She herself describes the nine types by means of animals, whose behavior is amazingly reminiscent of ours. Assigning animals or symbols to the individual Enneagram types is an obvious move. The Bible too continually uses comparisons, similes, and symbols. I will stick to the usual Enneagram numbers here and try to point up connections from a scriptural perspective. I am not trying to engineer these connections and then find "proof passages" to fit them. (I shall cite only a few that I have found and that seem appropriate to me; the reader may discover others, perhaps even better ones.) The idea, once again, is to establish, possibly to our astonishment, how pointedly the nine types have been characterized in the Bible, and how the Word of God shows the way to their full human development and redemption through Jesus Christ.

The basic feature of all the types is the condition for which the Bible uses the word "creature" or "being made." This has a double meaning: On the one hand, as the image of God ("God created man in his own image"), a human being reflects in his or her whole being the power (middle of the body), richness (head), and brilliance (heart) of God. On the other hand, as God's image man is not God himself, and thus limited and dependent. Hence in each of the various Enneagram types we can determine two things: In its status as an image of God each individual type reflects a power, a fullness, and a splendor that are built into it and that it may accept with joy and gratitude from the hand of its creator. But in its limitedness and dependency each type must become and remain aware that it has limits which it cannot transcend or overcome on its own. In dealing with my own limits I got help from the thought that the word "profile" can make even limitedness appetizing. Each type has its special profile precisely by being different from the others. From this double perspective the one-sidedness of our individual type points both to the creator, whose glory we radiate in this particular way, and to our dependence on *other* ways of making the creator visible. When this gets difficult, we have to invoke Paul's maxim of "forebearing one another" (Col. 3:13).

ONE

If we are looking for biblical expressions of this type, ONEs may consider their number "called" whenever Scripture speaks of ordering the world and creation, of goals, fulfillment, and perfection. The word "zeal" is the dynamism that governs ONEs; growing and letting others grow is the problem they have to struggle with. If we see in the person of the Apostle Paul a typical ONE, then we can glimpse from his experience, thoughts, and desires what the inner world, light, and shadows, the splendor and misery of ONEs look like, or how God's revelation, sin and guilt are illumined by Christian faith. The Letter to the Philippians gives eloquent expression to this mode of experience, as it is lived under the influence of Jesus's message and grace. In Philippians 3:6 Paul speaks of zeal for the Law. In Philippians 3:8 he tells us that he has given up everything "that I may gain Christ." In Philippians 3:14 he recounts how he presses on "toward the goal for the prize." Philippians 3:12–13 makes it clear how he connects his unconditional orientation to the goal with the path leading to it. He is well aware that there is an element of "not yet being there" that one first has to acknowledge in order to make the goal reachable. He feels that he is an example for others precisely because of his awareness of growth in the direction of the goal, which he has not yet reached, but strives for with all his power (Phil. 3:17).

It is important for ONEs to accept the invitation to patience (Eph. 4:2) and to grow and mature "to the measure of the stature of the fulness of Christ" (Eph. 4:13,15). Anger, the emotional expression of zeal, is "holy" only when it doesn't lead into sin, that is, doesn't solidify into resentment, the continual irritation that never fully comes out in the open: "Do not let the sun go down on your anger" (Eph. 4:26). In the Gospels the parables that speak of growth and the unfolding dynamism of the kingdom of heaven are the passages that must accompany ONEs on their human-spiritual path: Matthew 13:30 ("Let both grow together — the weeds and the wheat — until the harvest"); Matthew 13:32; Mark 4:32; Luke 13:19 ("and it grew and became a tree"); Mt. 13:33; Lk. 13:21 ("till it was all leavened"). In Mark 4:27–28 particular stress is laid on the hidden and "automatic" process of this growth, something that would have to apply the brakes to the high-handed zeal of ONEs. A further series of scriptural passages is written especially for ONEs: Matthew 7:1–2 ("Judge not!") or Romans 2:1–6 ("in passing judgment . . . you condemn yourselves"). When Matthew 23:3 speaks of the tension between saying and doing, this admonition of Jesus may be a direct appeal of Jesus to ONEs.

TWO

For TWOs the words of Scripture that count are those that speak of serving, caring, and giving. In the figure of the Good Shepherd TWOs encounter their biblical model, in other words, a way of behaving that they find in themselves as a natural drive and that they may live out as a talent. In John 10:1–18 this care is presented in its deepest dimension: Jesus's complete devotion to those entrusted to him, whose needs he is aware of, and to whom he can and will give life in abundance. At the washing of the feet (John 13:1–17), humble service is presented as an ideal for the disciples: "For I have given you an example, that you also should do as I have done to you. . . . If you know these things, blessed are you if you do them" (John 13:15, 17).

Giving plays a central role in Jesus's message: His giving his life for all people as his friends is the content of his mission. And so for the men and women following Jesus, giving and sacrificing are a fundamental element of his life. "God loves a cheerful giver," says 2 Corinthians 9:7. Of course individuals cannot give from their intrinsic resources, but only from the wealth that has been granted them. Only those who acknowledge their own needs and then bestow what they themselves have received can really be givers, helpers, and servers: "You received without paying, give without pay" (Matt. 10:8). Only those who let their feet be washed, can wash those of others, that is, serve them, as Jesus exemplarily did.

Jesus expressed his own needs: "Give me to drink" (John 4:7). "I thirst" (John 19:28). It's important for TWOs to accept their own helplessness, in other words to admit that that they themselves have to be redeemed and liberated. "All have sinned . . . " (Rom. 3:23). But God doesn't thrust his gifts upon us, and those who pass on God's gifts should not impose them on anyone: "And if anyone will not receive you or listen to your words, shake off the dust from your feet as you leave that house or town" (Matt. 10:14). But they should also not impose themselves: Luke 24:28 says that at Emmaus Jesus made as if to travel on. Jesus expressly asks the blind Bartimaeus, "What do you want me to do for you?" (Mark 10:51). The other must be able to decide what help he or she will accept. The specific root sin of TWOs is pride, in which people express their conviction that they are something, have something, or can do something that others aren't, don't have, or can't do.

In contrast to this is the "one another" principle, the mutual regard that is stressed in the Gospels and the other New Testament writings as the proper bearing among brothers and sisters. "He has scattered the proud" (Luke 1:51) and "God opposes the proud" (James 4:6; 1 Peter 5:5) are clear indications from Scripture to those who usurp the divine fullness of power through the posture of pride.

THREE

The basic concern of this Enneagram type is success. Growth, which is a problem for ONEs, is a principle of success for THREEs that functions perfectly. Hard work and persistence are indispensable for success. Many efforts by many people are necessary if there is to be anything to show for it. Success is by its very essence oriented to becoming "visible" and sheds a bright light on the person who brought it off. Success is a thoroughly positive-sounding and positively experienced state of affairs, and hence failure is a profoundly negative experience. In the Bible this concept is present everywhere in the image of bringing forth fruit. It resounds in the charge given to humans on the morning of creation: "Be fruitful" (Gen. 1:28).

Fertility of the soil, but above all fertility of the person is an ideal that God offers as a promise to men and women, to move them to go forth and engage in action: "And I will make of you a great nation . . . and make your name great, so that you will be a blessing," says God to Abraham (Gen. 12:2). Thus it is clear that unrealized ideals, sterility and failure, cause unspeakable suffering. "I am a woman sorely troubled . . . all along I have been speaking out of my great anxiety and vexation" (1 Sam. 1:15–16), as Hannah says to Eli. This theme runs through the entire Bible, but here it finds an answer that brings redemption for THREEs. Barrenness and failure turn into fruitfulness and success when they are accepted from the hand of God and held out to him: "I have labored in vain, I have spent my strength for nothing and vanity; yet surely my right is with the Lord, and my recompense with my God" (Isaiah 49:4). "Behold, my servant shall prosper, he shall be exalted and lifted up" (Isaiah 52:13). This expresses the true 'secret of success," which Jesus makes clear in the the image of vine (John 15:1–17). Bearing fruit is guaranteed for those who remain "in him," but impossible for those who want to act "apart from him:" (John 15:59). Arrogant lust for success and the wish to shine in splendid isolation in front of others is the root sin of THREEs: lying, deception, vanity. The story of Jacob (Gen. 25–49) may well serve as a biblical example of this, where wrong behavior is integrated into the history of salvation.

FOUR

This type too has a special message to convey to everyone. FOURs experience themselves as special, unique, one of a kind, unmistakable; and they have to live out the "splendor and misery" of their humanity from the standpoint of this personality. The splendor and misery are dramatically experienced among FOURs and expressively passed on to their environment. From the scriptural standpoint this Enneagram type is captured in the passages where the unmistakable uniqueness of the creature that God loves and cares for is spoken of. The biblical motif of "a"being called by name" (Isaiah 43:1: "I have called you by name, you are mine"; Isaiah 45:3: "It is I, the LORD, the God of Israel, who call you by name"; Isaiah 45:4: "I call you by your name, I surname you") is lived and "suffered" here in a model, but also compulsive fashion.

In the Revelation of John this gift to humans that FOURs live out is bound up with the relationship to Jesus: "To him who conquers . . . I will give a white stone, with a new name written on the stone, which no one knows except him who receives it" (Rev. 2:17). With Mary Magdalen, a FOUR, the name, the symbol for the wholly personal state of being responsive and spoken to, plays a redemptive role: She recognizes the risen Jesus when he calls her by name, and she becomes capable of receiving Jesus's order and carrying it out in her mission to "the brothers (and sisters)," to whom she communicates her own wholly personal experience.

What FOURs must struggle with is the fact that others too have this uniqueness in *their* own way, and that has to be acknowledged. In this sense "being ordinary" and "like the others' is hard, but to take seriously one's own uniqueness "with them," to grant them their own uniqueness instead of dissociating oneself from them in order to stand out, is the path of redemption. Jesus did not "cling" to his unique status, but was 'born in the likeness of men" (Phil. 2:7). He wished to be baptized by John "like all the others" (Matt. 14:15).

And in Luke 2:22–24 the unique child Jesus goes through what is prescribed by the Law (which applies to everybody). What TWOs deny or repress, FOURs emphasize excessively: their peculiar essence, even and especially in neediness, helplessness, and abandonment, which engender grief. But Jesus invites them to say a full yes to this" It is to your advantage that I go away, for if I do not go away, the Counselor will not come to you; but if I go I will send him to you" (John 16:7).

FIVE

Since the FIVE type is established in the head-center, the scriptural passages relating to this center's mode of experience are especially helpful. With FIVEs possession in the form of knowledge, awareness, discovery, and observation plays a supreme role. There are entire books in the Bible that address this need, which is necessary to FIVEs as a survival attitude: the book of Proverbs, Ecclesiastes, The Book of Wisdom, Sirach. Thus Sacred Scripture puts its stamp of approval upon this manner of living, experiencing, and reacting. But life-in-abundance, as offered to us through the Gospel, is possible only if we overcome the void, the ignorance, the failure to see the whole picture.

In the New Testament there are some suggestions as to how FIVEs should bring their profile to wholeness, in keeping with the saying of Paul: "To each is given the manifestation of the Spirit for the common good." Recognition of one's own gift is ascribed to the working of God's Spirit: "Now we have received not the spirit of the world, but the Spirit which is from God, that we might understand the gifts bestowed on us by God" (1 Cor. 2:12). So what we have to do is not struggle obsessively for knowledge, but accept it as a gift to be passed on. Here too Jesus is presented as a model: "For you know the grace of our Lord Jesus Christ, that though he was rich, yet for your sake he became poor, so that by his poverty you might become rich" (2 Cor. 8:9).

This wealth, this abundance, is to be viewed as the abundance of life (John 10:10), and in John 17:3 "eternal life" is linked to knowledge: "This is eternal life, that they know thee, the only true God and Jesus Christ whom thou hast sent." Jesus can let himself not know something: 'But of that day and hour no one knows, not even the angels of heaven, nor the Son, but the Father only" (Matt. 24:36). Omniscience is not the business of humans. But knowledge and understanding, which humans naturally long for, are constantly promised as a gift: "What I am doing you do not know now, but afterward you will understand" (John 13:7), says Jesus to Peter as he washes the feet of the disciples. James 1:5 expressly says that God gives wisdom: "If any of you lacks wisdom, let him ask God, who gives to all men generously." James 1:25 says, "But he who looks into the perfect law, the law of liberty, and perseveres . . . being no hearer that forgets but a doer who acts, he shall be blessed in his doing." For FIVEs this "doing' is giving, that is, the communicating of knowledge. That is why Sirach says: "She [wisdom] will exalt him above his neighbors, and will open his mouth in the midst of the assembly" (Sir. 15:5) and "For in wisdom must praise be uttered, and the Lord will make it prosper" (Sir. 15:10).

SIX

The need for security is deeply ingrained in SIXes. They get this security by orienting themselves toward authority, which offers itself to them in the form of external laws, instructions, and directives. Fidelity to this authority is the highest basic principle for SIXes. Fear/anxiety is not only their basic weakness, but their root sin. Since the Bible continually deals with these concepts, SIXes will feel "safest" under the mantle of the authority and instruction of Holy Scripture, where they will confuse their fear with fear of God. They will be especially glad to "work" with this fear and to argue about it, bothering and burdening others with this. Thus even Holy Scripture can become a pitfall to them, unless they grasp and accept its true authority. A verse from Psalm 40, "I delight to do thy will, O my God; thy law is within my heart" (Ps. 40:9) makes a very clear statement about the connections that SIXes are somewhat confused about. It is part of being human to acknowledge lawfulness and authority as a creature, to be aware that we live in a context and a structure that we don't control. But humans also have an autonomy, a uniqueness, and an inalienable core in themselves that can and must not be handed over to an outside authority. All of Psalm 118 is devoted to this theme, which Psalm 40, v. 9 tersely summarizes. Isaiah 51:4 says, "A law will come forth from me [God]";

but it is a law directed to a "people in whose heart is my law" (Isaiah 51:7). God, who is *the* authority for humans, his creatures, gives the promise and fulfills it in Christ: "I will put my law within them, and I will write it upon their hearts" (Jer. 31:33). Ezekiel expresses the same idea: "A new heart I will give you, and a new spirit I will put in you; and I will take out of your flesh the heart of stone and give you a heart of flesh. And I will put my spirit within you and cause you to to walk in my statutes, and be careful to observe my ordinances" (Ez. 36:26–27). Speaking of the "righteous," Psalm 37:31 says, 'The law of God is in his heart; his steps do not slip."

The security that the righteous seek and need comes from within, from hearts penetrated by God. The inner authority that men and women possess as a gift of God makes them free from bondage to external authority and the external law. But SIXes are tempted to renounce this inner authority that has been granted them, to repress it, and to abandon themselves "thoughtlessly" to external authority in order to find a security that it can't give them. In contrast we have the example of Mary who is at first "greatly troubled" at the address of the archangel Gabriel, but then ponders/reflects on "what sort of greeting this might be." Reflection leads her to inquire ("How shall this be?"). Only then does she make her free decision (Luke 1:29, 34, 38). The fear that SIXes bear within themselves is only fear of God when, as with Mary, it serves, so to speak, to make us completely awake, so as to accept the divine command rationally, and thus to come to a free decision. As for any lack of courage, sayings by Jesus such as "Courage! The victory is mine; I have conquered the world" (John 16:33, NEB) or, "Do not fear, only believe" (Mark 5:36) have vital importance for SIXes.

SEVEN

Since the profile of SEVENs is marked by gaiety and confidence, high spirits and *joie de vivre,* they will recognize themselves and find support in a great many passages of the Bible. Psalm 37:4–5 may be a shining example: "Take delight in the Lord, and he will give you the desires of your heart. Commit your way to the Lord; trust in him, and he will act." But right from the start it's clear that the joy the Bible speaks of has to be seen in relation to God. This is the joy in God himself that must permeate everything. When SEVENs remain dependent on creatures, on people and things or on themselves, they lack an undergirding foundation.

The temptation of SEVENs is to live cut off from this same divine foundation. That way they drift into superficiality and frivolousness, while losing the sense of reality that perceives and takes seriously the other side of life, pain and suffering. This connection is clearly brought out in Hebrews 12:2: "Looking to Jesus . . . who for the joy that was set before him endured the cross, despising the shame." Jesus gives us his joy, which makes our joy perfect: "These things I have spoken to you, that my joy may be in you, and that your joy may be full" (John 15:11).

So too the joy of (unredeemed) SEVENs, given to them by God as an aid to survival, becomes "perfect" through the joy bestowed by Jesus as life-in-abundance (John 10:10). Along with this joy that God gives through Jesus goes something else, as John 16:20–22 stresses: "You will weep and lament, but the world will rejoice; you will be sorrowful, but your sorrow will turn into joy. When a woman is in travail she has sorrow, because her hour has come; but when she is delivered of the child, she no longer remembers the anguish, for joy that a child is born into the world. So you have sorrow now, but I will see you again and your hearts will rejoice, and no one will take your joy from you."

In Galatians 5:22 joy is counted as a fruit of the spirit: "But the fruit of the Spirit is love, joy, peace. . . . " But the spirit of Jesus becomes "fruitful" in people only when they admit the whole truth. In the Beatitudes in the Sermon on the Mount (Matt. 5:3–12) or the Sermon on the Plain (Luke 6:20–26) this whole truth becomes clear, showing that joy and pain interpenetrate one another, as it were, throughout our earthly life. James 1:2–4 also points out that joy must be seen in conjunction with suffering: "Count it all joy, my brethren, when you meet various trials, for you know that the testing of your faith produces steadfastness. And let steadfastness have its full effect, that you may be perfect and complete, lacking in nothing." Thus SEVENs' compulsive avoidance of unhappiness is overcome in the redemptive acceptance of suffering and painful reality.

EIGHT

Might, power, strength, and force are concepts linked to type EIGHT. Many of the ways they behave can be explained and understood through this basic approach. And as anyone familiar with the Bible knows, these concepts run through the entire Bible. So EIGHTs too can readily recognize themselves in the Bible. Some readers like to make out EIGHTs in concrete biblical persons, but detecting this may be left to the individual's discretion. Once again the point here is to integrate EIGHT, with all its "splendor and misery," into the totality of the "nine faces of the soul" from a biblical perspective. In their role as images of God EIGHTs represent the creative and ruling power of God. God appears as Lord of the Cosmos and Humanity in many passages. Psalm 24 speaks of the "king of glory," "the Lord of hosts," "strong and mighty, the Lord mighty in battle.' 'The earth is the Lord's and the fullness thereof, the world and those who dwell therein" (Ps. 24:1). In Psalm 8 humans are placed near this divine ruler. God, whose name is 'majestic in all the earth, "whose glory above the heavens is chanted," (Ps. 8:1), who "founded a bulwark because of thy foes, to still the enemy and the avenger" (Ps. 8:2), has crowned man "with glory and honor" (Ps. 8:5) and "given him dominion over the works of thy hands" and "put all things under his feet" (Ps. 8:6). Thus being strong — which is what EIGHTs long for — is participation in the ruling dominion of the Creator himself.

But the danger for every creature is the temptation to take participation for sole possession, to arrogate divinity to itself. This arrogance is a characteristic feature of EIGHTs. God will not let his dominion be taken from him: "I am the Lord, and there is no other, besides me there is no God. . . . I form light and create darkness, I make weal and create woe, I am the Lord, who do all these things": (Isaiah 45:5–7). Sole possession of power by EIGHTs makes itself felt in their striving for justice or in their efforts in the struggle against injustice. Here too God reserves judgment for himself: "Vengeance is mine, and recompense" (Dt. 32:35). Ps. 37 describes how he takes care of justice and punishes wrong: "Fret not yourself because of the wicked, be not envious of wrongdoers!" (Ps. 37:1). "Refrain from anger, and forsake wrath; fret not yourself, it leads only to evil (Ps. 37:8). "Commit your way to the Lord; trust in him, and he will act. He will bring forth your vindication as the light, and your right as the noonday" (Ps.37:5–6).

This retribution, to which God alone is entitled, becomes effective in Christ as forgiveness for us, which Christ alone can grant, when we join in taking this step (from retribution to forgiveness), which God takes in Christ. This happens where, as in the case of Peter, an EIGHT's first reaction, to say no, turns into a responsive yes: "You shall never wash my feet. . . . Lord, not my feet only but also my hands and my head!" (John 13:8–9). This reacting-responding no-yes is expressly described in Matthew 21:29, where the one son responds to his father's request with, "I will not; . . . but afterward he repented and went." Jesus takes the "eye for an eye, tooth for a tooth," which aptly characterizes the way EIGHTs react, and brings it along to the response of non-resistance, which by turning "the other cheek" opens the way to forgiveness of the (unjust) blow "on the right cheek." The sight of the interaction of strength and weakness in 2 Corinthians 12:9–10 (" 'My grace is sufficient for you, for my power is made perfect in weakness.' . . . when I am weak, then I am strong") can help EIGHTs transform their hostility toward the weak into compassion, in other words to make the liberating move to TWO. In Jesus this interplay or intertwining of strength and weakness is fully realized. In Rev. 5 Jesus is characterized both as the "Lion of Judah" and as the "Lamb": The Lamb receives "power and wealth and wisdom and might and honor and glory and blessing" (Revelations 5:12). This passage also declares that the revelation of God's power, which EIGHTs may embody in their lives, reached its zenith in the resurrected Lord, who received "power over all flesh, to give eternal life to all whom thou hast given him" (John 17:2). As Jesus received his power not for domination, but for giving life, EIGHTs too have been given their power for showing compassion. Their reactive attitude of domination and control, which guarantees survival, must become a responsive attitude, a powerful transmission of life, in keeping with the level of "life-in-abundance" on which Christians should live.

NINE

Peace, contentment, tranquillity are characteristic concerns of NINEs. In their negative mode we know them as inactivity, indolence, sluggishness, laziness. This Enneagram type is also anchored in the Bible. Peace is a basic scriptural word. Like the "Fear not," peace is found all through the Old and New Testament. Thus many passages in Scripture can be discovered that can serve as encouragement, confirmation, stimulation, admonition, and warning to NINEs. The biblical *shalom*, the greeting pure and simple, is probably one of the most fascinating words in whose radiant landscape NINEs may see themselves. The quality of being an image of God that shines forth from NINEs is God as peace. In the Letter to the Ephesians Jesus is called "our peace" who "has broken down the dividing wall of hostility . . . so making peace . . . thereby bringing the hostility to an end" (Eph. 2:14, 15, 16). Perhaps this "exhortation" is a genuine encouragement to NINEs to *want* to be the gift that they are for others, even when they themselves don't notice it and refuse to believe it.

Since I have discovered myself to be a NINE — even the word "discover" is tied in with this Enneagram type — I can mention some personal experiences. For example, I'll never forget the time someone told me, "You scatter pearls as you walk along" (this was a FIVE!) "You're a gift to me," which I heard more than once (rather skeptically), is a statement that may well occur repeatedly whenever people meet, but for NINEs it's important to take it seriously, because they have a hard time with such "acceptances."

The expression "hidden treasures" (Is. 45:3) applies particularly to NINEs, because they have a compulsive inclination to hide or not to see. In the parable of the talents (Matt. 25:14–30; Luke 19: 11–27) NINEs, if they are honest, will recognize themselves in the man who gets one talent: "He who had received one talent went and dug in the ground and hid his master's money" (Matt. 25:18). He didn't notice that the money had been given to him in trust (in Luke 19:13 the nobleman says, "Trade with these till I come"). His reaction when he has to render an account to his master doesn't make sense: "Lord, here is your pound, which I kept laid away in a napkin; for I was afraid of you, because you are a severe man, you take up what you did not lay down, and reap what you did not sow" (Luke 19:20). The answer of his master is significant: "You wicked and slothful servant!" (Matt. 25:26); "You wicked servant!" (Luke 19:22); "You knew that I reap where I have not sowed, and gather where I have not winnowed? Then you ought to have invested my money with the bankers. . . . " (Matt. 25:26, 27).

We find a clear connection expressed here between laziness (sluggishness) or irresponsibility (ignoring the directions) and fear. NINEs display this in their inclination — which only increases their compulsiveness — toward their stress point SIX (root sin: fear/anxiety). A further typical passage from Scripture is John 5:5–14: the sick man at the Bethzatha pool. He has to be asked whether he even wants to be healed, since he doesn't do anything except wait for other people. If Jesus asks him about his wish to be made well, this means that here is where the man's sickness actually lies, because when he himself does something in response to Jesus's words ("Rise, take up your pallet, and walk"), he gets better after so many long years of "sickness" (lying around and waiting for others). "See, you are well! Sin no more, that nothing worse befall you," are Jesus's last words to him. This seems to be an allusion to laziness as the root sin of NINEs, because moving under his own power, which he felt responsibly bound to do, means his cure. It likewise clearly indicates the liberating movement toward THREE ("Trade with these!" (Luke 19:13).

ON DEALING WITH SCRIPTURE AND THE ENNEAGRAM

As a Help in Self-Knowledge

From what has been said thus far, it should be clear that the Enneagram and the Bible mutually illuminate one another, thus making possible a deeper understanding of both the message of the Bible and of the Enneagram, as a whole and in the individual types. The reader may also have become aware how many different standpoints the same things can be seen from. Surely some readers will not agree with my explanations, even though I think that I've found something valid and important for myself, something that has proved, and continues to prove, helpful for my personal and spiritual growth. The encounter with Holy Scripture, James 1:23 says, is like a glance into a mirror where I see myself. Likewise, if I have "located" myself through the encounter with the Enneagram, at least in clear outlines with some blurry spots remaining, then I can see myself even better in the mirror of God's word, with my strengths and weaknesses, my virtues and vices. But conversely too the profile of each Enneagram type, with both its positive and negative delineations, will be made clearer by the words and images of the Bible.

As an Aid to Prayer

A glance in the mirror proves fruitful for real self-knowledge only when it's a lingering glance that leads to change, or when hearing the word leads to action: "For if anyone is hearer of the word and not a doer, he is like a man who observes his natural face in the mirror and goes away and at once forgets what he was like" (James 1:23–24). But if we meditate on Holy Scripture with the self-knowledge that grows — at least in rough outline — out of working with the Enneagram, then James 1:25 will prove true: "But he who looks into the perfect law, the law of liberty, and perseveres, being no hearer that forgets but a doer that acts, he shall be blessed in his doing."

This also makes it clear that mere familiarity with the Enneagram type will have little effect, unless we are prompted by this knowledge to strive for "action," that is, for redemption and liberation through Jesus Christ, in other words plunging ourselves into "the perfect law of freedom." Discovery of our own type, that is, the way humanness is given us, both as gift and responsibility, and hence the way to the unfolding of our own personality, is a step toward the freedom that every one of us longs for and that is offered to us in Christ. Knowing about our own unredeemed, compulsive type provides us with powerful help for working on ourselves, and hence for transformation into the redeemed type by the encouragement, hope, and forgiveness that a prayerful encounter with the word of God gives us.

In searching for access to the kind of prayer most appropriate for the individual (in other words, how the process of prayer can begin) experience in giving the *Spiritual Exercises* has shown that knowledge of the three centers is of great importance.[2] Any detailed treatment of this point would go beyond the scope of this article, but I would nevertheless like to point out briefly how each of the centers (middle of the body-head-heart) has its own specific access to prayer:

— The middle of the body types (Peter), EIGHT-NINE-ONE experience the inner and outer world with equal strength, and move instinctively in both worlds (though often by themselves). They experience God in prayer within and without. Their best access to prayer is the prayer of silence in which one quiets the understanding, distances oneself from thoughts and feelings, and dwells in a state of pure attentiveness, emptiness, self-divestiture, and receptiveness.

— The head types (Thomas), FIVE-SIX-SEVEN have a large inner world and a limited outer world. They have a hard time being entirely in the world. Their own world of thoughts, plans, and dreams, but also of fear or anxiety, and their inherently strong feelings often remain within. They seek and meet God outside. Therefore the access to prayer most fitting for them is meditation centered on words and images, in which one lets oneself be grasped from outside, gets inspired from outside and finds the inner freedom that masters thoughts and feelings and directs one's attention to a specific object or image.

— With the heart types (Mary Magdalen), TWO-THREE-FOUR, the situation is reversed: They experience a large outer world and a small inner world of their own. They are constantly challenged from outside, torn out of themselves, and feel the invitation to commit themselves to others. They live under the scrutiny of others whose recognition they greatly need. They are often not entirely in touch with themselves, and so the feelings they express sometimes don't seem quite genuine. God meets them within themselves as the Lord of their longing, their feelings, their anxious solicitude. Thus their access to prayer is highly expressive praying during which they experience freedom and transparency by abandoning themselves to their own true self and entrusting themselves to the stream of energy that flows beneath roles, programming, conscious intention, and their own control.

As an Aid for Counselors and Retreat-Givers

Since bringing my knowledge of the Enneagram into the encounter with people whom I advise, I sometimes sense their amazement that I have touched the precise spot where their weakness lies or else where a change has just begun to set in. When appropriate, that is, when I have the impression that it will go over well, I mention the Enneagram to stir up interest and thereby stimulate the person to get further involved with it. But it's important that the people in question feel that this is helping them to get closer to themselves, even if it's painful.

In this process it's a genuine help to know that each type, in the sense of a limited image of God, may live out and bear witness to a quite specific message to others, and may also receive the messages of the others without having to surrender or deny themselves. It is all right for me to be the way I am, but others may also be the way they are. Where someone already knows his or her Enneagram type, "working" with it will naturally be a great help for hearing the personal message of the Bible, that is, for discovering one's unmistakably unique friendship with Jesus as a personal call and mission, and letting it become effective in encounters with others. "Discovering" and "encountering" are words that suggest a path or process: In the unfolding of the process of the *Spiritual Exercises* the Christian goes step by step along the way from enthusiasm over the gift God has given him or her, and liberation from compulsiveness and guilt through the death of Jesus, all the way to recognizing one's own call from Jesus and finding one's personal vocation. For each of these phases the Enneagram proves itself to be an solid school for prayer, as a help on the path of the *Spiritual Exercises*. It would be worthwhile to press the study of these connections still further.

As a Help in Life: Living with the Enneagram and the Bible

People who have discovered for themselves the "word of life" that Sacred Scripture aims to be, anyone who has sensed from his or her daily experience the truth of Isaiah 40:6–8 ("All flesh is grass, and all its beauty is like the flower of the field. The grass withers, the flower fades . . . but the word of our God will stand forever") and who connects 1 Peter 1:25 to Jesus's message ("That word is the good news which was preached to you"), will constantly keep this word in mind. They will continually let it shine into their everyday lives, into all their life-situations so as to interpret their own experience, which they will often find puzzling.

A similar thing happens to me with the Enneagram: It sheds a great deal of light on experiences with myself and others whom I meet, so that I can understand and accept reactions that I note in myself and others. Thus this knowledge influences my life and effectively works toward reconciliation with myself and others, toward self-acceptance, and readiness to bring what is "my own" into the community, so that the "special gift" (my Enneagram type), the "revelation of the Spirit," "may help others" (1 Cor. 12:11, 7). Everyone will discover for himself or herself the concrete areas where knowledge of one's own type in its typical (survival) reactions or the direction of the (life-in-abundance) response can be lived out. Just as in Bible-sharing sessions, where in community people share with one another what each has realized in personal meditation on the words of Holy Scripture, so the exchange of experiences with oneself on the basis of knowledge of one's Enneagram type in a group is exciting and fruitful for one's own way.

And just as there is a personal intercourse with the Bible, or as a person in Ignatius's *Exercises* seeks his personal call, to know the will of God for himself, so intercourse with the Enneagram also seems to me to have a quite personal quality corresponding to one's own type. Hence I feel it is necessary for anyone who speaks to others about the Enneagram be aware of and "confess" his or her own type. The discovery of one's type can be made "tasty" or "disgusting" to the other person depending upon whether one brings one's own "discovered" type into the encounter or denies it.

I would like to conclude my remarks with the thought that spells out my attitude toward the Enneagram. Just as I see the Bible as a gift to humanity, I see in the *Exercises* of Ignatius Loyola a gift to Christians and in the Enneagram a gift to exercitants and their directors.

Part IV

Personal Experiences

On Being One with Everybody:
A Journey through the Enneagram

Marion Küstenmacher

> "Is the path to Enlightenment
> difficult or easy?"
> "It is neither."
> "Why not?"
> "Because it isn't there."
> "Then how does one travel
> to the goal?"
> "One doesn't. This is a journey
> without distance. Stop traveling and
> you arrive."

—Anthony de Mello[1]

Travel is educational, they say. The people and places that we visit leave impressions behind in us, images. Before we leave we cling to promising prospects that are in any case much more beautiful than reality, and afterwards we cling to the vacation photos. We have learned to secure our impressions in the form of images. We're addicted to images, we put our faith in them, because we've forgotten a commandment so important that the Bible places it ahead of all the others: "You shall not make for yourself a graven image, or any likeness of anything that is in heaven above, or that is in the earth beneath, or that is in the water under the earth; you shall not bow down to them or serve them" (Ex. 20:4–5). This is a positively cosmic commandment, it embraces everything and excludes nothing. We are not allowed to misuse either the transcendent (God, heaven), nor the immanent (earth/human beings), nor anything "in the water under the earth" — the unconscious — by first possessing and then replacing it with our images.

Anyone who knows the Enneagram has an opportunity to visit nine landscapes of the soul. If you take this path, you should have the First

Commandment in your rucksack, in the back of your head. It's a sort of passport for admission to all nine countries. People who arrive "at the frontier"
with nothing but "prospectuses" — illusions, prejudices, evaluations borrowed
from parents, and the like — will find quite a few countries closed off to
them — often their own as well. Most of what we have from our country *is*
prospectuses. We continually send them like glossy picture postcards to those
who are planning to come visit us, and so we have largely forgotten that our
own country is much larger, more spacious, and more beautiful than our
modest, perfect, or stylized prospectus. These fancy brochures circulate
everywhere, they show our supposed "sights," which as a rule are as overrun
and unenjoyable as Venice in August. We're familiar with all of them:
perfection, helpfulness, efficiency, authenticity, knowledge, security,
righteousness, contentment.

Anyone who wants to travel in the Enneagram and receive visitors will
have to let go of these images and brochures. All of them, especially the ones
of us. One after the other. When I became acquainted with the Enneagram in
1988, I had the THREE prospectus in hand, ready for distribution: a mother
with an active career, always well-organized, efficient, successful. So I placed
myself at point THREE and looked around at the Enneagram from that point.
Since I had so many lovely mental images from previous "educational trips," I
quickly discovered the types at each point: There was this EIGHT, a union
leader who fought for justice at his plant but beat his stepdaughter at home.
Then there was this nice but boring NINE, who couldn't be stirred out of repose by injustice even if it cried to heaven, and who was literally sleeping her
entire life away. I met a strong ONE (female), whose moralizing and perfectionism stifled every joy in life. I saw a lovable TWO who overwhelmed others
with presents and ensnared them in her net like a spider. Alongside her was an
attractive THREE who lied through his teeth to himself and us, pretending that
his expensive brand-name mentality was his character. I got to know an
extravagant, but forever insecure FOUR who constantly looked people in the
eye — to see her own reflection. Then there was this cool, distant FIVE who
barricaded himself with his expertise behind his desk and lived off other
people's generosity. I saw a SIX, who now seemed modest, now a daredevil,
with fear and mistrust written all over his face. I met a witty, Epicurean
SEVEN, who whirled her way through life, making sure she never committed
to an in-depth relationship.

I saw the much-praised sights in the prospectuses. Some I liked, others felt
totally alien. I saw a lot of Potemkin villages, the first being my own. After a
while I noticed that I wasn't really on a journey; my finger was simply mean-
dering around a homemade picture-map. The adventure began when I let it all
go: my self assessment, my images of other types. At point THREE not a
whole lot happened to me. Was this blindness to my own case, or had I gotten
a wrong number? Many things about me also pointed to type ONE, but I had

always fought vehemently against it. I decided to take the First Commandment seriously and began a second journey minus images and prejudices.

First I went to point EIGHT, if only because I found these aggressive, noisy assailants the hardest of all to stand. And lo and behold, I got my passport for my own type. The aggressive energy of EIGHT was simply the open, honest variant of the angry gut energy suppressed by ONE. I always liked Shakespeare's shrewish Katharina who gets tamed with consistent love. That was my own energy. In the land of EIGHTs they can show you battle-readiness, incorruptibility, and the melting devotion of the strong for the tender and weak.

So point NINE was not my stress point (which it would be for THREE), but my wing. A rather lame, to be sure, or actually broken wing. As a workaholic ONE I knew only the negative variant: the collapse into exhaustion and the it's-all-the-same-to-me feeling. From my new wing I am now learning to catch my breath, take a rest, and keep the Sabbath. Our friends in the land of NINE are waiting for us with their tranquillity, peaceableness, gentleness, and the active power to bring about reconciliation.

From NINE I traveled on to TWO, the wing that I had already known from my false assessment as a THREE. As a mother some features of this type are familiar to me. In the land of the TWOs you can be warmed by solicitude and compassion. From TWOs I can learn to live in solidarity with my family and friends and to invite all strangers into this intimate circle.

In the land of the THREEs I'm now just a quest. I enjoy the energy you find at this point, which is so often missing in our Church. I sense how well the desire of ONEs for growth can work together with the energy and efficiency of THREEs. Like Jacob, THREEs can chase after the blessing, dream of angels, and wrestle with them. What a point! In the land of the THREEs you learn what a vision is.

At point FOUR I got sad. My stress point. The thin skin of ONEs gets punctured here. Self-doubt and melancholy. The problem was to realize my ONEish perfectionism through aesthetic means. The aversion to everything banal. Envy. But wonderful friends make their home at this point, and their sensitivity consoles me, their creativity challenges and animates me. Point FOUR waits for us with the gift of authenticity: To live this life as genuinely as possible.

The trip to point FIVE struck me as especially long. But I had the best memories from my student days in the FIVE world of the university, where you can indulge in thinking as much as your head desires. What can you learn from FIVEs? Sobriety and distance. In the land of the FIVEs you can let everything run through your head one more time, to distance yourself from your notions of the ideal, to see things more objectively. In the land of the FIVEs lives the wisdom that has renounced intellectual arrogance.

In the land of the SIXes I made the most amazing discoveries. No country has a more colorful or varied population. Nowhere do the women have such plucky charm. From SIXes we learn to serve a cause faithfully, without grabbing for the spotlight, or wanting to chuck everything and run at difficult moments. At this point the healthy SIX energy of trust and adult obedience awaits us.

The last point on my trip is point SEVEN, the consolation point of ONE. Wonderful — I'm married to a SEVEN. But simply to delegate joy to your partner would be wrong. Thus tense, serious ONEs can learn from the cheerful SEVENs to allow themselves more festivity and *joie de vivre*. Dancing, feasting, clowning around, enjoying — what a prospect for buttoned-down ONEs. In the land of the SEVENs blooms the joy of all those who have embraced and accepted their pain.

For many ONEs the tollgates just won't open. They stand there with their perfect ONE prospectuses and *work hard on themselves,* to integrate the consolation point, to avoid their stress point, to *improve* their understanding of the other eight types, and so become *more perfect.* And their angry wrinkles, their ramrod backs, and their stomach pains from all the unlived rage won't go away. Just the old ONE-trip that I keep falling for. One salutary, if not quite simple, contemplative exercise for us ONEs is to meditate on the words from the story of creation: "And God saw that it was good" (Gen. 1). Speaking for myself, I've noticed in reading these words how hard I find it to allow myself this pure satisfaction. I have to look at growing things outdoors. Not to intervene, just marvel. Simply let something be good, not having to change, rebuild, or improve anything . . .

The journey never ends, of course. It's a spiritual path: When you've left one point, you're on the way to the next. Every encounter is a chance to grow. Needless to say, you can also be underway without the Enneagram. I'm thankful that I know about it. It teaches me the special kind of attentiveness to myself and others that T. S. Eliot calls "concentration without elimination." Concentration, the highest attentiveness, and wonder, the greatest openness, come together in the Enneagram. The infinite variety of life shines forth and with it our original fellowship. The Enneagram is not a game of psychobabble with numbers, it's not pigeonholing or handing out brochures. It's an invitation to take a spiritual journey, and it gives us what all travelers need to be able to see: *the loving look at what really is.* You don't need anything more for this fearfully long journey without distances.

Is the path to enlightenment difficult or easy? Neither. Stop traveling, and you're there.

The Burden and Blessing of Being a SIX

Liesl Scheich

When you're a SIX, some brand of fear is always rolling off your assembly line. You're forever aware of things that could go wrong: The car could die just when you desperately need it; the street could be blocked off when you're rushing to an important appointment; you could get hospitalized just when a make-it-or-break-it project is almost done or when you're about to take a trip around the world.

You're afraid that this or that person will think you're a drag, that you basically can't impose on anyone, that if someone does praise you, it's only for "pedagogical reasons," that if someone does like you, it's only out of a sense of duty, out of Christian love of neighbor, or because you've knocked yourself out for them.

You're afraid to fail, afraid of making a fool of yourself, afraid of your own fear. In short, there's nothing you couldn't be afraid of.

When none of the things you feared occurs, then you can easily succumb to the danger of magical thinking: Your worst fears didn't materialize because you anticipated it in a thousand terrors. You've already endured all the bad parts, so that you didn't have to go through with it in reality. Meanwhile you're forgetting that most of these anxieties were manufactured by your own brain and had nothing to do with the real world.

This sort of life spent in fear is hard to bear. Fear and anxiety weigh on you with constant pressure. When the pressure gets too heavy, you try to shake it off, and then you often do things that actually provoke dangers that as a reasonable person you'd do better to avoid. You plunge into adventures of every kind, not knowing how they'll end, whether they're more or less dangerous to life and limb, or if you're only provoking people who in one way or another make you afraid. Or you take on jobs that you're basically not up to.

So many people consider you brave.

This flight into risky adventures lowers the pressure for the short term, but in the long run does no good, because nothing changes in your basic way of being. All you did was expose yourself to dangers you would have done better to dodge.

It may be natural for you to maneuver yourself into a blind alley. You panic, now you're really at the mercy of your fear — with no possibilities of escape. (The fact that you yourself are to blame doesn't make things any easier.)

When you can no longer escape this fear, and you accept your own powerlessness, then you have a chance, now that you're at the bottom of your fear, in the most hopeless abyss, to find your way to a trust that is greater than the fear, a trust that begins on the other side of powerlessness, a trust that relativizes the outcome of "history."

It's possible that you'll get help from outside, that through this trust you'll get new energies, that you'll be "saved." But it's also possible that this newly won confidence will carry you through failure. (This naturally holds true for all hopeless situations, not just the ones we ourselves are responsible for.)

This precious experience, that trust calms fear, leaves traces behind in you — though at first they're scarcely perceptible. And when fear overwhelms you at the next opportunity, you still have the distant memory. And perhaps you'll succeed very hesitantly in opposing fear with trust, in continually "practicing" trust in the face of all fear and mistrust.

At some point or other then you may be astonished to notice that you've been living quite naturally, all taken up with the demands of the moment. That will be like a gift, not something you have at your disposal, an existential state that you'll keep flipping in and out of. And yet something fundamental in your life has changed.

Continually finding the way out of fear into trust is a continual experience of redemption. Living permanently face to face with fear, conscious of it, unable to get away from it, this is the great burden of SIXes and yet their great opportunity. The fear is graspable, palpable, ever-present. But since you can't repress it, it can't carry on its dirty business in your unconscious. So this is the bright side, that "when anything is exposed by the light it becomes visible" (Eph. 5:13).

When you're a SIX, you'll be forever asking yourself: Who am I, really? You'll sense the most contradictory qualities in yourself. You'll sometimes have the feeling that you're at odds with yourself. You'll feel divided and torn; and then you'll feel that you can no longer endure this inner split, like a bow that"s been stretched too far and threatens to snap. The question, "Who am I?", will become unbearable.

But in the midst of this excruciating split it can happen that the opposites collapse into each other, that all at once a grand peace prevails, that the split turns into wholeness, that all the doubts and questions end, that everything is right, that you are God's beloved child, a whole person, sharing in the fullness of life.

You can live on these moments — when heaven and earth come tumbling down — and the memory of this wholeness and the longing for it will never leave you.

When you're a SIX, you yearn to be in sync with others, to belong to a group. You secretly hope that things will be clear, because you yourself have a hard time finding your way to inner clarity. You'd like to have help in making decisions, because your own inner voices continue to clash with one another, and you can make your mind up only with difficulty. You want security because you see yourself threatened by countless fears. You long for certainty about the path you should take, because everything in you is uncertain, everything seems directionless.

But deep within you you mistrust outer order. Because you're always aware of your own internal division, your weaknesses don't remain hidden very long to all the external authorities. So you begin to revolt against the group, the institution. The greater your longing was to find a "home" at long last, the more disappointedly you'll turn your back on this "place of refuge." And the higher your expectations were, the more inexorably you'll fight against everything that doesn't live up to them.

Thus for many reasons you don't succeed in following Christ, in living by the instructions of the Sermon on the Mount. And you focus all your hopes and expectations on the "Church," that is, on the men and women who "represent" it. Then you're disappointed when the "Church" doesn't act in accordance with its own lofty claims — namely to be based on Jesus Christ and to invoke him as its supreme authority — and doesn't meet your standards. Perhaps you'll notice at some point that you're behaving like a minor, a child waiting for directions from its parents, or a teenager rebelling against all orders.

Perhaps too you'll notice that you really aren't that weak child any more, needing protection and direction from whatever authorities. You'll discover your own strength, and perhaps you'll suddenly experience something like an inner permission to live this strength: "It's all right to be strong." If you've found your way to this trust in your own strength, then you no longer need to be fencing yourself in all the time. You can commit yourself to other people without being mistrustful and on your guard against being put into somebody's back pocket. You can say yes and no. You can adapt to others, you can pursue a goal together with them, but you can also say no, without immediately panicking about what the others will say. And without immediately worrying about no longer belonging.

Although you'll go on happily sticking up for people who belong to you, and you'd like to live in harmony with them, you'll be able to put up with distance and separation for the sake of your own truth. Maybe you'll also sooner or later find to your surprise that you have something to say to others, that they listen to your opinion, and come to you for advice.

Your ambivalence will be most evident in your relationships with other people. The major factors here will likely be insecurity and real or unreal anxieties — predominantly the latter. You long for intimacy, and at the same time you're terrified of it.

You'd like to trust, and at the same time you mistrust. You question the ulterior motives of anyone who's obliging to you or shows you any affection. You'd like to be loved and accepted for what you are, but since at bottom you can't accept yourself, you also don't trust others. In the background there's always the feeling that "I can't thrust myself on others, and before I expose myself to the danger of being rejected, I'll pull back."

Since you yourself aren't unequivocal and have great difficulties openly saying no (you do it after all, but surreptitiously), you also unconsciously impute your own brand of ambivalence to other people. You arm yourself internally against a no, a rejection that you sense is lurking somewhere in the background. Then you forestall this presumptive no by withdrawing.

In your heart of hearts there's nothing you yearn for so much as to be accepted and loved. But when you sense another person meeting you half-way with appreciation and interest, then you almost unavoidably call the whole thing into question. Does this person really mean me? Would she love me if she really knew me?

Then you involuntarily begin to put the other person — whom you really care a great deal for — on trial and, in a way, to provoke him or her. You do this with great anxiety in your heart, fearing to lose this person by your behavior, but something forces you to fight against the other's imagined ambivalence. You risk what's dear and valuable to you.

When you're a SIX, you have a particularly strong need to have the experience, at some point or other, of being loved unconditionally. You need people who give you the sense of liking you the way you are. Ultimately you need the experience, the faith, the undeserved gift that God loves you, because fear turns into trust only when face-to-face with an infinite Thou.

To find your way to trust is the only possibility for overcoming your ambivalence. Living on the strength of this acquired trust fundamentally changes everything, it's almost like being created anew.

You always were someone whom people could rely on, when it came to the crunch. You were a loyal friend, but this was often accompanied by ambivalent feelings. If you've now found your way to trust, all your relationships take on a new quality, a new atmosphere is born. You no longer expect friendship, affection, and love *because* of your loyal behavior — you take it as a gift. And on the other hand you give your friendship and love unquestioningly, as a matter of course, almost out of inner necessity, without wondering what will come of it — just because.

The Nine Types:
Personal Reports, Letters, and Testimonials

Selected and Arranged by
Marion Küstenmacher

Since the publication of Richard Rohr and Andreas Ebert's first book on the Enneagram (which I helped edit), we have received over a thousand letters, an average of ten per week. The offer we made in the early editions to do counselling by mail evidently spoke to such a profound need in readers that our little team of Enneagram counsellors was quickly overwhelmed with work. Like no other typology, the Enneagram seems to awaken an urge for personal exchange to verify and deepen the ideas people have read about.

The following excerpts from readers' letters are aimed at illustrating how tremendously open and vulnerable many of these readers are. Andreas Ebert chose these letters, while strictly observing confidentiality, and passed partial copies of them on to me. All personal data — age, occupation, gender, number of children — have been altered or omitted where there was any reason to fear the person might be identified.

The nine types were very disproportionately represented by our correspondents. The largest block of letter writers were NINEs, TWOs, and ONEs. But here, of course, you have to reckon with a certain percentage of false assessments; and some readers themselves hesitated between two numbers (NINE and FIVE, for instance) in evaluating themselves. Only a handful of SEVENs, EIGHTs, and FIVEs wrote us, and most of the FIVEs only wanted information about retreats or further reading, and revealed nothing about themselves. A few FIVEs whom we had asked for contributions to this book first agreed and then changed their mind. Not a single THREE took up the offer of counselling by mail; the accounts from THREEs cited below were those we requested and promptly received — one by and one about a THREE. The excepts from NINEs, THREEs, and SIXes are worth reading with care for anyone who wants to know about the center-energies.

All nine types invite us with their gifts to visit their point and enter into dialogue with them. Two correspondents have expressed this especially well, and so I'll quote them right at the beginning:

"I'm writing you because I felt joy deep down inside and the breadth and depth of the truths presented [in *Discovering the Enneagram*]. I've never read this sort of typology before. It gave me the impression of looking at people in all their variety and seeing them as still growing. In many other typologies the complexity of the person struck me as being artificially reduced to a tiny handful of types. All kinds of things have opened up within me, and I'm happily prepared for further discoveries. I think it's a book for living, not for reading."

"I'm very grateful to you for this book. It's been a long time since I read anything that was so much like a dialogue, I mean being in a concrete conversation with the book or its authors. Meanwhile all my friends have been *delighted* with the Enneagram, in the truest sense of the word."

Type ONE

"Interestingly, I always knew I was inclined to dogmatic insistence on being right. Only I was surprised sometimes that I had such a good feeling in my guts when it turned out that I *was* right. Russia has always been my favorite country. I have a picture of a Russian man at prayer in my office. I also like the Russian wedding ring (three rings in one, yellow gold, white gold, and red gold) — it made me think of my wings and their colors."

"It took me a while before I recognized myself as type ONE. Up till then I wasn't aware that I was 'governed' by aggression. But rage, anger, and irritation have been the source of energy in my life without my knowing it. For a good year now I've been using the Enneagram for guidance, and I've often had the feeling of coming apart at the seams. Till then I was on the whole satisfied, as a believing Christian, with my fellowship group, daily quiet time, volunteer work in the parish, going to church, and my children and career besides.

"I found it incredibly hard to let go of my self-image, because suddenly there was nothing there. Sometimes I even felt abandoned by God. And yet he didn't abandon me in this difficult time, but really gave me the grace to do penance for myself as a person. I couldn't get out of my head the motto you give ONEs in your book, 'All or nothing.' I risked breaking up my marriage when I realized how imperfect it was. I would have preferred 'nothing' to compromises! Thank God, my husband wouldn't agree to my proposal to separate. Some things have gotten really good, others I didn't tackle at all when I noticed that I couldn't give them the 100% treatment. So it keeps helping me as a ONE when I look on God as my father who loves unconditionally, who's interested in my *person* and not my *works*, the one who's already perfect in everything that he is and does. I have precious moments when I can lose myself in God. Then I get a feeling of boundless freedom — freedom from myself. I am a ONE and I always will be, but I hope that I've really made progress, that I'll stay on this path, and that I'll be granted patience and serenity."

"The description of ONEs was very consoling to me, since I'd spent years in counselling, wrestling with the temptation of *perfectionism* and the problems it causes. I *have* gotten much calmer over the years, and I can at least accept *others'* mistakes, but I keep running up against the same problem with my colleagues: Although I take pains to admit my mistakes and to show my weaknesses, and although I ask for criticism, I keep finding that the 'weaker' ones feel overwhelmed by me, consider me arrogant, and pull back from me. When I repeatedly meet with rejection, I very quickly get into melancholy-depressive moods (the stress-point of FOURs). My coworkers can't imagine how this can happen with such a 'strong' person as myself, and look stunned when I collapse."

"With a mild sense of shock I realized immediately that I belong to the ONEs. I wrote down my childhood memories, in order to find out my lifestyle, my pitfalls, unconscious goals, etc. Whenever I took liberties, was cocky, had fun and and felt good about it, or didn't do what others wanted, I got beaten, and hard. Today I administer these beatings to myself when I don't do what others want from me. When I see anyone having problems with me, I punish myself, direct my rage against myself, search myself for every mistake, and stop doing anything. Recently I went for counselling, because I was really desperate. Afterwards my advisor said he was getting an inferiority complex just talking to me. What garbage! Why is that it that other people feel inferior to me? There's nothing I can do that others can't do as well or even better — on the contrary, I can do much less. But I'm always getting told, 'You're so strong,' 'You're always right.'

"What does me good is going out dancing, jogging, hiking, climbing, being with friends, and horsing around. I allow myself all that when I'm finished, that is, when the house and garden are taken care of, and I'm not gnawing and brooding on unresolved conflicts."

Type TWO

"My life has typical TWO way stations: I've been a social-worker and counsellor, then I was trained in massage and physical therapy, and worked in an old age home, where I managed to push myself to the edge of exhaustion. . . . A total breakdown left me completely crippled for half a year. Thanks God I met a good doctor who told me: 'Your body is speaking loud and clear — don't give, just let yourself take!' . . . My dreams, which to me are the language of my soul, have long been presenting me with TWO-material. Through the Enneagram I got a new in-depth understanding. Thanks for the book; I'll pass it on to someone else."

"I'm not surprised that the book took me by storm. I'm a (female) TWO and it wasn't at all hard finding that out. After all some of the descriptions were so clear-cut that I thought for a while that Richard Rohr must have actually met me some time before. . . . I know many aspects of TWO as if they were a second skin. For example, my life depends on the way people around me think of me. I'm constantly looking for feedback, I can never get enough 'ratings' from strangers (of course, only as long as they're positive). I have a hard time relying on my own judgment. Sometimes I think I don't have any opinions at all about myself (at least no positive ones). But I did 'progress' to the point of getting a woman therapist to spend sixty minutes every four weeks listening to me tell my story. After six sessions I finally managed to look only at myself without calculating on the side what she might be thinking about me. Together we realized that in many situations I automatically took the other person's responsibility on myself — just as I had done with the therapist."

"Actually I've long been living in an over-strained condition (career as a social worker, children, working on a project for the unemployed), and I have great difficulties with being alone and taking a rest. As I child I was always being told: If you act so fresh, mother's going to die (she had heart trouble). My father loved us, but he couldn't show it the way I would have liked. . . . With the onset of puberty I began to have migraines, which got me all kinds of attention. When my father came home, he wasn't allowed to scold me because I either had been a great help to mother or I was lying in bed with a headache. When I finally got married after a long engagement, and my husband and I could sleep together, I warded off sex with terrible bladder infections. . . .

(Five months later...) "Meanwhile I'm learning that I don't always have to be the strong one, and I no longer have to hide my need for help. It was a very good time, and a brutally bad time. After one migraine attack I tried to get over it not with medicine (which I always used to keep my body from going over the edge) but with biofeedback. While trying this I had an exciting experience. In the training session we were supposed to concentrate on the gut and feel the warmth there; but when I did I felt a headache coming on. In the afternoon I went out to walk by myself, to pursue this lead. I knew that my migraine had somehow or other to do with my 'gut.'

"Suddenly it was like being hit by lightning — I was close to passing out. I've never felt anything like it. What had happened in my childhood that I remembered only in little fragments? I was overwhelmed by an uncontrollable fear of something inconceivable, but on the other hand I sensed that there was a way out of my dilemma here. The memories that poured over me weren't of facts but of fears. I became increasingly suspicious that my father might have sexually abused me in some way. That loving father, and above all that pious man! The next ten days were madness. I painted, dreamed, and the whole thing began to take shape: something terrible had happened in my childhood. . . . My husband was incredibly terrific to me during that time. He was constantly there for me — and he believed me.

(Three weeks later) . . . "Meanwhile I have the impression that I can live again, even though many things are still unresolved. My breakdown brings many opportunities along with it. It's not just for me, it's also good for my husband that I no longer play the superwoman that I actually never was. I'm glad when I see how real strength can be developed; and I can also accept my weaknesses more easily. I've 'slipped' many of my weak points onto my husband (like old sweaters), and he seems altogether different to me now. . . . I'm incredibly grateful that my phantoms have broken down, although it's sometimes hard not knowing how it will all turn out."

Type THREE

Roland Gehm writes:
"When I arrived at THREE, I heard a click. The very first image and the first lines made it clear enough: I was a THREE. Every line that followed confirmed this assumption; and I noticed how clear and distinct everything I was reading about myself seemed. It was not an unpleasant feeling. I knew about these qualities and hitherto I had found them quite useful — above all because many other people envied me for some of them (a friend who is a NINE, for example, envied my ability to sell myself). What wasn't so pleasant was the straightforward language describing these qualities. Not that they sounded didactic — loving was more like it — but they corrected my own definitions: the lying, the more-show-than-substance, the tinsel world, and the chameleon qualities struck me as unmistakably negative, not positive, as they had before. Earlier I would have called them 'purposefully optimized and situationally appropriate forms of personal expression,' or something highfalutin like that.

"I now know that I have the negative points of THREE 'harmonically' united; and I try to act accordingly. But this is where the main problem lies. Because most things run along so damned automatically that you don't notice it till it's too late: Here a little story with laundered truth, there an unobtrusively slick production, or a not entirely kosher super-sale — all things that go off without a hitch. So despite the Enneagram I haven't yet found my way to truthfulness — it will take quite a while to get that far.

"But it helps that I can longer hide from myself, and I'm increasingly aware of what's happening when I stumble into the THREE pitfall. I catch myself with my pants down, and I can't talk my way out of it. Whatever I do when I'm fully conscious, I've got to take full responsibility for it: My conscience is calling collect. In some situations, of course, I'm still so stuck and imprisoned in the old, bad patterns that I really can't help following their lead.

"A further problem comes from situations in which I don't know what's motivating me or don't have any access to an unequivocally honest answer for myself. Current example: these lines. Am I writing them because I've recognized my weaknesses and can clearly admit them to myself, and thus see this opening-up as a first important step? Or is it only a clever tactic: Am I putting them in as a sort of pseudo-opening-up, a fake confession in order to look absolutely fabulous in the eyes of a certain group? I don't know!

"In any event, the Enneagram has become a challenge to me, not just because I know myself better with it, but also because I'm learning something about others. Up till now I could accept many standpoints and perspectives only if they were 'relatively as right as mine'; but I couldn't really understand them. The Enneagram gives a fresh quality to my meeting and communicating with others."

Andreas Ebert reports:

"In the noontime break at a recent workshop a woman of about 60 came up to me and said: 'I'm a THREE. I always wanted to be an actress, and in way I did become an actress. In my life I've worn all the masks and tried out all the roles until three years ago. Within a year I lost my husband and my parents, and I myself got very sick. Everything broke down. I experienced something like one mask after another being stripped away. I felt my hostility toward God and the world. A couple of times I stood on the balcony and wanted to jump off, because everything seemed so meaningless. But a little voice in me held me back. I was afraid that if I lost my masks, in the end there'd be nothing there. Finally one day I was completely exhausted and totally empty. At that moment something new began. I suddenly noticed that there was something there. There were feelings, life, hope. But I wasn't producing all that myself. It was just there.'

"In the end she said: 'I've gone through hell. But I'd never want to be back where I used to be. Only now am I living. And something else happened to me: Now when I meet other people, I immediately see whether they're sincere or whether they're hiding something. They can't put anything over on me, because I know all the masks myself. Luckily, along with this gift God has given me a new love and compassion. I believe I can talk to people in a way that's helpful and good for them'."

Type FOUR

"These days the Enneagram is my 'daily bread.' I recognize myself — no mistake about it — in the flaming FOUR. Many ONEs have crossed my path up to now — I think I get the balance I need from them. . . . I'm a widow, and the pattern of my mourning was striking. I wanted to show the Church that 'she' can't mourn, but *I* certainly could — and I took on all the grief work by myself. There's a dazzling-but-dubious side of me that keeps breaking through; and because I'm ashamed of it, I retreat into myself. But at some point or other the peacock gets the upper hand. I keep clipping his tail feathers, but new ones grow back, as bright as before."

"I'm a FOUR, and it's true that FOURs have an uncanny sense of other people's moods and feelings, as well as for the atmosphere of certain places. It's terribly important to me to be something 'special,' not to be overlooked, and positively not to slip quickly into oblivion. It's extremely important to me that people recognize me even after X years of being away. When they do, it flatters me enormously and I feel tremendous. As a child I felt unwanted and discriminated against for years. I hadn't gotten the love I needed, and so I had to use my imagination to create my own sources of love. For two years now I've been mourning the love of my life, secretly hoping he'd come back. Nobody else can unleash the same feelings in me that he did, I compare every man I meet with him. Practically all my relationships have been with men who live far away, making an everyday love affair impossible. When I was on vacation with my current boyfriend (he lives 450 miles away), every day he got more and more on my nerves. I was bored and constantly had the feeling that I was running into a concrete wall. Yet until recently this strange weekend relationship was still something very special for me."

"I'm writing to you, although I'm afraid that I won't get the right treatment for my very personal problems. I'm also afraid that I'll get inappropriate advice from an incompetent person, because he or she might misunderstand me (I know, typical). And third, I'm afraid of uncomfortable change.

"I'm in the middle of a marital crisis that I set in motion by having an affair. I don't love my wife any more. For years now my thinking and feeling haven't been monogamous. In retrospect I see these years as a violation, a subjection, and an enslavement of myself. The longing for other women was at times more real than my wife's presence. For me adultery was a liberation from the slavery of having to love my wife, and only my wife, unconditionally. On the one hand I know that I'm taking my subjective feelings too seriously. On the other hand, I can't and won't give them up. It would end in chaos, I couldn't stand going through that again. For a long time I've fought my feelings with will power, but I still have hostile feelings, aggression, and hatred left over. I'm still very attached to my wife, but in the most negative sense imaginable."

Type FIVE

"The Enneagram has absolutely opened 'a door' for me. It was a tremendous help for me to recognize my reflection in type FIVE. I had always thought I was somehow 'abnormal'."

"My husband is an unmistakable FIVE. He's really working all the time, and beyond that, as he puts it, he loves our two children as *persons*, but not in the least as *his children*. That means they often disturb him. This hit me very hard, because I don't at all want to burden him with the babysitting. So I feel that I myself have to take care of it, which then puts the pressure on me."

Type SIX

"I believe I've recognized myself as a contraphobic SIX. I had a hard time with this, since I wasn't ready to face my conscious fear of life. SIXes, they say, can't develop basic trust because they had emotionally cold parents — this is quite true of me. In my family there was no room for feelings — they were considered disturbing. Not once did anyone simply take me in their arms — on the other hand I was unfairly punished by my father. I am very dependent on the infallible answers in the Bible. If you were to certify, in response to this letter, that the Bible has no absolute authority, my black-and-white world picture (sinners and the just) would be seriously shaken. But, as you see, I'm writing to you anyway and consciously taking this risk. Although I am a 'born again Christian,' I lack the certainty that I'm on the right track with my Christian world picture. I'm also notoriously mistrustful of both my superiors and my colleagues. Obeying the law is frightfully important to me. I can expatiate endlessly on the Law and the Gospel, and I see in the commandments God's precautionary measures."

From Andreas Ebert's letter in response:
"You're trying to get out of the Bible and Christian doctrine a system and a world picture that you can hold onto. But faith isn't clinging to an intellectual structure or system, it's a cordial, trusting, loving relationship with Jesus Christ. SIXes are in great danger of confusing the two. The authority of the Bible, which I'm not questioning, doesn't consist in providing infallible answers to all questions. Its authority lies in the living witness of living men and women who were impelled to pass on their powerful experiences with God. The Bible reaches its goal when it motivates us to involve ourselves with this same experience: with the risk of faith, which is more a letting go than a holding on. Faith offers us not security, but the freedom to be held and sheltered amidst fear and uncertainty. The good news for you is that God is different from

your father. It's not his 'authority' that saves you, but his love. Your uncertainty about your Christian world picture is an indication that you are on the way to a deeper and more personal understanding of faith."

"My image of God is certainly a central point. And it's a pretty well split: There is the very dear father (abba), whose tenderness I was allowed to feel on a few rare occasions in an almost physical sense, and likewise the brotherly Jesus. But in the background lurks a shadow, a sadistic Somebody who has it in for me, who creates countless problems, big and little, for me (if God is in control, then doesn't everything come from him?). When things go badly for me, this idolatrous caricature ventures forth. My lack of basic trust is probably connected with my childhood: the loss of my home and my father (I watched him being arrested by American soldiers), months in the hospital, where nurses and doctors — the only human beings I had any contact with — scarcely had time for me and caused me pain in the bargain. . . . This literally two-sided image of God was in urgent need of a cure, and that cure would liberate me too from much of my own inner division. This all became clear to me only when I wrote it down, and I'm deeply thankful to you for that."

"Family tradition trained me to be obedient, to do what was expected of me, and to show *external* humility (with high *internal* pretensions). Fear, faith in authority, and striving for security were fundamental features of my education. In the Enneagram I recognize myself as a SIX who always thinks he has to be a THREE (and fails in the attempt), but who wants to get closer to NINE. I have a very anxious attitude toward the Christian faith. I feel my own inner faith (often a longing for deep security) — but I don't have the courage, I'm too undecided, to take the first step."

Type SEVEN

"I never wanted to be a SEVEN"
A light-hearted intermezzo on the art of avoidance
by Johannes Minkus

"It took me almost ten months to realize that I am a SEVEN. First of all I actually wanted to be a NINE. Immediately after I first read about the nine Enneagram types, I felt I liked type NINE best of all. 'That's me,' I thought. I could well imagine myself lying in a hammock with a can of beer, letting the sun shine on my stomach. I also liked the idea that as a NINE I could save the world — if only I weren't so lazy.

"For around ten years I've envied people who can express their feelings effortlessly. Well, I had never had any problem showing joy and enthusiasm, but I didn't feel quite right about showing myself furious or aggressive. For that reason I was very happy to read that NINEs act 'from their gut.' At last I could toss my doubts in the trash can: I'm a NINE and so I can easily pour out my feelings.

"The collapse of all this came on a Friday after supper. My wife had been telling me about a typical SEVEN; and so I fished the Enneagram book out from under the bed, where it had been gathering dust for months. I've never liked SEVEN types, and actually wanted to read the section on SEVENs with an enjoyable sense of loathing. But as I read, it hit me: *I'm a SEVEN.* I'm one of these superficial head types.

"I flipped back and forth in the SEVEN section to find qualities that conclusively proved I wasn't a SEVEN after all — no luck.

"That whole weekend I felt depressed, My wife tried to console me: 'It's just a book,' she said. I would have been happy to believe it, but the problem was that between Saturday morning and Sunday night I discovered all sorts of typical SEVEN qualities in myself.

"For example, for Christmas my wife had given me a Walkman. I felt a deep sense of satisfaction as I laid the Walkman with brand new batteries in front of me on the table, and alongside it my five favorite cassettes. It was a wonderful feeling: If I wanted to, I could listen to any one of the cassettes. But I couldn't decide. I grabbed the remote control and switched on the TV: SEVENs love to have lots of options.

"I also remember a line that I like to use at the end of conversations with people contemplating baptism (I'm a minister): 'Well, I'm glad; I know everything that I have to know. Is there anything further we should discuss?' SEVENs love their self-image of being happy.

"Visiting the sick cost me a lot of energy, when I had to raise the issue of the patient's pain — in proper pastoral fashion. I would have much rather patted them on the shoulder and said, 'Everything will be back to normal. What a wonderful day it is today. . . . ' Getting close to pain is very hard for a SEVEN.

"I had similar difficulties in my therapy group. In itself it's a wonderful idea: Well-meaning group members help you see your problems from a different perspective. The unpleasant thing was that I was supposed to talk about my own problems and weaknesses. I tried to get out of it, but sometimes I had to do it. Fortunately when I get into such tight situations I almost always think of good jokes — which eases the tension. The woman group leader talked about 'escapism' and 'avoidance' — she probably didn't like jokes.

"But enough of these depressing stories. Let me end with one more secret recipe for a good mood. Spend an afternoon with another SEVEN enjoying the limitless possibilities of playing with a computer. You'll get 'good vibrations'."

"Do I Like Happiness Too Much?"
Experiences of a SEVEN
by Werner Küstenmacher

"When I first learned about the Enneagram, I was immediately told to my face that I was a SEVEN. I'm usually quite skeptical about models of personality and other attempts at explaining the world. But this time the Enneagram hit home.

"We are sinners — this truth has degenerated into a bromide that hardly stirs anyone any more. The Enneagram showed me that I have a favorite sin, a pitfall into which I keep stumbling. This experience was stunningly vivid. Above all if you start out by concentrating on this favorite sin and don't get distracted by too much speculation about wings, consolation and stress points.

"I had another experience: The first weeks after encountering my own pitfall were marked by an almost compulsive pleasure in repeatedly tasting its flavor to the full. I ate enormously, bought stuff, went far out of my way to avoid unpleasant things, and further expanded my system of giving myself little rewards. To recognize evil, it seems you have to get especially close to it one more time. On the other hand, this sort of draining-to-the-dregs syndrome is probably connected to the fact that you know you'll soon have to part with your favorite sin.

"I was fascinated by Rohr and Ebert's description of the nine root sins. Like many Christians, I used to make a detour around the concept of 'sin.' Is it really necessary to be confronted immediately by something so unpleasant? Couldn't it be put a little more nicely? I had also had problems with the breakdown of human vices into the usual mortal sins. The list never seemed complete. Fear and lying — they were exactly the two that had been missing. I felt that some of the classical sins had been framed too narrowly. Upon closer inspection I discovered I had them all.

"*Anger* — is that even a sin? I had thought of it rather as a passing emotional disturbance. But now I learned how self-destructive it is to take personally the mistakes and imperfections of other people. Hypersensitivity is a terrible pitfall: I can torment and overwhelm others with my desire for technical and social perfection: You don't see the mistake, you dumb jerk, but I do, I pay attention to the details. I know what dead ends I can drive into just to be right and not to have to admit mistakes.

"I couldn't understand *pride* until I translated it as 'egotism.' When disguised as love of neighbor, it's a terrifying weapon. How often I do good out of calculation!

"*Lying* strikes a nerve when I substitute for it the word "self-deception." I recall situations in which I kept lying until I believed it myself. And that was probably the main reason why I lied in the first place.

"I had classified *envy* as a subordinate motivation for certain actions: X has a bigger stereo system, so I have to one-up him. But envy gets bad precisely in matters that can't be changed even with a lot of money. 'I'm not up to it' — from there the road leads to depression and despair. But I was never much given to envy.

"I had always confused *stinginess* with thrift. But stingy people don't seem to be calculating what advantage their non-giving is to their financial or psychic bank accounts. Stinginess has become a principle in which the question of effective use is out of order. SEVEN and FIVE can be clean contrary to each other: I love to figure out why a luxury car might be more sensible than a subcompact (more pleasure, improved motivation, greater safety, higher resale value). FIVEs say: Even if that adds up (it generally doesn't, of course) it's still a waste of money.

"I always thought of *fear* as something that happens to you. In the Enneagram I learned that, just like joy, it's a product of our head. Fear is something quite calculating, almost the opposite of faith and trust. It's not trusting your own feelings and what's deepest within you, it's *thrusting* God away along with unpredictable human beings. I'm all too familiar with this over-controlled life.

"I don't know anybody who's *lustful* in the usual moral-theology-textbook sense. But I do know shameless people. They feel something like lust when they break through the fine, invisible frontier of shame that surrounds and protects us. We always make the mistake of considering the aggressor strong just because he dares to cross this border.

"Actually, it's always been clear to me that *laziness* is a sin. I've done everything possible to avoid it — thereby driving away the blessing that hangs over leisure and non-interference.

"'Gluttony' makes me think of an orgiastic medieval banquet, and this doesn't remotely touch me. But *intemperance* is another story. One brilliant definition for it is 'more is better.' This is the motto of the affluent society — which, by the way, I was always happy and grateful to belong to. I found other kinds of society suspect. I feel a small secret glow of satisfaction that the scarcity-ridden socialist economies are proving to be non-viable. I like to idealize head-directed reason: Perfect joy can flourish only in a society where people like one another and live in harmony with nature. Thus a society of SEVENs would have to work for peace, justice, and protection of the environment. Anyhow, it's the affluent societies that have discovered all this as a political goal, and are spending a lot of money and imagination to redress the sins of the past.

"If everybody was a SEVEN, this world would be wonderful. That I could formulate a sentence like that — at least on the sly — is a sure sign that I'm trapped deep down in my pitfall. Honestly, I feel pretty good in my SEVEN skin. I have the need to be happy, I really do, and now I'm happy, *basta*!

"Although I have seldom felt exactly like a lucky duck, things have always gone very well for me. I actually was always sure that I'd find a nice house, the right career, and the ideal wife. Did it really work out that way, or is it only my point of view? Did I always have enough money, or did I just rein in my demands so that the few pennies I had seemed a fortune? I can imagine another person feeling very unhappy in my skin.

"SEVENs avoid pain. That seemed self-evident to me, and I immediately discovered that I do too. But isn't everyone afraid of the dentist, or worried about lying helpless and twisted in pain on his or her deathbed? No, the pain avoidance of SEVENs sets in much earlier. They plan to avoid even the smallest unpleasantness. They run away, they don't think about it. I can do that myself: While watching a film about the misery of people in a poor country, I'll reflect that maybe the director is a FOUR and keeps hitting me with the most terrible and awful side of things. He shows me nothing or the quiet happiness or *joie de vivre* that the people feel.

"But wait, are the non-SEVENs the only ones who are really right? I was in Brazil once, where I visited families in the favela of Novo Hamburgo. These were people who got enormous joy out of life and were full of hope for better times. Among these hut-dwellers there was a solidarity that we First Worlders can only dream of. Since then I've been skeptical about secondhand feelings, like sympathy based on newspaper photos.

"The Enneagram draws its strength from concentrating on a single pitfall, one's own. Anyone who deals with it, will immediately find his or her best gift on the very same point. But I've also gradually learned to appreciate the Enneagram arrows too. I know that the emotionally anemic, withdrawn FIVEs have always given me the most comfort. I have had my most intense moments at times of absolute concentration: while preparing for a final exam or at a silent retreat at Taizé. For Gurdjieff, one of the most important transmitters of the Enneagram, the dynamics of the nine-point circle was important: Everything had to develop continually from ONE to TWO, from TWO to THREE, etc. Perhaps I have to go through the whole circle, as Jesus evidently did in his life? Is the Enneagram more dynamic than we think?

"By now the Enneagram has moved into the background for me. I feel it's a message from God designed to bring me nearer to him. It contains the command to set out on the path to him. Now I've read the message, laid it aside, and gone merrily on my way. It also contained the news that I would never do it without God. He had been at my side all along."

Type EIGHT

"My deepest thoughts, I believe, are those of an EIGHT. I've always wanted to present myself to the world as strong and good. At the moment I'm confronting myself in my *weakness*. It hurts a lot. What I urgently need is pastoral counseling. Just now I have the feeling that I'll never be able to get up again. I have quit my position as a company executive because I couldn't stand it any more watching the people die of stress. But I myself have dished out some pressure. Now I'm in a quiet job, which I earlier thought would be my salvation. But I'm more dissatisfied than before. Things were chaotic in the department that I took over, and I put it in order. I defended my people wherever I could. Now I work alone. I don't know whether I have the strength to begin all over again."

"What urges me to write is the aha-experience I had yesterday. It was like scales falling from my eyes, after I had been on the wrong track for a long time. I am an EIGHT. I clearly remembered all the experiences from my childhood and youth. As a child I was a gang leader, I was aggressive, I had the need to protect the weak, a well-defined sense of justice. I can also now see my sensuality in this context and the problems that I had to reconcile these needs with my being a Christian.

"It's now clear to me why I have to fight with fears, now that I am together with my husband. He's a NINE, and has shown me love, warmth, and kindness. He saw through my disguise, and with that I lost my long built up self-image of the strong woman, which has thrown me totally out of whack. I've had regular panic attacks. I thought about psychotherapy, but the idea of stripping to my skin in front of a perfect stranger has never appealed to me. Now finally I've found a point of departure in the Enneagram. I've lost myself and found myself, and I'm ready to clean up the chaos that controls me.

"What stunned me about the Enneagram is the fact that in all my seeking I was often unconsciously doing the the right thing to change myself for the better. For example, I try to accept people more the way they are, and to check my self-righteousness at the door. Slowly and painfully I'm learning to let other opinions stand without getting angry at the other person or declaring him a dope."

Type NINE

"I was once told by a THREE, whom I had always thought of as normal-to-redeemed, that it was impossible to take any path without a goal, that this would only be stagnation. You have to make decisions, she said, and I had obviously done that, or I wouldn't have any children. She couldn't believe me when I said I hadn't *decided*, I had just *gone along*.

"That could never happen to her! I felt totally miserable, because my admission looked like proof positive of shirking laziness. Compared with this strong personality I had to feel like a walking minus sign.

"I can never formulate a goal, I can't aim at goals in my life. What I used to define as openness and readiness to understand others might very well be a sign that I want to avoid taking my own stand. This rich gift of NINEs, being able to see the seemingly most diverse positions as valuable, becomes their peculiar dilemma.

"At such moments any certainty will do to get me out of my uncertainty. SIX *is* my stress point. But deep down I know that I'm cutting myself short, that I can find the truth only in accepting openness and uncertainty.

"In other words, I have to face and answer honestly the questions from THREEs about whether my attitude isn't really laziness. The THREE is my thorn in the flesh, to prevent me as a NINE from limiting myself to a pseudo-certainty (SIX)."

"The Enneagram comes in very handy to tell my story: Trapped in SIX, I was cut off from life, I could no longer breathe. But staying at NINE, setting up house there, in the long run means stagnation. If I didn't want to let life pass me by, forfeiting it, or rather sleeping it away, there was only one thing to do: head to THREE. Finding your way back to trust without knowing how things will concretely turn out was and is the way of integration."

"My father frequently drowned his sorrows in alcohol. My mother often quarrelled with him, and I was caught in the cross-fire. I'm very much afraid of punishment. Then I reach for an anesthetic (TV — which I have always seen as a relaxant) or food as a substitute for love, which is why I always have problems with my weight. It's hard for me to get going, I can't make decisions, I'm quickly exhausted. But just *doing things* isn't my redemption. Actually I have a lot of energy, but I have problems releasing it, just like my aggressions, which I can't live out because of fear. All this comes out in my skin (eczema and deep red flushes). The important thing for me is getting oriented toward THREE; I need clear goals so I don't get disoriented."

"One thing astonished me: When I bought your book, I came home that evening and lay down in bed (typical NINE: why sit when you can lie down?). I read and read. After midnight I wanted to get to sleep, which I can always do right away, but not this time. I assumed that what I had read must have excited me. Suddenly I had much too much energy. Now this keeps happening. Regardless of the time, day or night, as soon as I pick up the book, I immediately get charged with energy. So the book is already working as a power source."

"Since recognizing myself as a NINE, a lot of un-rest has come into my life, but with it have also come courage and readiness to know and accept myself. Thanks to Richard Rohr's books I keep seeing more clearly the need for deeper knowledge of yourself as the foundation for living faith. I have to confess that this is particularly difficult for me — I was never so painfully aware of my blind spots! I thought I was really a peaceable person, but the feeling was deceptive — because peace-making (with so much hidden cynicism and anger in my gut) is constantly being thwarted by insincerity (lack of humility). How to deal with this anger and cynicism? How often am I just entangled in paralyzing passivity? How many projects fail from lack of drive? When faced with extraordinary situations I take refuge in planning sessions, endless reflections, indecisiveness, or narcosis. Before I encountered the Enneagram I thought all this was fine, now it all irritates me. Life lies are raising their ugly head: My unreached goals were simply due to indolence. How painful it was to admit that!

"Whenever I have a free day, I anesthetize myself with movies, music, or reading. Everything leaves me dissatisfied. Acedia: I spend hours lingering with the sense that it's all nothing. On those days even the children get on my nerves. I'm actually glad when the daily routine liberates me from the paralysis.

"Of course, there are good things too. I get visits from many people seeking advice, they like to 'come to rest' with me. Many people appreciate talking with me. When I'm especially alert, I succeed in building bridges (over deep canyons), even at work. Now I'm very hopeful that with your help I can find the way to new forms of energetic love."

"For a long time I stood looking at the phenomena of my behavior without being able to figure it out. The Enneagram really uncovered for me what had been hidden — at least to my conscious mind. In school I wasn't especially good, primarily because I often felt *insufficiently challenged*. But you couldn't say that to the teachers, otherwise they just would have demanded more, and I didn't want that. Why should I slave away for something, when there was another, *simpler* way to get it.

"A further key experience was the recognition that I can't love. For over three years I hadn't dared to express my inner feelings in any way to a woman I met every week. Today I understand my unconscious NINE-logic: Why should I take the trouble to woo a woman, when it might be all for nothing?

"Another problem is all the specialization around us. I had a deep identity crisis because I realized that I'm not an expert in any one area. I can do something in a lot of areas, but I'm not really good or competent in any of them. So I'm in conflict with myself, because I find many things interesting and I *want* to do them, but I can't. The laziness lies buried so deeply beneath all this that I have no idea how to get at it. Comically enough, it always shows up with things that are absolutely pressing and not with things that can be put off. . . . On the other hand, I *don't feel at all lazy,* when I consider how much energy I can spend dodging deadlines or pressing chores (such as writing this letter).

"The Enneagram was like a mirror. I am working with it now, and I pray everyday for the three opportunities of NINEs. Since then God has made me notice many things, and I am beginning to learn, before I stumble into my pitfall, to seize my opportunity and overcome the pitfall. Most of the time it doesn't come off. So he leads me carefully and slowly to love, to courage and action, all of which hang together."

COUPLES AND THE ENNEAGRAM

"It was *the* aha-experience for both of us, but especially for my husband. It was actually finding our identity. . . . Never before in our our almost thirty-year-long marriage, with its continually renewed love and uncompromising fidelity, had we ever laughed — and talked — so much about ourselves. New doors have opened up in our relationship, and through our better mutual understanding we are getting to know a new freedom. We're grateful that this book was written."

ONE (m) and NINE (f): "Many years of marital agony, which almost ended in divorce, flashed before my eye. Until recently I always thought that I was her savior. But for some time now I know — and your book has confirmed me in this — that my *stiff-necked* idealism and my quest for perfection could most likely be broken down only by a state of soft, often plan-less and goal-less ease."

ONE (f) and NINE (m): "At first I couldn't find my type, until I ran into NINE — where every single sentence was right on target. I figured out where my wife fit in — only I was completely wrong. When she read the book, she immediately recognized herself as a ONE. Since then I understand our relationship much better, and I'm free to acknowledge my problems with life as typical and not unique weaknesses. As wing types we suit each other very well. We are completely different, but we have our common points of contact, the wings. That's also very good for the marriage; we now understand the reasons why friction arises between us.

"And one more thing: I used to think that my superiors were both cut from the same cloth. Thanks to the Enneagram I now know that two people with the same appearance can be completely different: One is a pure EIGHT, the other is a two on stress point EIGHT!"

ONE (f) and ONE (m) "It was strange. After the first superficial reading I took myself for a TWO. As I read more thoroughly I quickly discovered that my husband is a very typical ONE. That filled me with so much excitement and anger that I suddenly noticed that I myself am a typical ONE who always has to be right. I was completely ashamed. Even before reading the book I knew that we have the same weaknesses, especially our sensitivity. And it's hard, just as you say, to live with the same very high energy level. But perhaps you can imagine the Enneagram managed to relax me precisely on this point. Now I have the possibility of being more generous in allowing his anger, and I see more clearly than I can't do anything to change it."

SIX (m) and FOUR (f): "We we first met, my wife thought of herself as a 'born-again Christian'; at the time I was into drugs. After two years of testing one another we got married. In the meantime I gave up drugs and became even more religious than she was. But now she rejected my piety and said I had turned from a counter-cultural type into a crank. Only traces of her faith are left now, as far as I can see. She said today that she had been playacting for years and lying to herself. As you correctly say, I thought up far-fetched hypotheses about my partner's assumed motives. I don't trust myself, so I don't trust others. Since I always considered myself capable of committing adultery, I imputed the same thing to my wife. And in fact that actually happened. Since she doesn't want to give up this other relationship, I now find myself staring at a catastrophic wreck. But I believe that if I change myself, further changes can follow."

SIX (m) and SEVEN (f): "Your book seemed heaven-sent to me. But I've looked in vain for a connection between TWO and SIX (my husband). We love each other very much. But his sense of duty is often barely comprehensible to me. I myself don't have the courage to impose myself on my husband as I really am. I always act patient, amiable, understanding, caring. I never quarrel. And I'm beginning to doubt whether this is right and honest or an obstacle to intimacy and cordiality. For some years I have been suffering from rheumatism. I've read that rheumatism comes from repressed feelings of aggression that are then directed at one's own body. I can vouch for that from my own case. I have aggressive fantasies that I can't understand and that I'm ashamed of. But I'm unable to verbalize my aggression so I can deal with them. I'm just blocked.

"What does God say to me about handling my aggression? In the Old Testament and the 'revenge Psalms' I find texts about that. But Jesus? He stands before my soul as the patient one who endures everything, who encourages us to love our enemies. Up till now I had thought that the more selfless I was the closer I could get to Christ's commandment. And self-realization was not for me, instead it posed the danger of neglecting love of my neighbor. Would Jesus encourage me to be honestly aggressive?

"Until recently I didn't know what I should say in confession, what mistakes I should admit. At Mass I listened to the sermon while looking around at the people whose problems I believed were being addressed just then. I was always busy being responsible for others. I began to add up all I did for God and waited for him to recognize it. I also wanted the people in the parish to learn about this at some point. For a while now I have been trying to learn to become aware of my own needs. At first I found it extraordinarily hard. But now I have discovered that I yearn for silence, for time to read, to reflect, and even to dream."

[*Andreas Ebert:* "The previous letter, whose author considers herself a TWO, points more toward type SEVEN (cf. the social and self-preserving subtypes at SEVEN). Many phrases in the letter (reprinted here in abbreviated form) suggest that this woman belongs to the center of head types (whose basic theme is fear). The repressed feelings of aggression could suggest the EIGHT wing, which she did not live out in her parish or in her marriage with a SIX. The need for silence and rest mentioned at the end of the letter would speak for consolation point FIVE. In counselling the first task for her would be to find her way to her own center-energy (head or heart?), and from there to determine her own type."]

NINE (f) and EIGHT (m): "As a NINE I lived for years with an EIGHT who would keep on pounding me long after I was already flat on the floor. With the support of my friends I was able to end the relationship a year ago, but to this day I haven't recovered from it. In social situations I present myself as dead, probably to avoid conflicts and beatings. With my make-up I had no chance against an EIGHT, and I felt like a weakling. I have learned to believe in my weakness and lack of energy. Your book gave me courage, and it also helps me to understand what happened. Even as I read the first lines it was clear to me that I had finally found what I had been intuitively seeking for years."

THE ENNEAGRAM AND RELATIONSHIPS WITH GOD: RELIGIOUS SELF-DISCOVERY

"With your book you gave me a bit of self-knowledge, and that was a religious experience for me, because I would like to be religious again, contemplative, in search, looking for God."

"Your way of imparting knowledge and hope has given me a little — no, a great deal — of spiritual cheer. . . . Our liturgy really turned into a festival. Since up to that point I had been standing more on the edge of the Church, I first had to take a deep breath and swallow hard. . . . How wonderful that Jesus wants to help me out of the mess of my life. But to be able to accept this good news I first have to get rid of my old ways of thinking. . . . Where do I dump my anger at the Church, at the pastors who preach their job in the same theological-scholarly style, from the height of the pulpit? . . . Yes, I hunt and

and chase Christ, but I don't find him. Ah, now the circle is closing: Do you come to me? (Matt. 3:14–15) I can give up hunting. . . . Good, I'm always open to innovations. But who will free me from the fear I have of this step? So I get nowhere, and as if I were on a big merry-go-round I'm slowly getting dizzy and nauseated. And if I jump off? Who picks me up? . . . Seriously: Please help me, if you can, pray for me. And if you tell me that I shouldn't look for any help from outside and from people, because all the help is in myself, because God and Christ are in me, then I'll break down and cry, because I've lost the key for doing this sort of thing. I've looked through the keyhole, I know that that's how it is, but I can't open the door. Please, help me."

"Things that I knew well, but had never admitted to myself, were written down here and so they came into my consciousness. For the first time in five years I went back to confession. I believe it was the first real confession in my adult life, and it brought me enormous relief. . . . I spoke with friends about the book and we (four persons between forty and sixty) decided to work on ourselves with the help of the Enneagram."

"*He who is not with me is against me* — this is just what I'm seeking: to dismantle in myself everything that could be against Jesus. All the blockades, baseness, imperfections . . . I'm trying to learn with Jesus, who became a *human being*. Psychotherapy, which I've been going to for a year now, shows me that (as an old Oriental master demanded of his disciples) I am emptying my glass. But who will fill my cup? Only faith can do that. At all my previous stages I always had something like the feeling of a veil, behind which my abyss lay hidden. When I read about the Enneagram, I suddenly saw a ray of light break through the curtain. Now I feel as if I could push my curtain aside inch by inch, and somehow I know that behind it is a great light. . . . "

"The Enneagram has shattered my strong, idealistic, moralizing, and also cynical ONE-armor and set free the anger that drives me. What a pitiful game! In the final analysis it wasn't respect for God or man, it was all resistance and struggle so as not to be wounded. I cried and laughed at myself. It was a shock and a liberation. And now I stand before God, naked and bare, expelled from the false paradise, a sensitive, vulnerable child, who still clings only to Jesus Christ and dares to take his first tentative steps in freedom. My whole body is changing. I am becoming freer, softer, warmer (literally: my circulation is better!). I'm full of gratitude for the gift of community with the other types, and I recognize in it the body of Christ, to which I am allowed to belong. Reverence in the face of the wonderful work of God is perhaps the best word for my new condition."

"As a NINE I had very little emotional excitement and only rarely took pleasure in rejoicing and weeping. At the splendid liturgy on our Enneagram weekend, I sensed a holiness in me, so that as I tried to deliver my text, I couldn't speak, I had to cry. I cried for joy, and I'm happy that I could. I was so moved by this encounter, that I began to cry every time anyone started to speak to me. I could have cried the whole day — and I would have been happy. Some participants showed me that they were rejoicing with me, that they admired me, that I could cry — in front of other people for the first time in my life. I now realize that I can head toward my redemption with Jesus Christ, whom I have now let come to me and into me, and that it is my responsibility to contribute with my wife to the creation of a community. I believe that yesterday I became a Christian."

"By studying the Enneagram I have become more compassionate with myself, and even with the people whose 'style' gets on my nerves. . . . I think that if I don't continue working on myself, translating into everyday fact what has dawned on me, then it will be like one of the many spiritual books I read or the retreats where I get all edified by emotions and aha-experiences — but in the daily grind it all fizzles out. . . .

"The Enneagram is also a possible way to undo all the injuries and tear down the barriers to God and the Church, to take them apart, piece by piece, to receive God's love anew, and to return to the community of the Church. . . . Let's ask God that we can keep handling it with care and intelligence."

APPENDIX A

"The Regret No One Regrets"

A Meditation by Dieter Koller

Repentance can be a Monologue or a Dialogue

As the "face of God" the Enneagram helps me to become aware of myself. By its very nature truth exposes my hidden reality. But before this liberates me, it hurts and causes me shame: "Then the eyes of both were opened, and they knew that they were naked" (Gen. 3:7). I'm embarrassed to discover the game I've been playing for half my life. And now I'm in danger of using the Enneagram — quite contrary to its purpose — to go on with the game, whether in self-satisfaction or desperation: "And the man and his wife hid themselves from the presence of the Lord God among the trees of the garden" (Gen. 3:8). The moment I realize that I have been recognized and seen through, I run the risk of once again becoming blind to the face of God: "But the Lord God called to the man, and said to him, 'Where are you?'" (Gen. 3:9). What's at stake here is no longer a psychological truth, but a spiritual one.

There is something great about a person encountering himself or herself and looking squarely into the mirror of self-recognition. But it's something still greater or more profound when a person wants to encounter not just himself or herself, but the *not-I*, the *Totally Other*, the face of God.

Of course, it's crucial that we recognize this face of absolute truth as the *loving face of the God-man Jesus Christ* and not as the face of a fierce, unpredictable tyrant. I'm sure that many people have the same experience that I do: I keep forgetting that my psyche isn't the ultimate reality. But when I recall the hidden divine face, a new state of consciousness comes into being. I no longer find myself doing a monologue in front of the mirror of self-awareness. Rather I'm now before the face of God who understands everything, and I say to him: "Here I am. I repent. I'm starting over!"

What's the difference? It's the difference between *monologue* and *dialogue*. In my experience dialogue triggers the creative processes in me more quickly and deeply than monologue does. In dialogue I experience love and a response to love. In dialogue, that is, in prayer that listens, completely different ideas and inspirations come to me. True, I continually forget this inner dialogue and fall back into pure egocentricity. But when I remember the possibility and necessity of coming "before God," I get ashamed of having been so *forgetful of being.* And then I'm glad to have found my way home to my *primal image.* Only then do I realize my condition as a *likeness,* my dignity as the *image of God.* Forgetfulness of God, which we so readily succumb to, leads us to illusory goals. The Book of Ecclesiastes calls this "vanity." *Vanity* is the direct result of delusory pride, which the Bible and Christian tradition consider the destructive essence of Satan.

Attentiveness before God Leads to a Series of Realizations

As a matter of fact the Enneagram itself can be made to serve a refined culture of vanity. Biblical wisdom, however, says, "The fear of the Lord is the beginning of knowledge" (Prov. 1:7). "Fear of the Lord" is a much misused and misunderstood phrase. It can cause problems, especially for people whose minds have been stamped with a strict and authoritarian image of God. Such anxiety and resistance falls away once we can discover and accept the fact that "fear of God" simply means *inner attentiveness.*

Attentiveness — in contrast to thoughtlessness and forgetfulness — is the prerequisite for all learning and knowing. The wholly self-centered person may climb to lofty heights of self-knowledge, but the wisdom of the Bible would still call this "vanity" or "nothingness." Attentiveness before God hastens the process of realization, so that I can discover more quickly that the construct I've spent half my life skillfully assembling is actually a pitfall, I've missed the goal I was shooting for. "Missing the mark" is actually the original meaning of the Hebrew word *chatat* (sin), a term from archery.[1]

Attentiveness before God causes me to experience, not monological self-consolation, but the creative force of forgiveness. Absolution is an essential component of dialogue. For this reason we have to ask whether the Enneagram can reach its goal without *personal confession* and *absolution* (in whatever form).[2]

Attentiveness before God permeates the *bitterness* of repentance with the *sweetness* of divine love. In the third stanza of his hymn, "I Wish to Love Thee, My Strength," Johann Scheffler (1657) writes:

> Ah, so late have I known thee,
> Thou high-praised beauty,
> And did not call you mine before,
> Thou highest good and one true rest,
> I am saddened and grieved,
> That I came so late to love thee.[3]

The distress voiced here is not sentimental and doesn't remain hung up in fruitless guilt feelings. This is the "godly grief" that Paul says "produces a repentance that leads to salvation, and brings no regret, but worldly grief produces death" (2 Cor.7:10). Divinely instilled repentance saves and frees us from our self-laid traps.

By contrast purely "secular" repentance locks us into the fatal pitfall of *self-pity, self-contempt,* or *self-punishment.* Granted, Erich Kästner is on target when he writes in his epigram "To the Mouse in the Trap":

> You're running in circles, looking for a hole?
> You're running in vain. Come on, face it.
> Think it over. There's only one way out:
> Go within yourself![4]

But it can be dangerous to go within ourselves, if we don't at the same time go to the God of love.[5] It can be equally dangerous and one-dimensional to go to God without going within ourselves. In that case we misuse God to confirm the self-destructive state we're in.

In applying the Enneagram psychology and theology must — as in so many other areas — probe and question one another. Otherwise we get either psychological or theological fundamentalism, both of which flee from the *whole* truth.

REPENTANCE: A WAY OUT OF THE TRAP

Can We Talk about Repentance?

I would prefer not writing about repentance until I had it *completely* behind me, but I'm still right in the middle of it. I have a long way ahead of me, even though I've already come face-to-face with some outlines of my type, along with some of its roots and specific pitfalls. Do I even have enough life ahead of me to project myself sympathetically and unsparingly into all nine points of the Enneagram? It's a long way! And I've already carelessly squandered decades.

The most widely read book of meditations from the Middle Ages to today is the *Imitation of Christ* by Thomas à Kempis (1441). In the very first chapter of the edition I have (Frankfurt, 1670), Thomas writes: "I would rather feel compunction and repentance within me than be able to say and expound on what repentance is . . . apart from loving God everything is mere nothingness and vanity." These words come from the heart, and they touch me. But because I suspect that "repentance" is a lifelong task for every awake person, I'm writing these preliminary lines.

Fritz Perls, the Gestalt therapist, used to say that, "There is no end to integration." He meant that we never finish the job of bringing home the split-off and withered levels of the soul and making up for unlived life. Repentance is an inexhaustible vital process. Repentance is the hidden overriding theme of every life story.

How Can We Repent?

Repentance is the continual refusal to identify with the false "I," the ego that has laboriously established itself from our childhood days and that is incessantly and involuntarily — no, voluntarily — looking for confirmation and satisfaction. In repentance I distance myself from this demanding little child in me. I seek to identify instead with the attentive and honest observer in me who *perceives* and *impartially* views the machinations of the "ape" (as the Zen masters call the false ego).

The eastern Desert Fathers characterize the use of this capacity for observation, which every human being in every culture is born with, as *sobriety*. In the silence of the desert they became stone-cold sober, and they noticed how foggy-minded, drunk, over-zealous, lazy, and out of touch with themselves they had been up till then. Anyone who fails to use his or her innate perceptual ability will forever remain neurotically immature, completely identified with all sorts of involuntary behavior, thoughts, and feelings. This is the opposite of sobriety. But people who stop what they're doing and maintain some distance from themselves will be shocked — and sobered.

Nicephorus the Hermit, a thirteenth-century monk from Mt. Athos, writes:

> Listen carefully to me. Attentiveness is the sign of completed repentance. . . . Attentiveness is the resting of the spirit, becoming quiet or silent, which is the gift given the soul by God's compassion. It is the purification of thoughts, the temple where we remember God, and the source of strength for enduring trials.[6]

Here attentiveness makes another appearance. *First* it stands guard at the gates of the physical *body*. What and how am I seeing, hearing, smelling, tasting, eating, and drinking now?

Second, attentiveness stands guard at the more inward gates of the *psyche*. What feelings and emotions are trying to overwhelm me now?

Attentiveness is the *third* guard at the innermost gates of the *spirit*. What judgments, prejudices, comparisons, imputations, intentions, memories, and wishes are trying to dominate me now?

Attentiveness preserves me from constantly running into these traps. Repentance helps me climb out of the pitfall after I've fallen into it.

Can Repentance Come Too Late?

Whenever I brought home bad grades, my father used to say to me, "Regret is a limping messenger." This old German saying might have comforted me, if I hadn't fallen into the trap of resignation: "It's just too late, it makes no sense." Instead I should have listened to the message of the limping messenger: "I come late but with enough time to start over." Nothing is more beautiful than a sober fresh start, free of illusions.

Jacob, the (self-)deceiver, who reached a state of blessed prosperity through cunning and tricks (cf. type THREE), wrestles on the border of his old homeland with a strange man. Is it a demon? Is it an angel? Is it his shadow? Is it God? He struggles that night — successfully — for the blessing, but he receives a blow on his hip-joint and will walk with a limp for the rest of his life. That is the symbol of repentance, a sober regret that one doesn't regret. As Jesus says, it is better to enter life limping than to march self-confidently on both feet into the abyss of self-deception (cf. Mt. 18:8).

On the night before Good Friday, without being asked, Peter had sworn fidelity to his master. Oaths and bets are typical of people who are arrogant in their imaginary knowledge. Shortly thereafter Peter three times denies that he knows Jesus. The cockcrow sobers him up, and he weeps bitterly. In morning sun of Easter, on the shore of the Sea of Galilee, Christ will ask him three times, "Peter, do you love me?" The third time he becomes sad ("grieved"). Modestly and without illusions he says, "Lord, you know everything; you know that I love you." Now he is ripe for the new beginning: "Feed my sheep." Thus repentance arrives, not too late but in the nick of time. It undergirds the wisdom of the second half of life, when one can no longer "gird oneself" so easily, but lets oneself be girded and guided by a higher wisdom (John 21:15–19).

Thus repentance is a smart move by a person who notices that the house where he or she has lived is falling apart. Up till now it may have been perfectly habitable, but now I have to exit quickly before it comes crashing down on me. This so-called midlife crisis (why couldn't it last from thirty to sixty?) can bring about the necessary restructuring of our concept of life, thanks to the *regret one doesn't regret.* It looks as if repentance might be our greatest human achievement. So should we be proud when it "succeeds"?

Repentance as a Gift of God

Anyone who has "gotten into" repentance knows that, "God has granted repentance unto life" (Acts 18:18). So repentance is ultimately a gift of God, I can't do it, but only ask God for it. In one of his pastoral letters the Russian spiritual director Igumen Nikon (active during the Khrushchev regime, when religion was still persecuted in the Soviet Union) writes: "Devoutly ask God, the Lord, for the greatest and most necessary of all gifts: to see your own sins and to weep over them. Whoever has this gift has everything."[7]

A young man recently told me that he had prayed very earnestly: "Lord, show me who I really am, show me my sins." Two weeks later his prayer received a stunning answer. In fact this prayer is guaranteed to get a quick response, because it's a sign that the psyche is ripe and ready to receive the truth. Of course, you can also sleep through the opportunity to convert. Only wide awake, sober people see what "unfinished business" (Perls) is on the docket. As long as we're alive, the redemption we've postponed can be recovered from our pitfall.

Although I'm a Lutheran, I believe with the Catholic Church that the process of purification and transformation can also continue after death. In Purgatory, the antechamber of Paradise, unfinished repentance is completed. Heaven means the infinite unfolding of eternal life. Hell is — here and now — frozen growth, entrenched neurosis. Russian *startsi* called repentance a *second baptism.*

PSEUDO-REPENTANCE IS A SECOND PITFALL

Having recognized their pitfall, some people run headlong away from it, but straight into a new pitfall — a kind of repentance that brings with it nothing but more futility: "Worldly grief produces death" (2 Cor. 7:10).

Pseudo-Rebirth

This is comparable to a false pregnancy. A person has collected new Christian knowledge, thereby "converting" — and becoming puffed up. With pharisaical pathos such people conjure up their new awareness and condemn their old life: "Now I know it, now I have it. Hold still, brother, while I take the splinter out of your eye." The more inflated this state of mind, the blinder it will be to the beam in its own eye. Some people change only their *consciousness*, but not their *being*. There's a lack of sobriety here (which may be the danger with repentance in FIVEs).

Contrition

Sometimes people simply can't forgive themselves for anything. Self-laceration, self-punishment, and self-flagellation are signs of an injured self-love. Bitter remorse is not a sign of sobriety (this sort of pseudo-repentance may occur especially with EIGHTs).

Guilt Feelings

These arise instead of genuine realization of guilt. They are nothing more than projected resentment against oneself or others. Clear and sober (self-)accusation is repressed and buried away out of dishonesty or fear (a SIX might possibly act this way). Only when clear and justified charges are presented can a clear reconciliation ensue. Never-ending guilt feelings, by contrast, are a sign of insufficient sobriety.

Self-Pity

In the controversial film *The Last Temptation of Christ,* there is a striking scene where out in the wilderness Jesus draws a throng around himself, squats down in the middle and decides he won't leave the spot until he knows exactly what in his life situation is a genuine call and what is a mere seductive appeal. In his hour of trial Jesus hears a consoling voice: "You poor Jesus, you have such a hard time." But the voice comes from the mouth of a black snake crawling out of a sand dune. Jesus recognizes the temptation to self-pity, and says only, "Satan!" At once the snake dissolves in a flash of Luciferian fire.

Thomas à Kempis says: "Outward consolation is no small obstacle to inner and divine consolation." And:

It is good for us to encounter troubles and adversities from time to time, for trouble often compels a man to search his own heart. It reminds him that he is in exile here, and that he can put his trust in nothing in this world. . . . For we more readily turn to God as our inward witness, when men despise us and think no good of us.[8]

Weltschmerz

The "sadness of the world" echoes in the favorite saying of one of my relatives, which he often delivers in an ironic tone: "Oh, it's all so terribly sad." The enduring grief of resignation sometimes looks like ultimate wisdom, but it's really just the viewpoint of a disappointed person who has put on dark glasses instead of being glad to have escaped so many disappointments (perhaps this is the typical pseudo-repentance of a FOUR).

Fleeting Repentance

Could this be a danger for SEVENs? The prophet Hosea accurately describes it when he says, "Your love is like a morning cloud, like the dew that goes early away" (Hos. 6:4). As opposed to this, *The Last Temptation of Christ* shows a Jesus who is filled with lifelong radical repentance in the spirit of attentiveness, and thus — usually at the last moment — escapes all temptations.

Frozen Repentance

In the Hassgau region of Lower Franconia where I live there is a mountain cave where there used to be a shrine to the god Donar. During the rites of initiation you had to crawl on your belly through a long and very narrow passageway into the interior of the cave. I once tried it, but when I got into this birth canal I was immediately frightened and quickly crawled back. I claimed that I wanted to spare my clothes and my skin, but as a matter of fact it just got too narrow and too dark for me. With this attitude of avoidance we let precious years slip away. I continually meet people who are standing right in front of the "narrow gate" and are afraid of doing what would help them: going through it (Matt. 7:13).

Thomas Merton speaks in his autobiography of the "darkness of a strange half-conscious partial conversion"[9] that he had as a student in Cambridge. It seems to me that Protestantism too has largely become a conversion movement that is frozen in place. In the beginning there was Luther's first thesis of October 31, 1517: "When our Lord and Master Jesus Christ says, 'Do penance,' he wants the whole life of believers to be an unceasing repentance." The Reformation began as a pastoral movement in the confessional! It was a departure from the holy compulsions and the facile pseudo-pieties of the Middle Ages. But it wound up going back either to an anxiety-creating compulsive piety or to a system of "cheap grace" (Bonhoeffer), a theory of grace that seduced the psyche into total passivity and false childishness. Hymns that beg the Lord to "take my hand"[10] have become more popular than Paul's charge to, "Work out your own salvation with fear and trembling [that is, with painstaking attentiveness]; for God is at work in you, both to will and to work for his good pleasure" (Phil. 2:12–13). This paradoxical principle brings us back to the . . .

REGRET THAT NO ONE REGRETS

A feeling of pain is the sign of fruitful repentance at work. I am continually impressed by the unsparing honesty with which great autobiographies describe the blindness of the first half of life.

In *The Seven Storey Mountain* Thomas Merton looks back on his student years with shame and rage. A propos of working on *Dante*, he recalls:

> In the winter term we had begun with the Inferno. . . . And now, in the Christian Lent, which I was observing without merit and without reason, for the sake of a sport which I had grown to detest because I was so unsuccessful in it, we were climbing from circle to circle in Purgatory. . . . I suppose it would have been too much to expect some kind of application of his ideas to myself, in the moral order, just because I happened to have a sort of esthetic sensitiveness to them. No, it seems to me that I was armored and locked in within my own defectible and blinded self by seven layers of imperviousness, the capital sins which only the fires of Purgatory or of Divine Love (they are about the same) can burn away. But now I was free to keep away from the attack of those flames merely by averting my will from them: and it was by now permanently and habitually turned away and immunized. I had done all that I could to make my heart untouchable by charity and had fortified it, as I hoped, impregnably in my own impenetrable selfishness.[11]

The first western autobiography and at the same time the first psychological self-portrait in world literature comes from the pen of St. Augustine. This is the story of a conversion that began with childhood. The whole book is formulated as a dialogue in the face of love. This is how Augustine describes the last days before his spiritual breakthrough, which occurred in Milan in the year 386:

> Thus I was sick at heart and in torment, accusing myself with a new intensity of bitterness, twisting and turning in my chain in the hope that it might be utterly broken, for what held me was so small a thing! But it still held me. And You stood in the secret places of my soul. . . . For I kept saying within myself: 'Let it be now, let it be now,' and by the mere words I had begun to move toward the resolution. I almost made it, yet I did not quite make it. . . . I did not touch it or hold it. I still shrank from dying unto death and living unto life. The lower condition which had grown habitual was more powerful than the better condition which I had not tried. The nearer the point of time came in which I was to become different, the more it struck me with horror, but it did not force me utterly back nor turn me utterly away, but held me there between the two.
>
> Those trifles of all trifles, and vanities of vanities, my one-time mistresses, held me back, plucking at my garment of flesh and murmuring softly, "Are you sending us away?"[12]

The decisive breakthrough finally took place through the creative power of a passage from the Letter to the Romans.

The awakening of the inborn inner observer does not bring about a rebirth all by itself. The spirit of God is needed, as *Paul* says, "It is the Spirit himself bearing witness with our spirit that we are children of God" (Rom. 8:16). The sober *inner witness* needs the *witness from God*. That is how we come to the breakthrough to truth, which first brings shame but then happiness.

The Painful and Blissful Encounter with Truth

My life-lie is unmasked, and my false old ego dies away. That hurts. But at the same time the *new person* rejoices. That is why Igumen Nikon says, in keeping with the tradition of the Desert Fathers:

> You write all the time of your present or future sufferings. . . . In his love God wishes our redemption. For this reason he doesn't permit any sufferings that are beyond our strength and are not absolutely necessary. In fact suffering is necessary, but people can't realize this until they . . . purify themselves . . . through repentance. . . . As often as we may fall again, we do not falter, we repent and carry on the struggle. Thus we can draw profit even from a fall.[13]

Without suffering we would never recite the "publican's prayer," which has such central importance in the Eastern Church: "Lord, be merciful to me, a sinner!" *Nikon* can even write: "Whoever rejects a reproach, whether justified or not, rejects his salvation."[14] Because "The measure of spiritual growth of a person is his humility. The higher he stands in the spirit, the humbler he will be."[15]

I myself recently "fell among demons" in an unsuspecting moment. This phrase is used by the *startsi* of the Eastern Church to characterize the activity of unredeemed passions, which, they believe, are located in our nerve endings. In distinguished company, under the influence of tobacco smoke and good Franconian wine, I got into a disgraceful argument, which was followed by a migraine. In discussing the incident my spiritual advisor simply said: "How good that you experienced that. It brings you to truth and humility." And in fact I did feel a kind of "blessed regret one does not regret." Our greatest mistakes and most wrong-headed attitudes can lead us to the deepest spiritual maturity.

Once we have experienced this, we regret neither our repentance nor, looking back on the event, our guilt. This bold statement comes from the ancient liturgy of the Easter vigil, where the "Exultet" proclaims: "O truly necessary sin of Adam. . . . O happy fault (*felix culpa*) that merited so great a redeemer!"

In this way the Enneagram, through the practice of *consistent repentance* can lead us before the face of Christ. And to the degree that this face is reflected in ours, our redemption proceeds apace.

APPENDIX B

The Enneagram Types Test

The statements on the following pages describe ways of behaving, attitudes, feelings, or general observations. Using a scale from 0 to 6 indicate to what degree any statement applies to you, and thus is "typical" of you. 0 = completely disagree, 6 = completely agree, 1 through 5 = the various stages between the two extremes. Before you mark your answer, consider the broad, overarching patterns of your life. On the whole, does this statement fit me or not?

Reflect quietly for a moment, but don't brood for a long time over assigning one point more or less. The important thing is to register your spontaneous reaction as to whether the statement is "typical" of you and your life. There are no "right" or "wrong" answers. Please answer *all* the questions. Even if a statement doesn't entirely apply to you, please check off the number on the 1–6 scale that seems the most appropriate to you.

Once you have answered all the questions, turn to the next section and read the directions: "Evaluating the Test Results."

Please answer all 115 questions, then bend back each page on the dotted line and enter your numbers

1.	Life goes better if you look on the positive side instead of dwelling on the negative.	0 1 2 3 4 5 6
2.	I can observe emotionally tense situations while keeping a sober distance from it all.	0 1 2 3 4 5 6
3.	I like to work within the framework of an institution.	0 1 2 3 4 5 6
4.	It's important to make an impression.	0 1 2 3 4 5 6
5.	I would like to be independent.	0 1 2 3 4 5 6
6.	The most important thing for me is that the people around me feel good.	0 1 2 3 4 5 6
7.	For me it's important to plan the future, so that I know what's heading my way.	0 1 2 3 4 5 6
8.	When someone needs my help, I'm ready to put all my energy to work for him or her.	0 1 2 3 4 5 6
9.	I want to live emotionally, passionately, with all my senses — even if it hurts.	0 1 2 3 4 5 6
10.	I have a hard time putting up with imperfections, whether in myself or in others.	0 1 2 3 4 5 6
11.	Status and success play a large role in my life.	0 1 2 3 4 5 6
12.	In love the most important things are being fair and behaving decently.	0 1 2 3 4 5 6
13.	I can readily adjust to the demands of a new situation.	0 1 2 3 4 5 6
14.	I'm on the side of marginal groups, people oppressed and discriminated against (refugees, Third World children, minorities, etc.).	0 1 2 3 4 5 6
15.	Life is like a drama in which I'm both actor and spectator.	0 1 2 3 4 5 6
16.	For the sake of advancing my career I'm prepared to neglect my marriage, family, or friends.	0 1 2 3 4 5 6
17.	I'm often bothered by a bad conscience.	0 1 2 3 4 5 6
18.	I have the impression that the so-called "authorities" are incompetent, but I usually hesitate to take action against them.	0 1 2 3 4 5 6
19.	I like to let things run their course — lots of times problems just take care of themselves.	0 1 2 3 4 5 6
20.	I have to know where I belong.	0 1 2 3 4 5 6

Please enter your ratings here

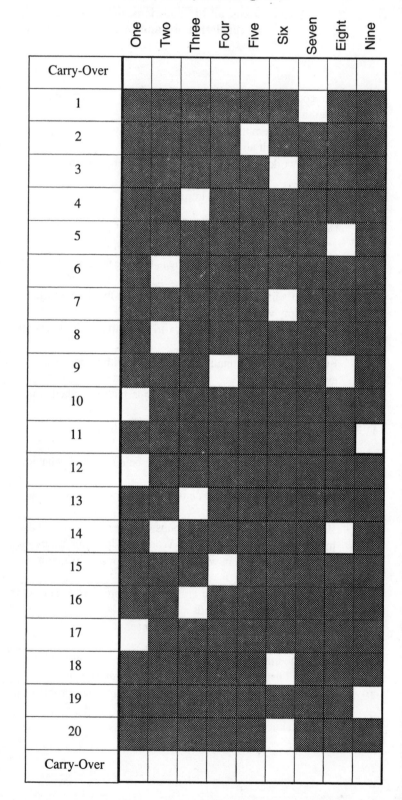

21.	I enjoy getting attention from other people and being in the lime-light.	0 1 2 3 4 5 6
22.	I often suppress my anger.	0 1 2 3 4 5 6
23.	I have the feeling that I can never be completely fulfilled.	0 1 2 3 4 5 6
24.	I often sense what's going on inside others before they say it out loud.	0 1 2 3 4 5 6
25.	Whatever I'm doing, I usually do it with enthusiasm.	0 1 2 3 4 5 6
26.	I have to know someone very well before I'll let him or her share in my private life.	0 1 2 3 4 5 6
27.	It's important for me that something always be "going on."	0 1 2 3 4 5 6
28.	It's easy for me to share.	0 1 2 3 4 5 6
29.	I like to express complex connections with simple images.	0 1 2 3 4 5 6
30.	Sometimes I feel overwhelmed by a nameless anxiety.	0 1 2 3 4 5 6
31.	When projects or relationships get too boring or do nothing for me, I abandon them.	0 1 2 3 4 5 6
32.	Even at games the most important thing for me is winning.	0 1 2 3 4 5 6
33.	I can become enthusiastic over new and unusual ideas.	0 1 2 3 4 5 6
34.	Many people pour their hearts out to me.	0 1 2 3 4 5 6
35.	I avoid divergent, attention-getting behavior.	0 1 2 3 4 5 6
36.	I am especially sensitive.	0 1 2 3 4 5 6
37.	In contradictory cases both sides often strike me as equally right.	0 1 2 3 4 5 6
38.	I feel there's something about me that sets me apart from other people.	0 1 2 3 4 5 6
39.	When life gives me lemons, I make lemonade.	0 1 2 3 4 5 6
40.	I often don't put my good ideas down on paper, and projects that I have in my head often stay put in the planning stage.	0 1 2 3 4 5 6

Please enter your ratings here

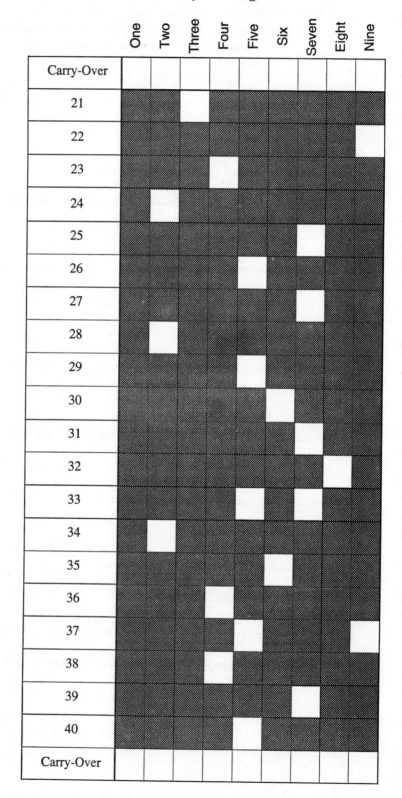

41.	I would rather disparage myself than show my abilities.	0 1 2 3 4 5 6
42.	I find contact with many people or intimacy (even when it's nice) stressful. Afterwards I need some time to be alone and "tank up."	0 1 2 3 4 5 6
43.	When one of my friends has a problem, I speak to him or her about it.	0 1 2 3 4 5 6
44.	People complain that in personal relationships I'm too dramatic.	0 1 2 3 4 5 6
45.	It's important to "sell" yourself.	0 1 2 3 4 5 6
46.	I believe that other people misunderstand my deepest feelings.	0 1 2 3 4 5 6
47.	I spontaneously express my anger, and then, as far as I'm concerned, the case is closed.	0 1 2 3 4 5 6
48.	Deep down I don't really feel quite "at home" anywhere.	0 1 2 3 4 5 6
49.	Life is competition.	0 1 2 3 4 5 6
50.	I don't make a move until I've thought through all the possible consequences.	0 1 2 3 4 5 6
51.	I like to call the shots.	0 1 2 3 4 5 6
52.	I have the tendency to do myself in with criticism and depressing thoughts.	0 1 2 3 4 5 6
53.	Other people sometimes say it's hard to live with me because I'm so "strong."	0 1 2 3 4 5 6
54.	Sometimes I'm gripped by a feeling of amazement and gratitude for the miracle of life.	0 1 2 3 4 5 6
55.	I'm very concerned about the health, education, and welfare of my friends.	0 1 2 3 4 5 6
56.	I have a hard time putting up with tension.	0 1 2 3 4 5 6
57.	Sometimes I step outside of myself and judge myself.	0 1 2 3 4 5 6
58.	I feel good when I can just "swim along" with the people in the community.	0 1 2 3 4 5 6
59.	I don't have any problems saying no.	0 1 2 3 4 5 6
60.	I like to use the telephone, and I make a lot of calls.	0 1 2 3 4 5 6

Please enter your ratings here

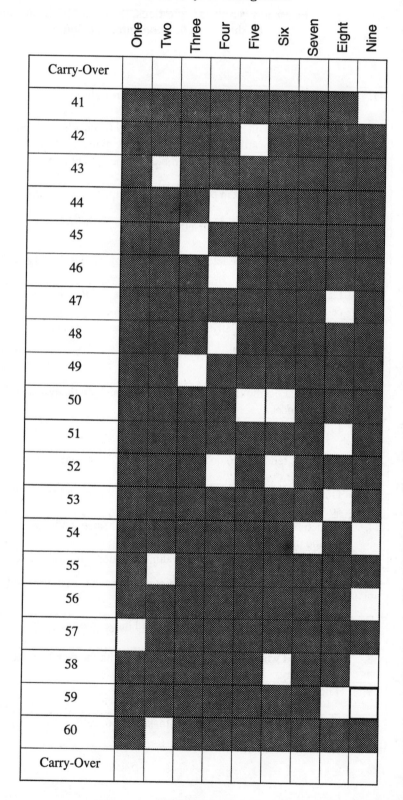

61.	It makes no difference to me when the majority disagrees with me.	0 1 2 3 4 5 6
62.	When I think a law makes no sense, I have no scruples about breaking it.	0 1 2 3 4 5 6
63.	Other people say I talk fast.	0 1 2 3 4 5 6
64.	I like to negotiate and make deals.	0 1 2 3 4 5 6
65.	I know how to motivate people and waken their enthusiasm for a cause.	0 1 2 3 4 5 6
66.	It's important to me to perfect my abilities (whether academic, physical, cultural, or professional).	0 1 2 3 4 5 6
67.	I'm prepared to put up with disadvantages rather than sacrifice my personal standards.	0 1 2 3 4 5 6
68.	Other people like to be in my company.	0 1 2 3 4 5 6
69.	Sometimes I get lost in the details (e.g., while straightening up), and I suddenly notice that hours have gone by.	0 1 2 3 4 5 6
70.	When someone pretends to be high and mighty, then I go and take him down a peg.	0 1 2 3 4 5 6
71.	I want the appearance I present to be natural, but chic and stylish at the same time	0 1 2 3 4 5 6
72.	A lot of my conversations are about work.	0 1 2 3 4 5 6
73.	I like to engage others in verbal duels with quick and witty repartee.	0 1 2 3 4 5 6
74.	I have a talent for organization.	0 1 2 3 4 5 6
75.	I've always been especially concerned about justice.	0 1 2 3 4 5 6
76.	In my house everything has to have its place.	0 1 2 3 4 5 6
77.	Any time something happens my feelings are often "blocked," so that they seem to limp behind the event.	0 1 2 3 4 5 6
78.	In my thoughts I often criticize myself.	0 1 2 3 4 5 6
79.	I often reverse my decisions shortly after making them, because I notice that I actually want something else.	0 1 2 3 4 5 6
80.	I often feel muscular tension (especially in my neck, shoulders, and jaw).	0 1 2 3 4 5 6

Please enter your ratings here

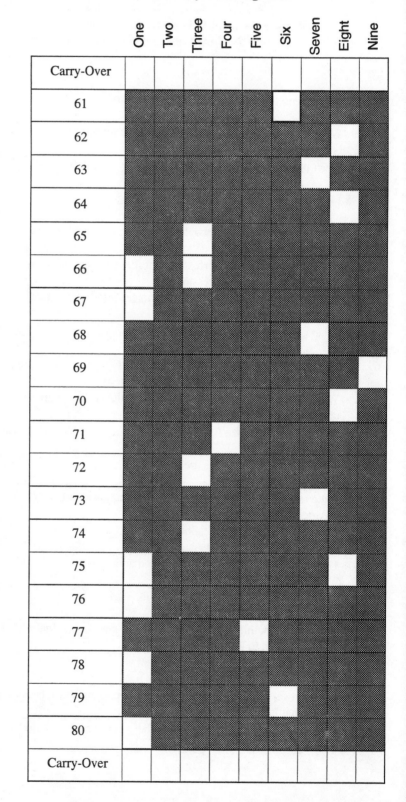

	One	Two	Three	Four	Five	Six	Seven	Eight	Nine
Carry-Over									
61						☐			
62								☐	
63							☐		
64								☐	
65			☐						
66	☐		☐						
67	☐								
68							☐		
69									☐
70								☐	
71				☐					
72			☐						
73							☐		
74			☐						
75								☐	
76	☐								
77					☐				
78	☐								
79						☐			
80	☐								
Carry-Over									

81.	I like to browse in bookstores and libraries.	0 1 2 3 4 5 6
82.	In my imagination scenes often take place where something bad happens.	0 1 2 3 4 5 6
83.	When my friends are in need, I outdo myself and dare to take on things that I wouldn't normally be able to.	0 1 2 3 4 5 6
84.	I need my own study or at least my own corner to withdraw to, when everything gets just too much.	0 1 2 3 4 5 6
85.	Others consider me athletic and attractive.	0 1 2 3 4 5 6
86.	I have an eye for shaping and designing rooms.	0 1 2 3 4 5 6
87.	I value having a good atmosphere at work.	0 1 2 3 4 5 6
88.	I get very concerned over the personal needs and problems of other people.	0 1 2 3 4 5 6
89.	I have always dreamed of becoming a painter, poet, singer, or something like that.	0 1 2 3 4 5 6
90.	It's important to me to see things as objectively as possible.	0 1 2 3 4 5 6
91.	I like to travel.	0 1 2 3 4 5 6
92.	Some people consider me a workaholic.	0 1 2 3 4 5 6
93.	Helpfulness comes natural to me.	0 1 2 3 4 5 6
94.	I have a large circle of friends.	0 1 2 3 4 5 6
95.	I have many different fields of interest.	0 1 2 3 4 5 6
96.	Others often feel criticized by me.	0 1 2 3 4 5 6
97.	It's important to me to see the big picture and to recognize the patterns and structures in it.	0 1 2 3 4 5 6
98.	When a conflict can't be readily settled, I prefer to back off.	0 1 2 3 4 5 6
99.	An unfriendly remark can often stick in my skin like an arrow, tormenting me all day long.	0 1 2 3 4 5 6
100.	I often hammer out plans for the future so I'll forfeit as few of the many opportunities as possible.	0 1 2 3 4 5 6

Please enter your ratings here

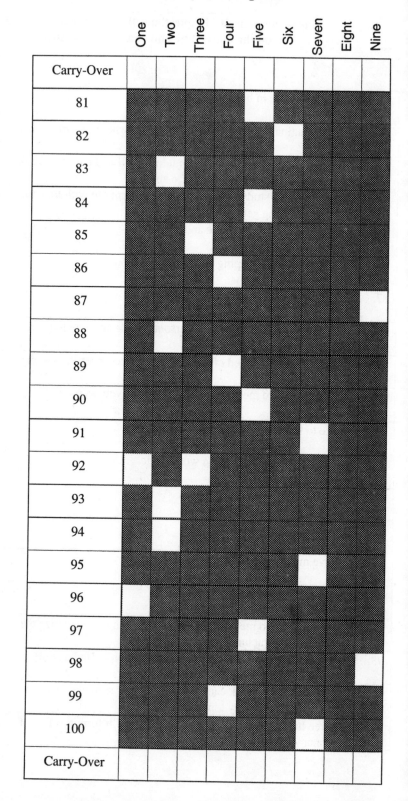

**Please answer all 115 questions, then bend back each page
on the dotted line and enter your numbers**

101.	I like to be alone.	0 1 2 3 4 5 6
102.	I seldom take the initiative.	0 1 2 3 4 5 6
103.	I often fight or argue just to get a clear picture of the situation.	0 1 2 3 4 5 6
104.	Fairly often I treat myself to things that are actually too expensive for me.	0 1 2 3 4 5 6
105.	I find it hard to disconnect, relax, and simply enjoy.	0 1 2 3 4 5 6
106.	I'm often overcome by self-doubt.	0 1 2 3 4 5 6
107.	When I have a job to do, my feelings have to wait.	0 1 2 3 4 5 6
108.	I live completely for my partner, my family, my friends.	0 1 2 3 4 5 6
109.	I have no use for idling or loafing around in my daily routine.	0 1 2 3 4 5 6
110.	I try to avoid conflicts at all costs.	0 1 2 3 4 5 6
111.	In my relationships I'm more the hammer than the anvil.	0 1 2 3 4 5 6
112.	I'm often not sure whether the affection other people have for me is sincere, or if they just like me because I'm nice to them.	0 1 2 3 4 5 6
113.	If I didn't withdraw every now and then, I'm afraid I might "lose myself."	0 1 2 3 4 5 6
114.	I like to express my feelings artistically (in music, painting, acting, literature, etc.).	0 1 2 3 4 5 6
115.	I'm often under time pressures.	0 1 2 3 4 5 6

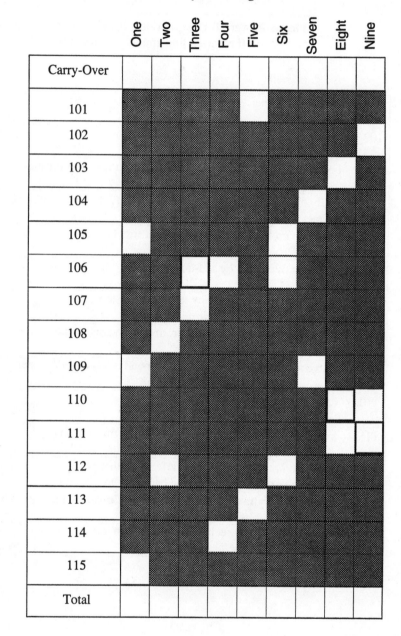

EVALUATING THE TEST

Four steps are needed to evaluate the Enneagram Types test.

1. Fold each page back on the dotted line so that the numbers 0–6 face the grid of little boxes. Each question is supposed to reflect one (or more) Enneagram type(s), and the corresponding boxes are white. Enter the rating you gave each statement in the appropriate white box. For example, question 1 reflects type SEVEN. If you've checked off 3 here, enter a 3 in the white box. N.B.: In the case of boxes edged in black you have to reverse the number as follows:

$$\downarrow \bigg| \quad \begin{array}{ccccccc} 0 & 1 & 2 & 3 & 4 & 5 & 6 \\ 6 & 5 & 4 & 3 & 2 & 1 & 0 \end{array} \quad \bigg| \uparrow$$

Thus, if you checked off 0 as your original response, enter a 6, if you checked off 6, enter zero, etc.

2. Add up the numbers for each type to get your subtotal.

3. Now most of the work is done. Look in the *norm table* and find out how many *standard values* from 0 to 9 you get for the individual types with your subtotal. Example: If you have 45 points in your subtotal for type THREE, check the norm table to see which standard value 45 corresponds to for THREEs. 45 is in between 42 and 47, which results in a standard value of 5.

4. Finally enter these standard values into your "Enneagram profile."

INTERPRETING YOUR RESULTS

On the Enneagram profile: Some people get below-average values with almost all the types, because on principle they don't readily agree with certain statements and ways of behaving. Others, by contrast, will get above-average values for most of the types.

So it's a matter of comparison. Which type do I clearly sympathize more with? Or, equally interesting: Which types do I assign very low ratings to? There might be qualities there that I lack and that could be important for me. The standard value of 5 shows the average result obtained: Around 50% of all people will end up with standard values of 4,5, or 6. Standard values over 6 or under 4 are correspondingly less frequent. Are you surprised or disappointed by your test results, or did they confirm your assessment of yourself?

A test is always just one step in the process of getting to know oneself better, by discovering, as in a mirror, something new or different about oneself. In this sense the Enneagram profile is not a conclusive "finding," but a snapshot that sheds light on how I rate myself at the moment.

A propos of self-assessment: It might be quite informative to ask a spouse, friend, or acquaintance to fill out the test to answer the question of how he or she sees *me*, what in his or her opinion is "typical" of me or "fits me." Other people often have a clearer view than we do of what is "typical" about us. Comparing assessments by ourselves and others might provide material for some rich and valuable discussions.

None of us is simply *one* type. We have parts of all of them in us, even if there are people whose attitudes and ways of behaving match almost perfectly a type described by the Enneagram. The crucial thing is to discover what's "typical" of me, to learn to see my strengths and weaknesses, and thereby deal better with myself and the world.

The Enneagram Types Test is designed to be an aid — but above all an encouragement to commit oneself further to the process of self-knowledge, change, and maturity.

TABLE OF NORMS

Standard Value	ONE	TWO	THREE	FOUR	FIVE	SIX	SEVEN	EIGHT	NINE
0	0-25	0-32	0-20	0-18	0-35	0-17	0-31	0-21	0-30
1	26-31	33-37	21-26	19-25	36-41	18-24	32-36	22-27	31-36
2	32-37	38-43	27-31	26-31	42-46	25-30	37-41	28-33	37-41
3	38-42	44-48	32-36	32-38	47-51	31-37	42-46	34-39	42-47
4	43-48	49-53	37-41	39-44	52-56	38-43	47-50	40-45	48-52
5	49-54	54-59	42-47	45-51	57-62	44-50	51-56	46-52	53-58
6	55-60	60-65	48-52	52-58	63-67	51-57	57-61	53-58	59-63
7	61-66	66-71	53-58	59-64	68-72	58-64	62-66	59-64	64-68
8	67-72	72-76	59-63	65-71	73-77	65-70	67-71	65-71	69-74
9	73-90	77-90	64-90	72-90	78-90	71-90	72-90	72-90	75-90

ENNEAGRAM PROFILE

Standard Value									
9	•	•	•	•	•	•	•	•	•
8	•	•	•	•	•	•	•	•	•
7	•	•	•	•	•	•	•	•	•
6	•	•	•	•	•	•	•	•	•
5	•	•	•	•	•	•	•	•	•
4	•	•	•	•	•	•	•	•	•
3	•	•	•	•	•	•	•	•	•
2	•	•	•	•	•	•	•	•	•
1	•	•	•	•	•	•	•	•	•
0	•	•	•	•	•	•	•	•	•
TYPE	ONE	TWO	THREE	FOUR	FIVE	SIX	SEVEN	EIGHT	NINE

General Remarks on Test Results

It's not easy to say something enlightening about your test results. A test — especially a questionnaire constructed according to scientific criteria like the Enneagram Types Test[*] — registers and evaluates the individual features of a person against the background of quantitative, statistical data. That is why there are average values, standard values, etc.

But for this very reason the "objective" test results need a counterweight; they have to be read and classified in a wholly "subjective" light. The decisive factor in interpreting and understanding the test is correlating it to the person, the unique individual, with his or her history and current life situation.

In clinical psychology, as a rule, "personality tests" are used only in combination with conversations with the client and other information (for example, current behavior). Anyone who has experience with tests knows that by itself a test merely provides an inadequate impression of a person's problems, possibilities, and qualities. But used together with other data the results of a test can be enlightening and helpful, because, like a photo, it captures for an instant correlations that are otherwise constantly moving and changing, and hence quite confusing.

On the one hand, therefore, I would encourage you not to overvalue the test. It's a *snapshot*. It doesn't cast you in bronze; it sheds light on a momentary situation and how *you yourself* present yourself in it. You now have in hand a "self-portrait" — and you know from experience that pictures can be blurry or "touched up," that we like the way we look in some pictures and not in others.

On the other hand, I want to encourage you not to dismiss the results too quickly, particularly if the test turned out differently from what you may have expected. That might indicate that there are totally different aspects alive inside you that you previously failed to notice. This might prompt you to ask others what living with you is like. The test becomes significant only when it's connection with other information.

Some observations that I have repeatedly made in evaluating personality tests can perhaps be of help in better understanding your test results.

---

[*]The German version of the ETT (Enneagram Types Test) has been designed in accordance with empirical-scientific criteria. The data it produces have been checked by means of factor and cluster analysis. In addition, it has been validated with another recognized personality test (FPI-R) and standardized on a German random sample. To satisfy strict empirical criteria this same procedure should be followed for the English-language edition. Till then, however, the ETT, even in this merely translated version, is a valuable and informative practical tool.

There are people who in response to almost every question in the Enneagram Types Test check off 3, that is, the middle. There can be different reasons for this. Often they are people who try to be very thorough, who weigh everything carefully and want, as far as possible, to avoid "mistakes." With respect to themselves as well, where their image is concerned, the way they present themselves, they want to do everything "right." They have a hard time deciding between "on the one hand" and "on the other." When they'd like to endorse a statement, they immediately think of another situation in which they might act altogether differently.

Again, there are people to whom the opinion of those around them is very important. On each question they reflect on what *the others* might think about it. And then since one person would answer one way and another person another, they "diplomatically" choose the middle ground.

There are certainly very different possibilities of interpretation. But the crucial point is that — regardless what number we opt for — the way we answer is also a part of our personality. It's embedded in us and reflects our desires and fears, perhaps even our fear of being pinned down to one type or of somehow or other being "seen through."

In most cases this leads to no one type's getting especially high numbers, but standard values under 2 are also rare.

The test results are valuable in that they reflect the qualities of our personality precisely through the way we have responded to the test questions.

In testing we also repeatedly observe consistently high standard values. On the one hand there are people who agree with almost every statement, at least at first. They readily identify with all possible statements, sometimes even contradictory ones, whether out of insecurity or because their personalities aren't as sharply defined as other people's. They have a hard time saying, "That's me — and that's not me."

On the other hand, there also people who are "stingy" with their test numbers. They seldom take the leap over the middle of the point scale. The upshot is that they get low standard values in all types, and differences can't be clearly indicated.

The above remarks are, of course, painted with a very broad and general brush. I am merely pointing to basic tendencies that may influence the way a person fills out the questionnaire.

Now to aspects more specifically Enneagram-related: The Enneagram Types Test registers certain *qualities* that are ascribed to the Enneagram types.

The types themselves are made up of *combinations* of these qualities, so that it's not surprising if, for example, a SIX also has high numbers under point TWO, because both types are similar, insofar as they are notably social in their orientation — though for different motives.

Thus it can happen that your test shows equally high numbers for types that according to Enneagram theory actually have nothing to do with one another, in other words, are neither "wings," "stress points," or "consolation points."

Hence if you have high numbers for one type, you can be sure that many things link you to the qualities and convictions of this type. But whether you *are* this type is something that no test in the world can reveal, only your own deep conviction and insight, if you have "recognized" yourself at one point or other.

Studies of the Enneagram — and psychological research in general confirms this — show that only about half of all people tested can be clearly assigned to one type.

There simply are people whom this system "fits," and others who always end up "in between" the types. For example, they feel at home in type TWO, FOUR, or SIX, depending upon what stage of life they're in or which people they're living with.

Another important thing here is that you continue to ask questions — not to learn once and for all what your type is, but to understand what your qualities and peculiarities are. Only then will it be possible to discover your most essential gifts and to avoid, at least every now and then, the "pitfalls" that you usually stumble into.

What's important is not the *formal* classification in one type, but the *substantial* connection between oneself and the type.

To take another example, someone might get high numbers for both type THREE and type EIGHT. This could be because this person identifies with qualities described as "perseverance," "a sense of reality," and "competitiveness." These are qualities that characterize both types. The results, then, could be summed in the following statement: "Evidently I identify at the moment with qualities that occur more frequently in types THREE and EIGHT."

At this point it would be appropriate to read over the type descriptions (in my opinion these are the heart of all Enneagram books) once again and check if you really feel "at home" in your type.

Because it might be that I am actually a ONE or a SIX, but my life situation just so happens to make heavy demands on me for "perseverance" and "competitiveness." Or is it my *wish* that is being expressed in these high numbers? Our identification with a type often has more to do with our internal and external "models" than we want to admit. (The observations made at the beginning of this book about the "distribution" of the types confirms this speculation.)

A further hint for understanding one's own Enneagram profile is to take a look where you have only a *few* or *no* points. Often such "gaps" define our behavior more than the strongly developed sides. Perhaps this is exactly where my stress point or consolation point is, in other words something of particular importance for my own development.

SELF-IMAGE AND OUTSIDE ASSESSMENT

Our "self-assessment" is always subject to certain influences. Most people tend to present themselves in the best possible light — even, and above all, to themselves.

Furthermore we are not so willing to abandon an opinion once we've settled on it, and thus a NINE will try to look like a NINE in his or her test results.

Our anxieties and desires also have considerable influence on our perception, precisely when the subject is ourselves.

Just as the human eye has a "blind spot" in the middle of the retina, we can also have an incorrect perception of our central qualities.

That is why an outside assessment is at times quite informative. Others can usually see us more objectively, or at least with more distance. The "typical" features of a person often catch other people's attention more quickly and clearly than the person in question.

This is in the nature of the business. Every "typecasting" requires a certain distance, as I argued at some length in the section on typologies. Thus if I am uncertain about my type, the assessment of another person who knows me well can be a great help. Just the comparison itself between self-assessment and outside assessment can provide a lot of food for thought.

FIVEs, for example, have the gift of appearing cool, even when they're positively bursting inside with excitement. They don't do this consciously, and so they're occasionally quite surprised that people around them don't notice their feelings, when they themselves feel all churned up and at loose ends in their inner core.

Of course, different people will always have different perceptions, and the key is not who's "right" or who has a better "fix" on the other person's type. The important thing to remember is that experiences and perceptions contribute to fashioning an accurate picture, which includes our "shadows." It often becomes clear that we involuntarily present ourselves to the outside world much differently from the way we feel inside.

Notes

PART I
FOUNDATIONS

The Enneagram: Vulnerable Community
Richard Rohr

1. Cf. the contribution to this book by Andreas Ebert, "The Enneagram and the Church," especially pp. 141 ff.

Empirical Studies of the Enneagram:
Foundations and Comparisons
Markus Becker

1. Don Richard Riso, *Personality Types: Using the Enneagram for Self Discovery* (Boston: Houghton Mifflin, 1987), p. 10.
2. Riso, p. 13.
3. Charles Tart, ed., *Transpersonal Psychology* (El Cerrito, Calif.: Psychological Processes, 1983), p. 285.
4. Tart, p. 293.
5. P. D. Ouspensky, *In Search of the Miraculous* (New York: Harcourt, Brace, and World, 1949), p. 11.
6. Ouspensky, p. 153.
7. *Enneagram Educator* I, 1988, 4: "and there met a man whose identity he promised to keep a secret."
8. Ibid.
9. John G. Bennett, *Enneagram Studies* (York Beach, Maine: Coombe Springs Press, 1983).
10. Riso, p. 17.
11. Riso, p. 25.
12. Riso, p. 26.
13. Jaxon-Bear, E., *Die neun Zahlen des Lebens* (Munich, 1989), p. 40.
14. Richard Rohr and Andreas Ebert, *Discovering the Enneagram: An Ancient Tool for a New Spiritual Journey,* tr. Peter Heinegg (New York: Crossroad, 1990), p. 184.
15. Riso, p. 220.
16. Jaxon-Bear, p. 52.
17. Jaxon-Bear, p. 96.
18. Rohr/Ebert, p. 26.

19. Riso, pp. 30-31.

20. Jaxon-Bear, p. 111.

21. Jaxon-Bear, p. 133.

22. Rohr/Ebert, p. 22.

23. Jaxon-Bear, p. 167.

24. Riso, p. 239.

25. Jaxon-Bear, p. 167.

26. Jaxon-Bear, p. 192.

27 Rohr/Ebert, p. 27.

28. We might ask whether confusion isn't a deliberate effect of this model. Through confusion old thought patterns can be cracked open, and new possibilities of seeing oneself opened up. This might be comparable to treatment methods using hypnosis to create an altered state of consciousness and thereby get around the ruts of familiar patterns of thought and experience, so as to find new cognitive strategies and solutions.

29. Jaxon-Bear, p. 111.

30. Galen (ca. 200–130 B.C.), the last great physician of classical antiquity, took the doctrine of the "humors" and expanded it.

31. Following Revenstorf, *Persönlichkeit* (Munich, 1982), p. 137.

32. Amelang/Bartussek, *Differentielle Psychologie und Persönlichkeits-forschung* (Stuttgart, 1990), p. 270.

33. Amelang/Bartussek, p. 270.

34. Psalm 1:6. The highly formulaic language of the Psalms loves to hark back to these stereotypes in ever new variations.

35. Revenstorf, p. 33.

36. Dorsch, *Psychologisches Wörterbuch* (Bern, 1982) p. 704.

37. Amelang/Bartussek, p. 274.

38. Duane Schultz, *Theories of Personality* (Belmont, Calif.: Brooks/Cole), pp. 169–70.

39. Revenstorf, p. 33.

40. Dorsch, p. 704.

41. Revenstorf, p. 71.

42. *Enneagram Educator* I, 1989, 5.

43. Amelang/Bartussek, p. 257.

44. Riso, pp. 321–43.

45. Following Riso, p. 326.

46 Following Riso, p. 329.

47. Riso, p. 331.

48. J. P. Wagner, *A Descriptive Reliability and Validity Study of the Enneagram* (Chicago, 1981), p. 168.

49. Wagner, p. 192.

50. Following Riso, p. 322.

51. Riso, p. 333.

52. Riso, p. 323.
53. Riso, p. 331.
54. Riso, p. 332.
55. Rohr/Ebert, p. 197.
56. Rohr/Ebert, p. 93.
57. Rohr/Ebert, p. 93.

PART II
PSYCHOLOGICAL ASPECTS

The Enneagram and Focusing:
A "Map" and a "Path" for Personal Change
Hans Neidhardt

1. F. Köhne and J. Wiltschko, "Focusing — des Körpers eigene Psychotherapie," companion text to the video (Mediateam, Talackerstrasse 20, 8100 Garmisch-Partenkirchen).

2. Köhne/Wiltschko, p. 8.

3. Deutsches Ausbildungsinstitut für Focusing-Therapie (DAF), Marktstrasse 8, 8000 Munich 40.

4. Christian Wulf, "Das Enneagram — eine dynamische Landkarte der Seele," *Geist und Leben* 64/91.

5. Jaxon-Bear, pp. 65–66.

6. J. Wiltschko, "Strukturgebundene Prozesse. Ausbildungsmaterialen des DAF" (unpublished).

7. Margaret Frings Keyes, *Emotions and the Enneagram: Working Through Your Shadow Life Script* (Muir Beach, Calif.: Molysdatur Publications, 1990).

8. Cf., for example, M. and R. Goulding, *Neuentscheidung — ein Modell der Psychotherapie* (Stuttgart: Klenn-Cotta, 1986).

9. In an earlier essay I took a fairly polemical swipe at the "false labeling" that hinders development (H. Neihardt: "Wege und Holzwege in der Arbeit mit dem Enneagram," circular of the Ecumenical Work Group on the Enneagram, 1/91).

10. Jaxon-Bear, p. 32.

11. M. Siems, *Dein Körper weiss die Antwort — Focusing als Methode der Selbsterfahrung* (Hamburg: Rowohlt, 1983), p. 53.

12. Ron Kurtz, *Body-Centered Psychotherapy: The Hakomi Method* (Mendocino, Calif.: LifeRhythm, 1990), pp. 38–39. "Hakomi" is a Hopi word that means roughly, "Who are you?" "What is your world?" or "Who are you in relation to these many worlds?"

13. L. M. Moeller, *Die Wahrheit beginnt zu zweit* (Hamburg: Rowohlt, 1987), p. 166.

14. Jaxon-Bear, p. 33.

Biospiritual, Development-Oriented
Work with the Enneagram
Klaus Renn

1. Meister Eckhart, *Deutsche Predigten und Traktate* (Munich, 1963), p. 63.

2. Thus far I have been using terms such as "type," "ego," "psychic apparatus," "number," "fixation," and "superficial identity" as seemingly synonomous. I hope this will leave the reader more room for his or her own ideas and conceptual formations. There is no one "right" scientific term. Nevertheless in more detailed work we really should agree on a common language.

3. Alan Watts, *This Is It: And Other Essays on Zen and Spiritual Experience* (New York: Vintage, 1973), p. 18.

4. Piero Ferrucci, *Werde was du bist* (Hamburg: Rowohlt, 1986), p. 80.

5. Welwood, "Das holographische Weltbild und die Struktur der Erfahrungen," in *Das holographische Weltbild* (Munich: Scherz, 1986).

6. For a much more thorough treatment of this see Peter Campbell and Edwin McMahon, *Biospiritualität* (Munich: Claudius, 1992).

7. Welwood, p. 138.

8. See also Eugene Gendlin, *Let Your Body Interpret Your Dreams* (Wilmette, Ill.: Chiron, 1986).

9. See also P. D. Ouspensky, *The Psychology of Man's Possible Evolution* (New York: Random House, 1977).

10. Humberto Maturana and Francisco Varela, *Der Baum der Erkenntnis. Die biologischen Wurzeln des menschlichen Erkennens* (Munich: Goldmann, 1990).

11. Ken Wilber, Jack Engler, Daniel Brown, *Psychologie der Befreiung* (Munich: Scherz, 1990).

PART III
PERSPECTIVES FOR SPIRITUALITY AND THE CHURCH

The Enneagram: On Working with
a Spiritual Theory of Personality
Christian Wulf

1. The article presented here in shortened form first appeared in *Geist und Leben*, vol. 1/91, 64–75. Sources used include the following: M. Beesing, R. Nogosek, and P. O'Leary, *The Enneagram: A Journey of Self-Discovery* (Denville, N.J.: Dimension Books, 1984); J. G. Bennett, *Enneagram Studies* (York Beach, Maine: Coombe Springs Press, 1983); Sam Keen, "Interview

with Oscar Ichazo," *Psychology Today,* July 1973, reprinted in *Interviews with Oscar Ichazo,* ed. John Bleibreu (New York: Arica Institute Press, 1982); R. Nogosek, *Nine Portraits of Jesus: Discovering Jesus Through the Enneagram* (Denville, N.J.: Dimension Books, 1987); H. Palmer, *The Enneagram: Understanding Yourself and the People Around You* (New York: Harper & Row, 1988).

The Nine Faces of the Soul of Christ
Dietrich Koller

1. Hanna Wolf, *Jesus der Mann* (Stuttgart, 1977), pp. 80 ff: "Jesus, the man without animus."
2. *Die Bekenntnisschriften der evangelisch-lutherischen Kirche* (Göttingen, 1976), p. 1039. "Konkordienformel, Solida Declaratio VII. De persona Christi," p. 87.
3. Ibid.
4. Ibid.

The Enneagram:
Possibilities and Dangers for Pastoral Care
Dirk Meine

1. Heinz Häfner, *Schulderleben und Gewissen* (Stuttgart, 1956), p. 56. Häfner characterizes this as "subjective value-design."
2. Rohr/Ebert, p. 5.
3. An example: A person with the helper syndrome (a TWO) gets guilt feelings when he lets others go, setting them free instead of helping them.
4. C. G. Jung uses the term "persona" for this situation: the mask with which we adapt to parental or social pressure to play certain roles, and to repress, by driving them into the unconscious, the undeveloped, inferior, evil, and destructive elements inside us. See Helmut Harsch, *Das Schuldproblem in Theologie und Tiefenpsychologie* (Heidelberg, 1965).
5. Häfner, op. cit.
6. Christian Wulf.
7. Rohr/Ebert, p. 30.
8. Rohr/Ebert, p. 47. Rohr speaks of the "Rumpelstiltskin effect," using the Grimms' fairy tale to illustrate the underlying psychological state of affairs. See also Goethe's *Faust*: "Your real being no less than your fame / Is often shown, sirs, by your name, / Which is not hard to analyze / When one calls you the Liar, Destroyer, God of Flies...I understand your noble duty; / Too weak for great destruction, you / Attempt it on a minor scale," I, ll. 1331–34, 1359–60, tr. Walter Kaufman (Garden City, N.Y.: Doubleday, 1961), pp. 159, 161.

9. Cf. the contribution to this book by Dietrich Koller.

10. Cf. John 20:17, 27; Matt. 19:21; Luke 19:8–9.

11. Rohr/Ebert, p. 11.

12. Wolfhart Pannenberg, *Christliche Spiritualität* (Göttingen, 1986), p. 7.

13. Rohr/Ebert, p. xv. The Enneagram does not provide any final answers, only limited truths and partial aspects of human nature. It can't save us. Eli Jaxon-Bear takes a different position in *Die neun Zahlen des Lebens* (Munich, 1989), pp. 248–49. Jaxon-Bear sees the Enneagram as a handbook that makes us conscious of all the answers, laying down rules that lead us to the gates of immortality.

14. Rohr/Ebert, pp. 15 ff.

15. Rohr/Ebert, pp. 8–10. There have been many highly subjective and distorted additions to the literature on the Enneagram during this period. But they also provide a certain enrichment through the varied experiences they document, and the bottom line is that the Enneagram "adds up," because it has survived.

16. Rohr, *Das Enneagram Video* (Munich: Claudius, 1990), ordering number 62 150.

17. Rohr/Ebert, p. 23.

18. Dietrich Bonhoeffer, *Gemeinsames Leben* (Munich, 15th ed., 1976), p. 101.

19. Ibid.

20. Rohr, *Video.*

21. The term "spirituality" has become vague, not least of all because of "inflationary" overuse. It describes the internal experientiality and penetration of personal actions in life — and is consciously related to or dependent on transcendent/external spiritual forces — theologically speaking: God.

22. Rohr, *Video.*

23. Rohr/Ebert, p. 16.

24. Seminar participant in Wallerfangen.

25. Rohr/Ebert, p. 31. But in his video Rohr admits that he feels a personal aversion to types THREE and SIX (and FIVE). Unfortunately this feeling also found negative expression in the description of those types in his book.

26. Rohr/Ebert, p. xii.

27. Rohr/Ebert, pp. 203–9; and because "redemption" occurs exclusively in the realm of the divine, the Enneagram completes the psychological categories of "immature-average-mature."

28. Just compare the way psychoanalysis deals with guilt feelings that can be traced back to childhood trauma, for which parents, teachers, etc., are "guilty." But their responsibility too is transferred to the person shaped by those parents and teachers.

29. Rohr, *Video.*

30. Rohr/Ebert, p. 14, but while this may hold true for beginning with the Enneagram, how many people will never get past this stage without counseling?

31. Rohr/Ebert, p. 124.

32. Appendix A, above, p. 210.

33. Ibid.

34. Ibid., p. 211.

35. Wilhelm Knackstedt, who is in charge of ideological issues for the Landeskirche in Hanover, conducted an experiment in his high school class: Every student was presented with what was purportedly his or her personal horoscope and asked to examine it. In fact all of the students were given the same version. Nevertheless practically every one of the students recognized himself or herself in the horoscope.

36. Rohr/Ebert, pp. 133, 143: the international distribution of wealth as a structural sin.

37. Cf. Andreas Ebert's contribution to this book.

38. Bernd Moeller, *Geschichte des Christentums in Grundzügen* (Göttingen, 1983), pp. 89–90, describes this dangerous process around the time of the great transition under Constantine.

39. Riso, p. 45: "We can learn to be healthy." Cf. the blurb for Rohr's video: "This book can be your key to freedom. . . . If we work away through our 'pitfalls' . . . we find a cleansed landscape, a purified power, our best and true self." — The Enneagram is also an item on the market, and it wants to be sold.

40. Cf. Markus Becker's contribution to this book.

41. I am thinking especially of the dogmatic statement that "Everyone is precisely one type." In my opinion the Enneagram does not stand or fall with this claim, even if it does lend the system particular weight. It's considerably more difficult to judge the (heretical) notion that in the final analysis even the number nine might be dispensable. But this is purely hypothetical, because there is no practical alternative to it.

42. Rohr/Ebert, pp. 193–94. Paul Tillich, *Systematische Theologie,* vol. 3 (Berlin/New York, 1987), 4th ed., 57: Hidden motives can render even a seemingly heroic sacrifice dubious.

43. Rohr/Ebert, p. 29: Our gifts can become a curse.

44. Rudolf Bultmann, *Theologie des Neuen Testaments* (Tübingen, 1984), pp. 217–21.

45. Paul Tillich, *Systematische Theologie,* I, 312; II, 2, 14–15.

46. Rohr/Ebert, p. xii.

47. Rohr/Ebert, p. 181.

48. Dietrich Koller rightly warns about this in the Appendix.

49. Rohr/Ebert, p. xiv.

50. Manfred Seitz, *Praxis des Glaubens* (Göttingen, 1985), p. 72. By faith Seitz doesn't mean dogmatic orthodoxy, but a constantly challenged relationship with God.

51. The special field of counseling the handicapped, "ergotherapy" with children and old people, etc., naturally uses different "linguistic" means.

52. Hans-Joachim Thilo, *Beratende Seelsorge* (Göttingen, 1986), pp. 7–8.

53. Joachim Scharfenberg, *Seelsorge als Gespräch* (Göttingen, 1983), pp. 73–74. See also Christian Wulf, *Geist und Leben,* 73; cf. Rohr/Ebert, pp. 133–34, 139, where the presumed limits of SEVENS in counselling are described.

54. The guilty ego can't believe that it can find love, even with its shadow side, that "despite everything" there is justification. Häfner, p. 60.

55. Rohr/Ebert, p. 96. This is softened in the American version to, "Nobody else *had* the idea of articulating protest," etc.

56. Rohr/Ebert, p. 142.

57. Rolf Dieter Seemann, Protestant pastor and Enneagram group leader.

58. Häfner, pp. 62–63, where "health" is used in a relative sense, with no binding definition.

The Enneagram and the Church:
Impulses for Building Community
Andreas Ebert

1. For example, consider the position taken by the church press secretaries (the Church probably looks for THREEs for such jobs too) in response to the critical questions of the "people" that were polled on the occasion of a public opinion poll in Germany recently. The spokesman for the Protestant churches claimed, for example, that power "in our church is based solely on the word, on dialogue, not on money . . . " or "In the Church money is wasted less than anywhere else." The spokesman for the Catholic German Bishops Conference stressed: "We deal very responsibly with money." And in another place: "As far as human dignity is concerned, women have always been given equal rights." Dozens of proofs could be cited to show that these statements are at the least embellished truths. Such rhetorical cosmetic surgery on the truth belongs to the typical verbal pattern of THREEs.

2. It would be worthwhile to point the spotlight of the Enneagram on the form and content of church services. Questions on this score can only be suggested here: Where in our liturgies is there room for the call to conversion and the proclamation of God's unconditional love (ONE)? What is the situation with the need for intimacy, communication, and encounter (TWO)? Is the form of our services attractive and appealing to outsiders as well (THREE)? What place do music, spontaneity, creativity, dramatic effects, and symbolism have in the liturgy (FOUR)? What value is placed on sober information? Is our

people's need to maintain their distance respected (FIVE)? Do we preserve traditions? Are the form and content of the liturgy readily recognizable (SIX)? Do our services give us and others joy? Do they welcome children and families (SEVEN)? Is there clarity, confrontation, and challenge in the sermons (EIGHT)? Can we stand longish stretches of rest and silence, in which people can come to themselves (NINE)? Such and similar considerations can make a decisive contribuion to reshaping Christian worship.

3. Examples of initiation groups are courses in which information about religion is passed on. Still more important, however, is the introduction to the experience of being a Christian and of community. The end result of a religion course should be not just increased knowledge of the faith, but an experience that makes it possible for the participants to make a conscious decision for or against active community life. In the face of the breakdown already mentioned of tradition in the parish churches, I believe that religion courses for adult volunteers are one of the most promising forms of work in the Church today. An important part of such courses is also the coming to terms with negative and disappointing experiences of the Church (the Church as non–community or as compulsion) and intellectual doubts about the faith.

4. "Growth groups" can be, for example, Bible study or fellowship groups, in which people from different walks of life get together regularly to do three things: to share in the life of others (exchange), to confront the Bible in common, and to meditate/pray. In the growth group people practice commitment to and responsibility for others. In the course of time trust can grow, vulnerability and sincerity become possible. In discussing the Bible one's own religious ideas will heard by others and enriched by their remarks. Through common prayer for one another and for causes that are larger than the group (families, community, political problems) awareness grows for our global ties, our worldwide responsibilities and for the presence of God among all people and in all things.

5. Discipleship groups hear the "call" to active and energetic self-dedication. This can be for missionary, service, or social concerns, and ranges from helping foreign children with their school work to participation in a citizens' initiative for protecting the environment. In these groups the main focus is not so much on making sure of one's faith as on the consequences of faith.

6. Thus the — not quite felicitously chosen — pair of basic terms of the "Missionary Double Strategy" as formulated in 1984 by the Parish Committee of the United Lutheran Churches of Germany. Christian Möller has rightly criticized these terms taken from the domain of technology and has proposed instead the biological-organic image of the "diastolic" and "systolic" rhythms of the heart, which also capture the simultaneity of both movements.

7.   Cf. Ernesto Cardenal, *The Gospel in Soletiname,* tr. Donald D. Walsh, 4 vols. (Maryknoll: Orbis Books, 1982).

8.   "Non gaff ghen caelum, hie unden hastus, Postmoderne Religion und ein Buch von Hermann Timm," in *lutherische monatshefte,* XXX, n. 6, June, 1991, 256.

The Enneagram and the Bible
Wolfgang Müller

1.   Monastery of St. Clare, 1310 Dellwood Ave., Memphis, Tenn., 1990.

2.   This is brought out in Barbara Metz and John Burchill, *The Enneagram and Prayer: Discovering Our True Selves Before God* (Denville, N.J.: Dimension Books, 1987).

On Being One with Everyone:
A Journey Through the Enneagram
Marion Küstenmacher

1.   Anthony de Mello, *A Minute Wisdom* (Garden City, N.Y.: Double-day, 1986), p. 50.

Appendix A

"The Regret No One Regrets"
Dietrich Koller

1.   Consider the importance that archery technique has in Zen Buddhism. Complete concentration on an external target is a symbol of the inner concentration and attentiveness involved in every serious spiritual path.

2.   Many Catholics have had bad experiences with confession. Most Protestants have never practiced it. In 1939 as part of the illegal seminar on preaching he gave for the *Confessing Church* Dietrich Bonhoeffer wrote a brief introduction to the practice of personal confession, which is contained in his little book *Gemeinsames Leben* (19th ed., Munich, 1983), pp. 95–104. These few pages may the best single piece ever written on this subject; they can help to remove misunderstanding and anxiety surrounding it.

3.   *Evangelisches Kirchengesangbuch* (EKG), p. 254, 3.

4.   Erich Kästner, *Gesammelte Schriften für Erwachsene* (Munich/Zurich, 1969), I, 325.

5.   The wisdom of a Berlin joke pointedly recognizes this: Two friends meet, and one says, "Mann, geh doch mal in dich!" (Man, go into yourself

[= search your conscience]. To which the other replies, "Da war ick schon; da ist ooch nischt los!" ["I've already been there — no problem!"])

6.   *Kleine Philokalie* (Zurich-Einsiedeln-Cologne, 1976), p. 129.

7.   Igumen Nikon, *Briefe eines russischen Starzen an seine geistliche Kinder* (Freiburg, 1988), p. 50.

8.   Thomas à Kempis, *The Imitation of Christ,* tr. Leo Sherley-Price (Harmondsworth: Penguin, 1983), pp. 36, 39.

9.   Thomas Merton, *The Seven Storey Mountain* (New York: Harcourt, Brace, and World), 1948), p. 181.

10. To cite a hymn by Julie von Hausmann (1862), EKG (Bavaria), p. 679.

11. Merton, pp. 122–23.

12. Augustine, *Confessions*, tr. Frank Sheed (London: Sheed & Ward, 1943), pp. 166–67.

13. *Briefe eines russischen Starzen an seine geistliche Kinder,* pp. 79 ff.

14. Ibid., p. 92.

15. Ibid., p. 81.

Books on the Enneagram

Beesing, Maria; Nogosek, Robert J.; and O'Leary, Patrick. *The Enneagram: A Journey of Self-Discovery*. Denville, N.J.: Dimension Books, 1984.

Keyes, Margaret Frings. *Emotions and the Enneagram: Working Through Your Shadow Life Script*. Muir Beach, Calif.: Molysdatur Publications, 1990.

Metz, Barbara and Burchill, John. *The Enneagram and Prayer: Discovering Our True Selves Before God*. Denville, N.J.: Dimension Books, 1987.

Nogosek, Robert. *Nine Portraits of Jesus: Discovering Jesus Through the Enneagram*. Denville, N.J.: Dimension Books, 1987.

Palmer, Helen. *The Enneagram: Understanding Yourself and the People Around You*. New York: Harper & Row, 1988.

Riso, Don Richard. *Personality Types: Using the Enneagram for Self-Discovery*. Boston: Houghton Mifflin, 1987.

Rohr, Richard, and Ebert, Andreas. Translated by Peter Heinegg. *Discovering the Enneagram: An Ancient Tool for a New Spiritual Journey*. New York: Crossroad, 1990.

Contributors

MARKUS BECKER: Born in Hanover (1958). Studied Protestant Theology (university examination, 1987) and Psychology (examination, 1991) at the University of Tübingen. Certified psychologist at a clinic for psychosomatic medicine in Frankfurt. Has participated in conferences on expanding experience of oneself and God. Has also worked as a therapist in Schöntal.

ANDREAS EBERT: Born in Berlin (1952). Studied Protestant Theology at Neuendettelsau, Tübingen, Würzburg, and Heidelberg. Co-founder and pastor of the base community of Lorenzer Laken in Nuremberg. Deputy director of the Lutheran Community Theological College in Celle. Translator and author. President of the Ecumenical Enneagram Work Group in Germany.

DIETRICH KOLLER: Born in Neuendettelsau (1931). Studied Protestant Theology at Neuendettelsau, Tübingen, and Erlangen. Pastor. From 1970–74 full-time (part-time since 1979) staff member of the Schloss Craheim Ecumenical Life Center. Author of books and plays. Trained in Gestalt Counselling at the Institute for Integrative Gestalt Therapy in Würzburg, and in Pastoral Theology. Retreat master and member of the Ecumenical Enneagram Work Group.

MARION KÜSTENMACHER: Born in Würzburg (1956): Strongly influenced by work on the staff of the "Tearoom" base community in Würzburg. Studied Germanistics and Protestant Theology in Munich and Tübingen. State certification (1982). Since 1983 a reader at Claudius Verlag. Member of the Ecumenical Enneagram Work Group, introductory seminars and workshops on the Enneagram.

DIRK MEINE: Born in 1960. Studied Protestant Theology in Göttingen and Tübingen. Second theological degree (1991). Vicar of the Hanover *Landkirche* in Hanover. His article is an abbreviated summary of his thesis submitted for the second ecclesiastical examination.

WOLFGANG MÜLLER, S.J.: Born in Freiburg (1936). Studied Catholic theology and philosophy in Freiburg, Munich, Pullach, and Frankfurt. Entered the

Jesuit order in 1958. Teacher of religion in Ravensburg and St. Blasien (Switzerland) from 1969 to 1974. Worked for the Community of Christian Life (GCL) in Munich, mainly giving the *Spiritual Exercises,* from 1974 to 1985. On administrative assignment for the Jesuits in Munich and Rome from 1985 to 1990. Studied in Zimbabwe (1990–91). Since 1990 he has again been giving retreats and courses with the GCL.

HANS NEIDHARDT: Born in Bayreuth (1952). Studied Psychology in Würzburg. During this period worked on the leadership team of the "test tube community" in Würzburg. Certification in Psychology. Clinical psychologist, person-centered psychotherapist, Focusing trainer. Until 1987 director of the Würzburg Telephone Counselling Center, then founder of the Center for Psychological Practice and Therapy in Bayreuth. Advisory member of the Ecumenical Enneagram Work Group.

KLAUS RENN: Born in 1953. Certification in Social Pedagogy. Focusing therapy trainer and apprentice therapist at the German Training Institute for Focusing Therapy. Coordinator at the Focusing Institute of Chicago. Works in private practice.

RICHARD ROHR, O.F.M.: born in Topeka, Kansas (1943). Ordained a priest in 1970. Founder of the Christian lay community New Jerusalem in Cincinnati (1981). Since 1986 has worked to build up the Center for Action and Contemplation in Albuquerque. Internally known speaker, retreat master, and best-selling author.

LIESL SCHEICH: Born in 1933. Studied education at the Bergstrasse Youth Center in Munich. Primary school teacher in the Rheingau. Since 1973 a teacher in Höchsty/Odenwald. Member of the Council of the Diocese of Mainz.

CHRISTIAN WULF: Born in 1954. Studied education in Hamburg and Mainz, Ed. D. (1986). In charge of intensive pastoral care at the Retreat House in Dieburg. Retreat master and meditation director. Enneagram seminar leader. Founding member and member of the board of directors of the Ecumenical Enneagram Work Group.